Social Insurance in Transition

SOCIAL INSURANCE
IN TRANSITION

An Economic Analysis

JOHN CREEDY

and

RICHARD DISNEY

CLARENDON PRESS·OXFORD

1985

89-00004337

Oxford University Press, Walton Street, Oxford OX2 6DP
Oxford   New York   Toronto
Delhi   Bombay   Calcutta   Madras   Karachi
Kuala Lumpur   Singapore   Hong Kong   Tokyo
Nairobi   Dar es Salaam   Cape Town
Melbourne   Auckland
and associated companies in
Beirut   Berlin   Ibadan   Nicosia

Oxford is a trade mark of Oxford University Press

Published in the United States
by Oxford University Press, New York

© *John Creedy and Richard Disney 1985*

HD
7165
·C726
1985

British Library Cataloguing in Publication Data

Creedy, John, 1949–
    Social insurance in transition: an economic analysis
    1. Social security——Great Britain
    I. Title   II. Disney, Richard
    338.4'7'368400941   HD7165

    ISBN 0-19-877228-9
    ISBN 0-19-877227-0 Pbk

Library of Congress Cataloging in Publication Data

Creedy, John, 1949–
    Social insurance in transition.

    Bibliography: p.
    Includes index.
    1. Social security——Great Britain.   I. Disney,
    Richard.   II. Title.
    HD7165.C726   1985   368.4'00941   85-10564
    ISBN 0-19-877228-9
    ISBN 0-19-877227-0 (pbk.)

Set by Colset Pte Ltd, Singapore

Printed in Great Britain at
the University Press, Oxford
by David Stanford
Printer to the University

Acknowledgements

The preparation of this book has been a pleasant experience for both of us, and we should like the acknowledge the following for their help. For discussions and comment at various stages we are grateful to Erika Szyszczak (Kent) and Norman Gemmell (Durham), who also kindly allowed us to use results from joint research. A jointly written book of this kind necessarily involves much typing, and especially retyping, only ended by deadlines. We should like to thank Frances Rhodes and Sue Davies (Kent), and Kathryn Cowton (Durham), for their splendid work. A penultimate draft was read by Alan Carruth and Graeme Macdonald (Kent), whose helpful comments led us to make significant improvements in the exposition. As always, none of the above can be held responsible for any errors or shortcomings of this book. We should also like to thank the editors of the *Scottish Journal of Political Economy*, the *Journal of Economic Studies*, and the *Oxford Bulletin of Economics and Statistics* for permission to reproduce tables and figures, and the Department of Health and Social Security for permission to use their data.

Contents

PART 3

Unemployment and Sickness

PART 4

Tax-and-Transfer Schemes

PART 5

Social Insurance in Transition

List of Figures

List of Tables

Introduction

It is now widely accepted that the state has a major role to play in ensuring that people have sufficient resources to deal with those contingencies which reduce, either temporarily or permanently, their capacity to obtain income on their own account. These contingencies include unemployment, sickness and invalidity, and old age. The major role of the state in Britain is illustrated by the fact that public expenditure on social security in 1984–5 exceeded £37 billion; over 30 per cent of centrally financed government expenditure.

Nevertheless there is rather less agreement concerning the best form of state intervention to provide social security, and the appropriate extent of state provision. In the present economic and political environment, the latter concern has been given a major emphasis, with state provision increasingly questioned in the light of overall reductions in government spending and a debate concerning the optimal extent of social, relative to private, provision over a wide range of economic activities.

The form of state social security provision which developed in the United Kingdom from the turn of this century, reaching its apotheosis in the Beveridge Report (Beveridge, 1942) and the subsequent post-war legislation, was embodied in the concept of 'social insurance'. In brief, social insurance was based on the idea that the state should operate a quasi-insurance system, exacting compulsory 'contributions' from the working population in order to finance the payment of benefits when certain contingencies occurred: notably unemployment, sickness, and old age. It has been argued, most recently by Dilnot, Kay, and Morris (1984), that this conception of social insurance was fatally flawed from the start. It is easy to see that a scheme of social insurance is not the only form of state social security provision that might be envisaged; for example the state could alternatively finance a range of income transfers entirely out of general taxation. Indeed there developed in the United Kingdom, side by side with the social insurance system, a variety of other income transfers; these include means-tested social security benefits such as Supplementary

Benefit and Family Income Supplement. The complexity of state provision, stemming partly from the operation of several distinct forms of intervention, has served as a focal point for much criticism.

In the past ten years, sweeping changes have occurred in the social security system in the United Kingdom, including the introduction of a new and complex pension scheme, changes in the level of and eligibility for unemployment benefits, the institution of a new scheme of short-term earnings replacement for the sick, and significant administrative changes in the operation of the means-tested sector. The system has in fact been in a state of flux right from the start, but as the title of this book suggests, the extent to which these recent changes have altered the whole character of social insurance provision in the United Kingdom suggests that the system is no nearer to a generally accepted steady state. Indeed the major reforms of the past decade have if anything intensified expressions of dissatisfaction with the social security system, both as a whole and in its constituent parts. For example, the Institute for Fiscal Studies, the National Consumer Council, and many witnesses to the Treasury and Civil Service Committee Sub-Committee (1983a) have all recently been seeking radical reforms of the whole tax and transfer system. Furthermore in May 1984 the government instituted a series of Social Security Reviews in order to examine the operation of various parts of the social security system in the light of overall government budget constraints and it is likely that further changes will occur in the not too distant future.

The present book represents a further contribution to this debate. Unlike some recent contributions, however, its central concern is not simply to propose another 'blueprint' for the reform of the social security system. Rather it seeks to examine in depth the operation of the social security system in the United Kingdom from the point of view of economic theory. It uses as a framework a set of general economic criteria by which to judge the extent and nature of state provision. The book therefore attempts to provide a rational analysis of the issues, rather than proposing a scheme which necessarily embodies a set of value-judgements. Since the concept of social insurance underpins much of the system, it is natural to commence the analysis by starting with a treatment of risk. Chapter 1 therefore posits the existence of risk, reflected in contingencies such as unemployment and sickness, as being a major factor determining the extent and kind of state social insurance provision.

Now the extent to which the state, as opposed to the private sector, should insure these risks, and the nature of this insurance offered by the state, is conventionally conditioned by four motives for state intervention: market failure, paternalism, redistribution, and revenue raising, with the relative administrative efficiency of public and private provision as an additional factor (see, for example, Diamond 1977). These motives are described in more detail in Chapter 1 and then used in ensuing chapters. It will be seen that in considering the motives for state intervention, differences in policy choices can arise both because people take different views about economic behaviour and the effects of policies, and/or because they adopt different basic value-judgements. Since a full rationalization of government policy is seldom, if ever, given at the time, the evaluation of policies is fraught with difficulties. However, the analysis of Chapter 1 is used in an attempt to assess the extent to which actual state intervention in the United Kingdom appears to have been motivated by, or at least is consistent with, one or more of these criteria. This approach underlies Chapter 2, but also underpins much of Part 2, which discusses the provision of pensions, and Part 3, which examines the schemes of unemployment and sickness insurance operating in the United Kingdom.

The procedure may be illustrated by the example of the radical change in state pension provision in the United Kingdom in the mid-1970s. From public pronouncements, the motive of redistribution *within* age cohorts seems to have underlain the introduction of the new state earnings-related pension scheme in 1978, although previous extensions of state pensions in the United Kingdom have been motivated by each of the suggested criteria at one time or another. Yet, as Part 2 shows, a careful analysis of the post-1978 scheme, using a precise definition of redistribution, shows that the redistributive content of the scheme is very limited. Several possible conclusions follow from this. These include the possibility that the actual motives behind its introduction were somewhat different from public pronouncements on the subject; for example actual motives may have included a desire to extend the tax base in return for promises of better benefits in the future (a revenue-raising motive) or in order to promote a higher savings rate (the paternalist motive). Another possibility is that the originators of the scheme actually had insufficient information and an inadequate conceptual analysis with which to form any judgement as to whether the scheme was redistributive or not.

It is clearly necessary to consider the nature of the policies to be adopted, *given* the nature of certain basic value-judgements. It is important to consider, for example, the extent to which trade-offs among policy objectives must be made. A number of alternatives are therefore examined, although a complete 'optimization model', which may for example specify the optimal policy choice, given a fully specified social welfare function in terms of individual utilities, has not been used. A more basic approach has been used which nevertheless allows a number of simple policies to be compared. Taking the pension scheme as the example again, the question may be posed as: given a desire to secure redistribution within generations, what kind of state pension scheme would be appropriate subject to low administrative costs? It is apparent that the solution would not be the present scheme but one in which, broadly speaking, flat rate benefits were financed by a progressive tax schedule. Even with a desire to limit the degree of redistribution, it is·again not apparent that the 1978 scheme would represent the optimal solution. To take another example, this time from Part 3: it is almost impossible for a state unemployment insurance scheme to replicate the working of a private insurance scheme. It is likely that a state unemployment insurance scheme will of necessity contain a high degree of risk-pooling and consequently some degree of systematic redistribution. Measures to limit redistribution will therefore have, and indeed have had, serious repercussions, especially concerning eligibility for benefits and increasing reliance of claimants on the administratively costly means-tested sector. Again rational policy analysis might, depending on the precise trade-offs, suggest acceptance of a greater degree of systematic redistribution in the social insurance scheme, if administrative efficiency is held to be a major aim.

It will be apparent from this brief discussion why this book is not primarily motivated by the desire to promote, or justify, a single overall reform of the social security system, even though in the course of the book it will be argued that there are many aspects of the present scheme which do not consistently meet the criteria of Chapter 1, and that there seems to have been a lack of foresight in the design of several of its parts. The primary motive of the book is analytical rather than polemical. As in other fields, however, general opinion concerning social security follows 'fashions' at any point in time and in recent years the trend, reflected for example in the Treasury and Civil Service Committee Sub-Committee reports and evidence, and described in the recent book by Hemming (1984), has been towards an emphasis on the issues of poverty alleviation, labour supply, incentives, and the operations of the 'unemployment trap' and 'poverty trap'. This fashion has perhaps been underpinned by a shift in the perception of social security, away from the Beveridge conception of social security as a framework of social insurance against specific contingencies and towards social security as part of a system of taxes and transfers, although this view too has its antecedents such as Rhys-Williams (1942, reprinted in 1953) and Friedman (1962). These issues, most notably the operation of the tax and transfer system as a whole, are important and are covered in Part 4 of the present book. As will be apparent from the preceding discussion, however, the same criteria which are used to appraise components of the social insurance system should also be relevant in examining the tax and transfer system as a whole and possible modifications to it. Thus even apparently laudable aims such as, on the one hand, abolishing the 'poverty trap', or on the other hand concentrating resources solely on the poorest, should take account of the trade-off between different criteria which is essential in social security analysis and should be explicit in their rejection, if that is the consequence, of other motives underlying state intervention.

In Part 5, the themes of the book are restated, drawing on the conclusions of Parts 2 to 4. As outlined previously, the use of these motives as evaluative criteria permits a detailed appraisal of the operation of the social security system as a whole and its constituent parts. Their use suggests that there are parts of the social security system which are extremely difficult to justify whatever motive or combination of motives are held by the analyst. As indicated earlier, the social security system is unlikely to be in anything other than a state of transition. There is no simple solution to any of the many perceived problems, but progress can only be made with a more precise awareness of the nature of the issues involved.

PART 1

Social Insurance: Theory and History

1
A Framework of Analysis

Risk is a pervasive feature of economic life; it exists in credit markets, in rental markets, and of course in labour markets. The combination of risk with a widespread aversion to risk, and its often unpleasant consequences, naturally leads to a demand for insurance. The simplest type of insurance, self-insurance, involves individuals making an effort to try to prevent the particularly unpleasant events (such as taking basic precautions against fire and theft), combined with personal saving in order to provide a precautionary stock of resources to meet exigencies. Self-insurance, while undoubtedly very important, may not be sufficient to meet the demand for insurance, especially where the costs are high and individuals are very risk averse. There is often an incentive for groups of individuals who face similar types of risk to devise a form of risk-sharing. Such sharing, or pooling, of risks obviously requires the preparation of special contracts. This has not proved to be too difficult when there is a large amount of information about the nature of the risks involved and the parties to the contract have plenty of information about one another. For example, life insurance could not develop until the statistical analysis of mortality rates had been well established. It is not surprising that risk-sharing insurance schemes developed in situations where the event occurs with fairly high frequency, but where the costs are relatively low. The contrast between fire and theft insurance and insurance against wars, plagues, and natural disasters is quite clear.

The statements in the preceding paragraph are uncontroversial; risk is widespread and risk-averse individuals have a high demand for insurance. The issue which leads to considerable controversy is that of the extent to which the state should attempt to meet the demand for insurance. If, further, it is accepted that the state should supply insurance, the extremely difficult problem of deciding on the appropriate form of contract still remains. The purpose of this book is to examine a limited number of risks—those associated with unemployment, sickness, and the risk of being unable to support oneself in old age (through for example disability, skill obsolescence, or having inadequate non-labour income). It therefore concentrates on the three main areas of social insurance, namely unemployment, sickness, and pensions. It may be noted that the provision of a retirement pension after a specified age may not seem the obvious response to the risk stated in the previous sentence.

These three areas of social insurance continue to attract a great deal of debate and heated controversy. There is much room for disagreement, not only in terms of basic value-judgements, but also about empirical matters where it is difficult, if not impossible, to provide clear evidence. There is often much confusion, in the sense that people who hold similar value-judgements may disagree strongly about the appropriate policy because they hold different views about the orders of magnitude of relevant empirical details. They may not always realize the precise sources of their disagreement however, because of the complexity of the issues and the amount of 'heat' which is often generated in debates. For similar reasons, people who hold different basic value-judgements may sometimes find themselves in agreement about the courses of action they feel governments should take.

Because of the sensitive nature of the subject, it is important to stress that the present book attempts to provide a *rational* analysis of policy issues. The approach is based on the view that economic analysis has a vital role to play in policy debates, by examining the implications of adopting alternative value-judgements, and indicating precisely which empirical issues are most important. Policy inevitably involves a difficult choice among conflicting objectives, and the role of the professional economist is to clarify the nature of the trade-offs which must be made. The level of policy debate is improved when the value-judgements, which cannot be avoided, are made as explicit as possible. Economists often complain that policy-makers rarely, if ever, provide a coherent rationalization of their policies. While it may be answered that this complaint reflects a naïve view of the complexities of decision-taking, power struggles, and political compromise, it can nevertheless still be argued that a rational economic analysis can make an important contribution to debate, while recognizing the limitations of the perspective offered by a single discipline.

It should not be too surprising that social insurance is still undergoing many transitions all over the world. The general acceptance by governments that there may be a role for social insurance has taken place in many countries only in the present century. Indeed, in 1893 Gladstone could still state that action to relieve unemployment was 'outside the legitimate sphere not merely of legislation but of parliamentary discussion' (quoted in Harris, 1972, p. 100). The charitable organizations gave much emphasis to self-help, and an important distinction was drawn between the 'deserving' and 'undeserving' poor. The operation of the Poor Law requires little discussion here, except perhaps to stress its emphasis on the incentive effects of poor relief, and the strict attempt to monitor the behaviour of recipients. However, it gradually came to be recognized that some risks were not diversifiable, and could not be accommodated by risk-sharing schemes among individuals. Mass unemployment, for example, came to be seen explicitly as a 'problem of industry', where individual risks are far from independent and identifiable in terms of individuals' characteristics. The development of social insurance schemes in Britain is examined in more detail in Chapter 2.

Social insurance expenditure has, however, grown considerably over a relatively short period of time. In most countries the real level of benefit provision is now considerably in excess of the amount which would be required to alleviate poverty (even using a generously defined 'poverty level'). Despite this, evidence is regularly presented to show that the insurance systems used have in fact failed to eliminate poverty. Although there is considerable room for disagreement about the concept and measurement of poverty, there seems little doubt that there is also much room for the improvement of the system. The debate has been focused sharply by recent emphasis on attempting to reduce public expenditure as a whole, and the social insurance budget has not remained immune from cuts.

Some idea of the important social insurance benefits in the United Kingdom is shown in Table 1.1. This gives a detailed breakdown of the various social insurance benefits in the three recent financial years: 1977–8, 1981–2, and 1984–5. It will be apparent that the totals are dominated by the payment of pensions, followed by Supplementary Benefit and Child Benefit, and then Unemployment and Invalidity Benefits. These benefits will be described in more detail as the argument develops. Benefits are divided into two kinds: contributory and non-contributory. The former are financed by the National Insurance contribution, a payroll tax nominally levied on employers and employees and supplemented by a subsidy from the central Exchequer. This system of financing is described in more detail in Part 4. The non-contributory benefits are financed out of general taxation receipts, which are dominated by taxes on income and expenditure. In

TABLE 1.1   *Expenditure on social insurance benefits*

Year	1977–8	£ million 1981–2	1984–5*
Contributory Benefits			
Retirement pension	6,613	12,227	15,539
Widows' benefits	466	691	798
Unemployment Benefit	629	1,702	1,538
Sickness Benefit	647	680	246
Invalidity Benefit	704	1,371	1,928
Industrial Injury Benefit	225	367	439
Maternity Allowance	76	158	191
Other benefits	17	19	20
Total	9,377	17,215	20,699
Non-Contributory Benefits			
Pension benefits (incl. war pension)	444	523	500
Attendance Allowance	143	330	500
Invalid Care Allowance	3	6	—
Non-contributory Invalidity Pension	44	130	200
Mobility Allowance	20	173	300
Supplementary pension	665	1,417	800
Supplementary allowance:			
long-term rate	338	822	1,482
short-term rate	1,072	2,600	3,883
Child Benefit	868	3,372	4,291
One-parent benefit	6	76	122
Family Income Supplement	25	66	131
Maternity Grant	15	16	18
Rent rebate	206	490	2,045
Rent allowance	39	64	416
Total	3,888	10,087	14,907
National Insurance administration (contributory benefits)	355	718	736
DHSS administration (non-contributory benefits)	237	427	629
Local authority administration (housing benefits)	25	45	86
Department of Employment administration**	35	77	149
Total programme	13,917	28,567	37.207

* Forecast.
** Costs of paying Supplementary allowance to unemployed; Unemployment Benefit is included under National Insurance administration.

Source: Chancellor of the Exchequer (1984) *The Government's Expenditure Plans 1984-5 to 1986-7*, Cmnd. 9143, vol. 2, HMSO, February.

1984–5 these items of social security expenditure comprised around 28 per cent of total centrally financed government expenditure and 12 per cent of Gross Domestic Product. Non-contributory benefits accounted for 14 per cent of expenditure financed from general Exchequer receipts.

The following section of this chapter provides a non-technical analysis of the role of social insurance, compared with private insurance. This provides a basic framework of analysis within which alternative policies are assessed. Analyses which show the conditions under which certain types of government intervention may be justified do not however necessarily explain why intervention has taken place in the past. The rationalization of policy *ex post* is fraught with many dangers. Some difficulties which arise in analysing the state are discussed briefly in section 1.2.

1.1 Economic Theory and Social Insurance

This section examines the main economic arguments involved in determining the appropriate extent and nature of social insurance provided by the state. The most natural first question to ask here concerns the extent to which demand for insurance is likely to be met by private markets. This is considered below under the heading of 'market failure', though it should immediately be noted that the existence of such a failure cannot *necessarily* support government intervention, since 'government failure' may also be likely. The early welfare economics literature perhaps too often compared an imperfect market with an omniscient government.

Secondly, it could be argued that the state should use social insurance for redistributive purposes. The most basic motive relates to the relief of poverty; the view that society, through social transfers, should ensure that everyone receives a guaranteed socially acceptable minimum level of income. But social insurance may be further motivated by the value-judgement that it should be used to produce much more systematic redistribution. As shown below, this raises some difficulty, especially where some systematic redistribution may arise as a result only of the desire to provide insurance. It may be worth noting here that the argument for 'pure' redistribution through compulsory state action has sometimes been supported on the grounds that it is Pareto-efficient where preferences are interdependent. Thus, if individuals wish to see income redistributed to the low paid, but suspect also that their sympathies are shared by others, there may be an incentive to conceal preferences and allow others to make the voluntary transfers. In this case redistribution is regarded as a public good, and individuals become 'free-riders'. Coercive transfers may therefore be Pareto-efficient, and increase the welfare of the rich as well as the poor (the rich would vote for a compulsory system which eliminates the free-riding inherent in charitable transfers). Such an argument is more fully developed in Mueller (1979).

A third argument for social insurance is that people will not make appropriate provision because they systematically underestimate their own risks. This motive, discussed below under the heading of 'paternalism', was explicit in much of the early literature of welfare economics, although some important charitable organizations did not accept this as a justification for state involvement, preferring instead to encourage greater awareness and self-help.

Fourthly, it has been suggested that an income support scheme which is presented as a form of social 'insurance' may be used by governments as a method of raising revenue. By linking income support to special ('earmarked') contributions, it may be possible to raise taxable capacity, even though individual contributions bear no relation to benefits received. The revenue-raising role of a pseudo-social insurance scheme may in some ways be related to the theory of 'fiscal illusion', associated with the name of Puviani (and discussed by Buchanan, 1967, and Wagner, 1976). This aspect is also examined in more detail below and in Part 4.

Finally, a comparison of state and private provision must involve an assessment of the administrative costs of each system. Some of these aspects are brought together in the final subsection below.

Market Failure

The types of market failure examined here concern situations in which the private market fails to meet the demand for insurance, so that some individuals are 'quantity constrained'. The private market should be interpreted in a wide sense, since insurance is provided not only by specialist insurance companies but also by employers who agree to pay constant wages in the face of varying demand conditions (following the theory of 'implicit contracts'). One interesting example may, however, be mentioned of a situation in which self-insurance may lead to *over*saving in aggregate. In high-risk but relatively low-cost situations, Pauly (1968) argued that a risk-sharing system can be more efficient by ensuring that the contracts reflect the *actual* probabilities of events occurring, rather than depending on the probabilities perceived by highly risk-averse individuals.

Several types of market failure can be identified. The first type occurs where the risk are *non-diversifiable*, so that risk-pooling would not be viable. Examples of these risks are those of war, mass unemployment, high inflation, and epidemics. A state could not in these cases provide genuine insurance contracts, but the value-judgement may be made that the state should provide support to those who suffer from such events, over which they could not be expected to have any control. This may well involve significant redistribution *ex post*, but is not really predicated by a deliberate redistributive policy, involving systematic transfers from the relatively rich to the relatively poor. Intergenerational redistribution may also be involved in those cases where the method chosen, to finance the payments to those who suffer, shifts the main burden of taxation to future generations (when debt is redeemed).

A second type of market failure arises from what is called *adverse selection*. This problem arises from population heterogeneity in the risks faced by individuals, combined with asymmetric information about those risks. For example an insurer would prefer, by risk-rating, to relate the individual premium to the probability of the outcome occurring to that individual. Thus a smoker or heavy drinker may face a higher premium in a scheme of sickness benefits, and a young driver of a sports car would pay much more for motor insurance than a middle-aged driver of a medium-sized saloon car. But in some cases it may be very difficult to identify individual risks, and even if the risks could be identified the screening costs may be very high. Insurance companies may therefore not attempt risk-rating, or may use only simple rules of thumb regarding easily identified characteristics, and would simply charge higher premiums for all contracts to meet the higher costs of insuring the high-risk individuals. (The use of this type of rule-of-thumb risk-rating is of course also relevant to theories of labour market segmentation.) However, those individuals who know that they face low risks will rapidly transfer to insurance companies which require lower premiums for the same cover. Thus where individuals initially have more information than the insurer about the risks they face, there will be an incentive to use more effective risk-rating, where possible. This may have the effect of raising the price of insurance to prohibitive levels for the high-risk individuals, particularly if high risks are associated with low income and wealth. If risk-rating is very difficult (even using extensive screening methods) then the use of more or less arbitrary rules may exclude some individuals altogether from the market for insurance.

The problem of adverse selection may then be used to support the role of a compulsory state scheme; that is, one from which the low-risk individuals could not contract out (otherwise the revenue would not be available to pay sufficient benefits). A counter-argument is that the state could operate risk-rating by having more access to information, and the high-premium people could be dealt with by separate income transfers, based on explicit value-judgements about the income redistribution (if high risks are generally associated with low incomes). Alternatively the redistribution inherent in risk-spreading in a heterogeneous population may be thought to be justified on insurance grounds. Indeed, where individuals themselves are also unaware of the differential risks they face, it is not difficult to show that (redistributive) insurance provides a Pareto improvement. This has been demonstrated by Varian (1980) for unemployment insurance, and by Smith (1982) for intergenerational transfers arising from pensions. However, if in fact individuals do have some idea of the risks they face (even though this information may be gained *ex post*), they are likely to perceive the government intervention as a redistributive policy. Great care must therefore be taken in dealing with insurance and redistributive motives in favour of state action. It will be suggested later in this book that the designers of state schemes in Britain, especially regarding unemployment insurance, have failed to consider adequately the problems arising from population heterogeneity. In the context of pensions the implications, for contracting out, of adverse selection also seem to have been given too little attention.

A third market failure arises from the problem of *moral hazard*; that is, the existence of insurance may affect the individual's behaviour such that less effort is taken to avoid the event. Moral hazard essentially arises because of asymmetric information about the actions of those purchasing insurance, since those actions cannot be monitored fully by the insurance company. For an extended treatment of this issue, see Stiglitz (1983). In private insurance schemes, methods such as the use of co-insurance or deductibles have been devised in an attempt to avoid this disincentive problem. In this context it is worth noting that the early private unemployment insurance schemes were operated by fairly homogeneous groups of workers in the same industry and locality, where information about benefit recipients' behaviour was much easier to monitor.

If the absence of private provision is judged to arise from moral hazard, this does not necessarily provide a justification for state intervention, since it cannot be implicitly assumed that the state, simply because it has more 'authority', can always monitor behaviour where private markets fail. However, the problem of moral hazard has usually preoccupied the debates on state support, whether in the form of the old Poor Law (which relied on 'less eligibility' and on close monitoring by the use of the workhouse), or in more modern forms of social insurance. Thus the payment of unemployment benefit has usually been linked with a 'work test', involving the use of labour exchanges, and individuals are disqualified from receiving benefits for a certain period if they are dismissed from their previous employment, leave voluntarily, or are on strike (though dependants continue to receive Supplementary Benefits). It is therefore interesting to note that, at a time when complaints about the incentive effects of the social insurance system are very high, new regulations have been introduced involving self-certification for limited periods of sickness, and the elimination of the need to register at an employment office or job centre (to be seen to be actively seeking employment). These recent changes have in fact been motivated by a strong desire to reduce administration costs, combined with considerable emphasis being placed on the effects of high (theoretical) replacement rates on labour supply incentives, to the neglect of eligibility conditions and direct attempts to monitor the behaviour of claimants. Administrative costs and theoretical replacement rates are not difficult to calculate, unlike the actual moral hazard effects of particular social insurance regimes, and it seems likely that policy has concentrated on the more 'visible' features in carrying out its objective of retrenchment.

There is an important risk which has not so far been mentioned; that is, the risk of being unable to support one's dependants, through unemployment, sickness, or because of other income reductions. It would perhaps be expected that the explicit analysis of this type of risk would have played a part in the design of regulations concerning Child Benefits and pensions for spouses, widows, and widowers. In this context the problem of moral hazard would also feature as a central issue, concerning for example the extent to which family formation is affected by the ability to shift part of the cost of support to the state scheme. Although family support schemes have in the past been suggested explicitly in order to stimulate population growth, Child Benefits are now usually examined entirely separately from social insurance, perhaps because of the extremely sensitive nature of the moral hazard aspects. Similarly, pension benefits for dependants provide a further example of the extent to which the term 'insurance' is a complete misnomer when applied to actual state pension schemes in existence. Treatment of the risks in an insurance framework is further complicated by the existence of large intra-family, intergenerational transfers.

In principle the 'failures' of the market for private insurance offer important reasons for seriously considering the use of a state insurance scheme even though, Stiglitz (1983) argues, an optimal state scheme would still involve quantity rationing where moral hazard exists. Nevertheless there are failures of other markets which may be thought to support a role for the state, in the context of retirement pensions and insurance against poverty in old age. An important case is the existence of a capital market which allows individuals to accumulate savings for self-insurance. Even the optimal provision of unemployment and sickness insurance will be conditioned by whether or not a capital market exists which facilitates short-term borrowing (see Flemming, 1978). For example, small investors may be unable to develop portfolios of investments which allow them to combine reasonable yields with security of capital value (Diamond, 1977). One feature is the absence of an array of indexed financial assets which allows investors to hedge against inflation. As Diamond points out, this market failure in itself might not lead the government to offer social insurance but rather to intervene in the capital market by offering index-linked assets. This has to some extent happened in the United Kingdom. However, a failure of indexation in the capital market will have implications also for the form of state social insurance. The private and state provision of indexed pensions will be examined in more detail in Chapter 4.

Redistribution

It has already been shown that an insurance scheme may imply some systematic redistribution if there is no risk-rating and if the population is heterogeneous with respect to risks faced by individuals. If, in addition, high risks are correlated with low earnings while in employment, then there will be some systematic redistribution from the relatively rich to the relatively poor, thereby reducing inequality. This type of redistribution may, in *ex ante* terms, be seen as a Pareto improvement. Some people may well support the view that social insurance should be designed to produce more explicit redistribution. Those in favour of much redistribution, depending on their value-judgements, may wish to employ any possible methods of redistribution which they believe are available. Others may nevertheless feel that a social insurance system does not provide a particularly effective mechanism of income redistribution, arguing that much more direct transfers from rich to poor could be devised. Here again is a situation in which the policy recommended depends to a considerable degree on judgements about empirical orders of magnitude, as well as on value-judgements held.

It is certainly true that redistribution through social insurance operates in a very indirect way when compared with other selective transfers. The relationship between the contributions to a state insurance scheme and the benefits received over a long period of time is very complex, and there is very little information available for studying this issue. There would of course be little point in considering only a very short-term measure of income. Changes in policy involve, for example, changes in eligibility conditions, regulations concerning averaging periods, exhaustion of benefits, earnings ceilings, and so on. The contributions and benefit formulae are only two of very many relevant factors, although this point does not seem to be widely appreciated. The redistributive aspects of unemployment, sickness, and pension schemes are therefore examined at length in this book. This issue involves many conceptual problems in addition to more technical data and measurement problems, and these aspects are also discussed.

Paternalism

The paternalist case for intervention argues that individuals, left to their own devices, will make inadequate provision for states of the world such as unemployment, sickness, child-rearing, or old age, even when insurance and capital markets exist which allow them to provide for such circumstances. A state social insurance system with compulsory contributions will force individuals to make some provision, and this motive therefore is also known as an argument for 'forced saving'. The paternalistic argument usually supports the state provision of a minimum income for individuals if certain states of the world occur. But the paternalistic argument finds it more difficult to justify benefits well above the minimum (such as earnings-related benefits) where there is a stronger possibility of forcing people to save more than they might (even with the benefit of hindsight). Furthermore, when there is a fully developed state social insurance system with compulsory saving, it is difficult to know what individuals would have saved had there been no state system. This problem leads Wilson (1980) to argue that the criterion for judging the social insurance system should be the scope it allows for individuals to express their preferences, for example as between flat-rate and earnings-related benefits.

Diamond (1977) puts forward a number of justifications for the paternalist argument. One is that individuals may be unable to obtain sufficient information as to the relevant probabilities. For example, individuals cannot predict the rate of unemployment in ten years' time. As another illustration, individuals may underinsure relative to the risk of high losses and overinsure relative to small losses, as Kunreuther (1976) and Slovic *et al.* (1977) found for earthquake and flood damage. In contrast, in Chapter 8 it is argued in the context of sickness insurance that if medical and media information give greater prominence to long-term illness (serious accidents, heart disease, or cancer) and less to repetitive illness (such as influenza, respiratory problems, or backache), the reverse may occur. In the case of pensions, myopia may simply lead to insufficient saving in early years of the working life, although individuals in this case have some chance to make adjustments later in life. Yet another approach to paternalism in the context of pensions, also used by Diamond (1977) in analysing the US pension scheme, is to use survey data to ask whether individuals appear to act in practice in a sensible way in their savings plans. While acknowledging the dangers of this approach, his own conclusion is that actual wealth–income ratios of the population cast doubt on the proposition that individuals would have followed sensible savings plans in the absence of social security. He therefore argues that paternalist intervention has raised social welfare.

A more general difficulty, already mentioned, is to determine the optimal level of social insurance provision to be offered by the paternalist state. For example, it cannot simply be assumed that there should be full earnings replacement for the unemployed. Taking a contrasting case, Sen (1973) argues that an invalid should be given more money than when healthy if his or her capacity to derive utility from a given income is impaired. However, both Wilson (1980) and Hemming (1984) point to an even more general case. If capacity to derive utility from income depends on the standard of living to which the person has become accustomed, this provides a case for relating benefits to past earnings. Such a scheme would, on other redistributive or even some other paternalist grounds, prove objectionable. It is difficult therefore to give a clear guide to optimal provision by this argument. Furthermore, the paternalistic case does not rest too easily with the usual assumption made in economic analysis that individuals themselves are the best judges of their welfare in various circumstances, so that they can be said to be better off in chosen positions. As mentioned above, the paternalist case for state social insurance has often been put very strongly, but considerable caution must be exercised before asserting that all that has been done paternally in the UK social insurance system has increased social welfare.

Fund-raising

It was suggested earlier that, by creating the 'insurance myth' that individuals are in some sense paying for their benefits in one period from contributions (earmarked taxes) in other periods, taxable capacity may be increased. It has not been difficult to create such an illusion especially where many individuals may believe that they are 'passing on' the burden of their contributions to others, even if those beliefs are mutually inconsistent. This point relates to the special problem of the extremely uncertain incidence of taxes which are in the form of National Insurance contributions levied on employees *and* employers. Furthermore, the way in which the income tax system interacts with the NI contributions system may not be clear to many taxpayers. Some of these aspects are examined in more detail in Part 4.

Table 1.1 shows that around 40 per cent of benefits were non-contributory and financed out of general taxation, but the remaining 60 per cent are financed by National Insurance contributions. These contributions are paid into the National Insurance Fund and the contribution rate is set each April in order to balance receipts and outgoings in the forthcoming year. Table 1.2. presents the accounts of the National Insurance Fund for the tax year 1981–2. However, although contribution rates are normally set such that the Fund balances each year, an unexpected increase in the rate of earnings growth may lead to a surplus of receipts over payments where benefit rates have already been fixed (the preceding November) and the contribution rate is a fixed proportion of earnings. In principle a surplus in one year can be offset by a lower contributions rate next year, but in practice this has not always happened in the UK. For example Fig. 1.1 shows the net surplus (deficit) of receipts relative to outgoings of the Fund in recent years and it will be seen that during the mid-1970s, net receipts exceeded outgoings for several years. This stemmed from a combination of rising earnings and the introduction of earnings-related contributions for the new state pension scheme (described in more detail in Part 3).

TABLE 1.2   *Receipts and payments of the National Insurance Fund 1981–2*

Receipts		Payments	
Contributions from employees		Unemployment Benefit	1,702
and employers	14,035	Sickness Benefit	680
Supplement from Exchequer	2,433	Invalidity Benefit	1,371
Net investment income	588	Retirement Pension	12,227
		Widows Benefits	691
		Other benefits	549
		Expenses*	707
		Other payments	120
Total	17,055		18,047

* Paid to the DHSS (for administering benefits other than Unemployment Benefit), the DE (for administering Unemployment Benefit), and other departments.

Source: DHSS, *Social Security Statistics* 1983, HMSO.

The existence of a partial 'fund' (which may itself help to create the illusion that a state scheme is based on insurance principles) provides a further reason why governments may be attracted by the use of 'insurance' contributions. Any surplus must be used by the Fund to purchase government securities. It is not invested in order to provide more generous benefit rates to 'members' of the scheme. It can be used directly as a means of financing government borrowing in a way which helps to support monetary policy. In contrast, when the Fund showed a substantial deficit in 1982, stemming from lower than expected inflation and rising unemployment, the government was quick to raise the contribution rate in order to balance the Fund. Indeed the employers' surcharge on National Insurance contributions, introduced in 1976 and abolished in 1984, was paid directly to the central Exchequer and was quite explicitly a revenue-raising device, in a period when the government was constrained in its ability to raise revenue by other means.

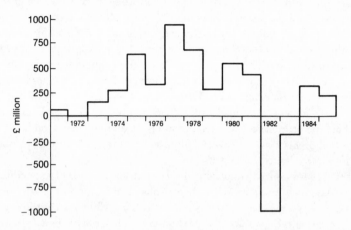

Fig. 1.1   *Excess (deficit) of receipts over payments of the National Insurance Fund 1971–85*

Notes: All values are current prices. Figures pre-1976 include Industrial Injuries Fund. 1985 (financial year 1984–5) represents estimated out-turn.

Source: DHSS *Social Security Statistics* 1983, HMSO. Report by Government Actuary, Cmnd. 8969, 1983, HMSO.

Administrative efficiency

Comparisons between the private and state provision of insurance often point to the low ratio of benefits to premiums generally offered in private schemes before the various tax advantages have been taken into account. There is little doubt that the selling costs associated with private insurance are extremely high, although to some extent these costs may be regarded as a justifiable cost of providing a greater diversity of policies and an ability to vary policies to suit the special needs of individuals. It is sometimes also suggested that state schemes can obtain significant economies of scale in addition to eliminating selling costs (though of course large costs of providing information would remain with a state scheme). Such economies may be relevant with regard to the collection and assessment of information about risks, and there may be economies of 'decision-taking'. A complete evaluation of the case for state provision would need to make an extensive study of these types of cost and benefit.

As with the other arguments discussed in this section, it cannot be taken for granted that state organization would succeed where private markets are judged to be less than 'perfect'. Relevant considerations include the actual objectives of the decision-takers and administrators in a state scheme; it is not obvious that they seek always to improve 'social welfare', however perceived. Some insights into these aspects has recently been provided by literature on the economics of bureaucracies (see, for example, Jackson, 1983). It is thus worth emphasizing that the idea of 'administrative efficiency' involves much wider issues than the straightforward examination of directly measurable costs, although this may not always be appreciated by those with the primary objective of cutting government expenditure.

It is also worth comparing the relative proportion of expenditure devoted to administration in the various components of the UK social security system. Recent figures from *Hansard* (23 February 1982) give administrative costs, as a proportion of benefits, of less than 3 per cent for a flat-rate universal benefit (Child Benefit), rising to 3 to 4 per cent for National Insurance, which relates eligibility to past contributions. This rises to 11 per cent for Supplementary Benefit, which involves means-testing, and to 15 per cent for some local authority means-tested benefits such as rent rebates. Before 1983 unemployment insurance benefits used to incur an even higher administrative cost, since each claim required registration both at the benefit office and job centre, but only one registration (at the benefit office) is now required.

1.2 The Analysis of the State

The preceding discussion, of arguments which are relevant to the question of the appropriate extent and nature of state intervention in social insurance, has involved a mixture of value-judgements and empirical issues, combined with conventional analysis of economic efficiency. Section 1.1 therefore provides a basic frame of reference around which an assessment of social insurance can be made. There is a wide range of combinations of value and empirical judgements which may consistently be held by individuals, and the framework may be used to provide a wide taxonomic analysis. Before considering some alternative state schemes, and details of the UK experience of social insurance, it is first necessary to say something about the use of the term 'the state' in this analysis.

In this chapter the institution of the state has essentially been treated as a vehicle for carrying out the required form of intervention. This may be suggested by a perceived deficiency of private provision, whether a market failure, lack of optimal redistribution, or some other motive. However, the fact that a case for state provision has been identified neither guarantees that the state will intervene in practice or that the actual form of state intervention is compatible with this motive. In essence, the state is perceived as an agent external to the economy, in the tradition of welfare economics. In effect, the state is brought in by the economist to intervene where the market economy is unable to fulfill certain social objectives satisfactorily.

There are a number of objections which can be made to this approach, which are worth examining briefly. The first objection has often been raised within the discipline of social administration, and argues that the perspective of the role of the state held by the economist effectively 'marginalizes' the role of the state. In this way it correspondingly overemphasizes the role of the market economy in producing a socially optimal allocation of economic resources. In contrast, it is argued, analysis should place a greater weight on the alternative set of values and methods of social organization embodied in the term 'welfare state'. Consequently social, or state, involvement should not be limited simply to whatever the market economy cannot provide. Now while it is true to say that many economists have argued for greater market provision of goods and services potentially or actually provided by the state, the above framework does allow a very wide range of degrees of state involvement and forms of state provision (depending particularly on the value assigned to the redistributive role of the state). Indeed, the economist would argue that criteria such as those outlined in this chapter must be used in assessing actual state provision and in pointing to various conflicts that may arise and choices that will have to be made. The possibility of a conflict, between the form of state involvement that is socially desirable and that which is economically sustainable, is a theme of increasing importance throughout the welfare state (see Gough, 1979). Furthermore, examination of state involvement by reference to these criteria may cast light on the discrepancy between the redistributive promise of the welfare state and the actual practice, noted recently by Le Grand (1982).

It must be emphasized that the present study does not attempt to develop a well-formulated *positive* theory of state behaviour; that is, an explanation of precisely why state intervention in social insurance provision in the United Kingdom has taken the form it has. Nevertheless, some cautious inferences will be drawn as the analysis proceeds. At a theoretical level, positive theories of state intervention can be developed in several frameworks. One is the public choice framework, summarized in Mueller (1979). A detailed description of public choice theories is beyond the scope of this book, but an illustration may cast some light on what such theories offer. One theory predicts that the tax system will tend to redistribute income from the rich not to the poorest but to middle-income groups. If redistribution takes place by a political process in which voters form coalitions according to their income position, and if majority voting is used to determine outcomes, it is the median or middle-income voters who wield the strongest effective power. Their choice of whether to join a coalition of the rich (preserving the status quo) or the poor (advocating redistribution) will determine which side eventually triumphs. It is worthwhile for both rich and poor to bribe the median voters to join their coalition and so median voters do well. This is of course a naïve model, but more sophisticated models can be developed to suggest that 'redistribution through selfishness' rather than generosity is compatible with observed redistribution (Culyer, 1980).

Other frameworks yield positive theories of state intervention; a number of perspectives are summarized in Room (1979). One is a Marxist perspective in which the 'welfare state' is seen, not as antithetical to the market economy, but as a necessary complementary factor. In this framework actual state intervention is conditioned by the need to reinforce or maintain the market economy itself (Gough, 1979; Ginsburg, 1979). However analysis of actual state provision in any one area using such analysis proves to be quite complex. For some successes and failures of such an approach in the context of unemployment insurance, see Disney (1982).

2
The Historical Background

Chapter 1 examined the main economic arguments relating to state social insurance provision. These were arranged under the main headings of market failure, redistribution, paternalism, revenue raising, and administrative efficiency. It has been suggested that there are many problems of attempting to rationalize, *ex post*, any social insurance system in a complex and changing political environment. For example, the existence of a sound economic argument in favour of a policy does not by itself provide any grounds for saying that the argument has any direct bearing on the policy decision. Recognizing this type of problem, the present chapter reviews the origins and development of state provision in the United Kingdom. It is argued that this type of exercise is useful in illustrating possible inconsistencies, and failures to allow for particular policy 'trade-offs', in past decision-taking. This chapter therefore does not actually attempt to test any 'positive' theory of the state, but to evaluate previous state actions in terms of a framework of economic analysis. Being 'wise after the event' is after all an important part of the process of learning, and should help to promote more rational analyses of policy options in the future.

State provision in the United Kingdom was conditioned by the existence of extensive private provision, some of which contained the kernel of the basic ideas of social insurance. This was in clear contrast to Germany, for example, where an early integrated and extensive social insurance system was introduced in the 1880s for explicitly paternalistic motives, and as a way of consolidating an autocratic state (Rimlinger, 1971). Motives in the United Kingdom will be seen to have varied from programme to programme. In section 2.1, state provision in the United Kingdom in three main areas of social insurance is examined. These are unemployment, sickness and invalidity, and pensions. Section 2.2 then reviews means-tested benefits and family benefits. Other expenditures and taxes are not discussed in detail here; an analysis of the historical development of many ideas in public finance which in turn underpinned state intervention through general tax and expenditure programmes is contained in Creedy (1984).

2.1 The Main Insurance Schemes

Unemployment insurance

State provision of unemployment insurance in the United Kingdom began in 1911 when compulsory insurance, financed by flat-rate contributions from employees, employers, and the central Exchequer, was introduced. Coverage was limited to several 'scheduled trades' which were perceived to be especially prone to cyclical unemployment, and benefits were flat-rate and limited in duration. Unemployment insurance had previously been organized through trade unions, although coverage was thereby limited largely to skilled and craft workers. In return for a weekly contribution when in employment, members of the union would receive a donation when out of work and in some cases, help in finding a new post. This took the form of payment of travelling expenses and the operation of labour exchanges through trade union branches. Benefits were often generous but limited in duration. Other normal provisions, later embodied in the state insurance scheme, included provisions for 'waiting days' and various other exclusions According to Beveridge (1930) the largest 100 unions paid £4 million in unemployment benefits in the ten-year period 1898–1907.

Those who were not membe s of insuring unions had two sources of poor relief. Some would rely on outside relief where available, under the Poor Law, while others (after the 1905 Unemployed Workmen Act) relied upon public works provided by local Distress Committees. Relief under the Poor Law and the 1905 Act was provided on the basis of 'less eligibility'; that is, benefits should not exceed the amount paid to the lowest paid labourer in employment.

The market failure motive might suggest that the 1911 Act would extend coverage to that part of the labour force not covered by trade union schemes. However in general this was not so; although trade unions only covered one quarter of manual industrial workers, state unemployment insurance was introduced in areas where there was already relatively strong union coverage. In fact the 1911 provisions were modelled on the existing trade union schemes in many important respects, notably eligibility requirements and duration limitations.

Indeed the state benefits could be paid through existing trade union schemes. The major difference was that the state scheme was still conditioned by 'less eligibility', although benefits could be 'topped up' by trade union schemes. In addition, an initial attempt was made to encourage experience-rating in the state scheme, whereby a refund of part of the employer's contribution was made to any employer who retained a workman for at least 45 weeks in a year. This provision was dropped in 1920 as it proved administratively costly.

The 1911 Act, by placing part of the notional incidence of finance on employers and the state, appeared to offer a wider tax base than simply relying on the contributions of workers, as in the trade union schemes. Nevertheless unions were well aware of the distinction between notional and effective incidence, and argued against the contribution by employers. They thought that such contributions would simply be shifted to employees, through lower wages, and instead advocated a larger Exchequer subsidy to the state scheme. The state insurance scheme was not explicitly concerned with redistribution, and by limiting coverage to several 'cyclical' trades and to the skilled working class, the degree of systematic redistribution was also narrow. However, the later analysis by Beveridge (1936) showed that there was systematic redistribution in the state scheme between net contributors and high-risk individuals. This had also proved to be the case in the trade union schemes, as shown in their pre-1914 statistical returns to the Board of Trade (Beveridge, 1930).

State involvement was conditioned by the insistence on a distinction between those unemployed through inferior 'personal characteristics' and those suffering the effects of the trade cycle (Harris, 1972). Although Beveridge (1930) clearly recognized that cyclical unemployment had a systematic effect throughout the labour market, and that those with the least skills and qualifications suffered the worst incidence of unemployment, the uninsured were *not* initially accepted into the state scheme. It was felt that such extensions would contradict the 'less eligibility' requirement. The 1911 Act was a compromise between those who wanted to extend coverage along the lines initiated by the trade unions and those who saw unemployment insurance, coupled with the introduction of employment exchanges, as a way of improving the functioning of the labour market and discouraging malingering (Gilbert, 1966; Yeo, 1979).

The 1916 extension of unemployment insurance added seven new 'war trades' to the list. This and later extensions were not concerned with redistribution or market failure but stemmed from the revenue-raising motive. The Treasury feared a sharp rise in unemployment insurance and poor relief claims, following rapid demobilization, and wished to extend contributory insurance into as many areas as possible. But it faced concerted opposition, particularly from trades such as textiles where unemployment had been relatively low and where alternative arrangements had evolved (such as work-sharing and guaranteed pay; see Whiteside, 1980). The contributory unemployment insurance scheme was finally extended into most parts of the labour market in 1920, but not before a concession was made in the form of the 'out-of-work donation', or 'dole'.

The out-of-work donation supplemented insurance benefits by extending the duration of benefits, introducing dependants' allowances, and paying the benefit irrespective of contributions. This stop-gap, non-contributory, non-means-tested benefit continued to exist under various guises, such as 'uncovenanted benefits' or 'transitional payments', throughout the 1920s (Burns, 1941). Their rationale was the high average level of unemployment which blurred the distinction between the 'cyclical' trades and structural unemployment, but the strain on the financial soundness of the Unemployment Insurance Fund was a continuing problem throughout the period. The Treasury was forced to supplement its contribution to the Fund over and above the provisions of the insurance scheme. Attempts were made to debar payments by enforcing other exclusions concerning the work test, but it was only in 1930, under the Unemployment Insurance Act, that the solution of financing these transitional payments out of general taxation was made.

The relatively generous level of the transitional payments has been suggested as a *cause* of the high inter-war unemployment in Britain in the controversial paper by Benjamin and Kochin (1979). This issue is examined in more detail in Chapter 12. The payments led to the next great crisis of the unemployment insurance scheme, when the 1931 Exchequer deficit included transitional payments of £19 million. The following political crisis led to budgetary measures which reduced the level of insurance benefits and, more significantly in the long term, implemented means-testing for non-contributory benefits. Means-testing had been placed in the hands of local authorities but several of them, at least in the view of the government, failed to enforce the test with sufficient vigour. Accordingly the 1934 Unemployment Act centralized the provision of such benefits in the hands of the Unemployment Assistance Board. This occurred despite intense opposition from some local authorities (Briggs and Deacon, 1973).

The inter-war period therefore revealed conflicts over the operation of the unemployment insurance system. These conflicts included the method of raising revenue, the acceptable degree of systematic redistribution within a contributory scheme, and the extent of market failure identified during an era of mass unemployment. These issues were of importance in influencing the Committee on Social Insurance and Allied Services (chaired by Beveridge) which reported in 1942. The committee believed that a contributory unemployment insurance scheme was only financially viable with a high level of employment. Their desire to establish a unified contributory insurance system for unemployment, ill-health, and old age depended on the establishment of benefits at a 'subsistence' level, and an explicit commitment by the government to full employment.

The 1944 White Paper and the subsequent 1946 National Insurance Act represented in many respects the high tide of the contributory insurance scheme. Many of the provisions in the 1946 Act paralleled earlier legislation, especially contribution requirements and various exclusions from benefit. Unemployment Benefits were payable for seven months and for up to a further year if the past contribution history has been satisfactory. In 1966 this was standardized for unemployment benefit at a maximum duration of one year. Unemployment Assistance was integrated into a general scheme of National Assistance for those with inadequate contributions. In 1966 this scheme was retitled the Supplementary Benefit scheme. The vestiges of 'less eligibility' remained, as unemployed claimants to Supplementary Benefit have only been able to claim the short-term rate of benefit, (which has been lower than the long-term rate since 1973). However, both contributory and non-contributory benefits include dependants' allowances.

The major post-war development was the general shift towards earnings-related benefits and contributions. The latter were introduced in 1961. Increased inducements to reallocate labour came in the form of redundancy payments in 1965, and in 1966 an Earnings Related Supplement for the first six months of receipt of Unemployment Benefit was introduced. This Supplement lasted only until 1980, when it was announced in the Budget that it would be phased out during 1982, although earnings-related contributions remain. A 5 per cent real reduction in the value of Unemployment Benefit in the 1980 Budget was introduced as an 'interim measure'. The rise in the average duration of unemployment, as the rate of unemployment rose to levels not seen since the early 1930s, led to an increasing proportion of the unemployed being in receipt of means-tested Supplementary Benefit rather than National Insurance benefits. In 1981–2, as Fig. 1.1 revealed, the National Insurance Fund went into sharp deficit for the first time since the 1930s. Benefit cuts and Fund deficits seemed to highlight the return of the types of problem experienced in the inter-war years.

Sickness and invalidity benefits

State provision of sickness and invalidity benefits began earlier than unemployment benefits. The 1897 Workmens Compensation Act introduced a compulsory scheme of contributory insurance for industrial accidents. In general however the history of sickness and invalidity insurance is the clearest example of state social insurance complementing and, in some cases, competing with private provision.

It is useful to start from the introduction of general state sickness insurance benefits in the 1911 National Insurance Act. Private benefits were at this time provided from two main sources. First, there were numerous Friendly Societies which in 1898 had 4.2 million members. These were voluntary organizations for the payment of benefits, such as sickness and invalidity insurance, funeral benefits and widows' and orphans' benefits, financed from individual contributions. This enormous growth of collective self-help stemmed from the Victorian period. Eligibility conditions and the organization of individual societies varied considerably, from merely 'collecting Societies' to full mutual aid associations in which there was explicit systematic redistribution among members (Gosden, 1973; Yeo, 1979).

In the early years of the twentieth century, some Friendly Societies were facing considerable difficulties, mainly due to the increasing longevity of the population. The improvement in public health in the late nineteenth century and the consequent decline in cholera and typhoid was balanced by increasing long-term disability and retirement due to ill-health. Ill-equipped with actuarial evidence and expertise, Friendly Societies found themselves facing a rundown in their financial resources. However, attempts to institute pension and invalidity schemes in the Societies proved to be a failure (Gilbert,

1966). In addition, the unskilled working class and working women were poorly covered.

Secondly, there were the 'industrial' insurance companies, such as Prudential Insurance, which offered various forms of life insurance and funeral benefits. The commercial sector probably had the greater coverage of the poorest households, with 30 million outstanding funeral benefit policies in 1910 and 70,000 full-time door-to-door collectors. However the number of outstanding policies suggests that many policies were allowed to lapse. This over-selling of policies and the 15 to 20 per cent of receipts which went in commission meant that, on average, no more than 37 per cent of insurance company receipts was paid to beneficiaries (Gilbert, 1965).

The rationale for state intervention in each case is therefore clear. The Friendly Societies faced actuarial difficulties which posed potential problems of market failure, while state provision had clear advantages over the commercial sector for reasons of administrative efficiency and in the establishment of optimal saving levels. The original government proposals extended Friendly Society coverage by a once-and-for-all subsidy plus a requirement that sickness insurance be compulsory and operated through these 'Approved Societies'. However, Gilbert (1965, 1966) has shown that the commercial interests were able to lobby the government successfully so that orphans' and widows' benefits and, most important, funeral benefits, were excluded from the scheme. Furthermore, the commercial insurance companies were also treated as Approved Societies for payment of benefit. The 1911 Act provided sickness benefits payable for 26 weeks, a disability benefit, and a medical benefit to general practitioners for treatment. These were all financed by a contributory system similar to that for unemployment insurance and operated through the Approved Societies. Essentially the scheme had become a state-subsidized compulsory insurance scheme, with Friendly Societies no longer having a fraternal role and becoming 'distributors' rather than 'producers' of welfare (see Yeo, 1979).

This scheme survived throughout the inter-war period. The establishment of pensions removed the problem caused by increased longevity. However, there was a differential incidence of claimants and contributors among different groups, especially between men and women and among different geographical regions. Gilbert (1970, pp. 257–8) has shown that the richer Societies were unwilling to share their surplus with poorer Societies, while the latter were forced to pay minimum benefits and to insure higher risks.

Since the Societies had become little more than government agencies, appeared to face adverse selection problems, and were unable to take full advantage of risk-sharing, the case for direct state intervention seems clear. At least it appeared clear to Beveridge, who devoted an appendix in the 1942 *Social Insurance Report* to showing the high administrative costs of running this scheme of compulsory insurance through Approved Societies (although these administrative costs were no higher than those later associated with the payment of Supplementary Benefit).

In 1946 the scheme of compulsory sickness insurance through Approved Societies ended. Instead the sickness and invalidity schemes were merged with unemployment and pension provision to provide a single, compulsory, contributory scheme paying flat-rate benefits. In the case of sickness benefits, this meant the inclusion of the self-employed and some non-manual groups previously exempt from the inter-war scheme. Disablement Benefit was abolished, Sickness Benefits could now be paid for an unlimited duration, and dependants' allowances were introduced. A maternity allowance was included to supplement the maternity grant and a funeral benefit was added.

As with the other National Insurance benefits, there was a shift towards earnings-related benefits after 1946. From 1966 to 1982 Earnings Related Supplement could be paid for the first six months of the sickness spell and from 1971 the more radical change took place of introducing Invalidity Benefits for spells lasting longer than six months. This last change stemmed from the refusal of the Conservative government to implement the National Superannuation scheme of the outgoing Labour administration, which included provision for earnings-related pensions for the long-term disabled as well as ordinary pensioners. A flat-rate invalidity pension was substituted for the planned earnings-related scheme, but the Invalidity Benefit was payable at the long-term (and subsequently higher) National Insurance rate, and included an additional Invalid Allowance

Coupled with the introduction of various non-contributory benefits in the mid-1970s, the trend in the 1970s was towards marginally more generous treatment of long-term incapacity. However, during this period state provision for the short-term sick was conditioned by the growth of occupational sick-pay schemes (described in more detail in Chapter 8). The market failure argument for state provision in the short-term became less convincing and from 1983 a new scheme has come into operation for the first eight weeks of a sickness spell. This scheme, Employer's Statutory Sick Pay (SSP), abolishes the contribution condition and makes employers responsible for payment of sick pay, although the amounts paid will normally be refunded by the government. Part of the administrative cost of the scheme is therefore shifted to employers. Coupled with the abolition of Earnings Related Supplement and a change in the eligibility conditions (see discussion of the spell-linking rule in Chapter 7), the effect has been to reduce the generosity of state short-term sickness benefits quite sharply. Privately administered, but state subsidized, provision has once more come to dominate insurance for the short-term sick.

Pensions

Unlike unemployment and sickness insurance, the first step towards state pensions followed a non-contributory means-tested path. For the reasons described earlier, Friendly Societies were in financial difficulty, although they did not always appreciate the nature of their problem. Many were therefore reluctant to raise their contribution rates, and it was difficult for others to do so because of competition among Societies. Yet as late as 1895 the majority of a Royal Commission had argued that the number of aged poor was declining and therefore contributory state pensions were unnecessary. In contrast, from the 1870s onwards, those arguing for state provision were split between believers in the contributory principle (who therefore essentially presented a paternalist case for intervention) and those who believed that the aged poor, including women and the unskilled, would be unable to afford the necessary contributions. The latter group therefore argued for a means-tested non-contributory pension financed out of general taxation; in other words for a degree of systematic redistribution (Thane, 1978). This group won the day when in 1908 the government introduced a non-contributory pension to all individuals aged over 70 subject to a means test and various tests of 'good character'. The potential threats to 'less eligibility' and the level of private saving were lessened by setting the benefit rate at an extremely low level, some 30 per cent lower than the 1911 contributory sickness and unemployment benefits. However, with benefit payments under the 1908 Act soon running at an annual level of over £6 million, this was to prove the only step along the non-contributory road.

After the 1914–18 War pensions were raised but further extension of state pensions was stifled by a deadlock between supporters of non-contributory pensions and advocates of contributory pensions. The former group included trade unions and major employers who agreed that further increases in flat-rate contributions would hit both wage-earners and employers. The latter group was led by the Treasury which wished to keep the scheme of National Insurance to raise further finance (Gilbert, 1970). The 1925 Contributory Pensions Act therefore established a compromise. All National Insurance contributors would pay an additional contribution which would guarantee a basic pension at the age of 65, and would then be entitled to receive the non-contributory pension at age 70. There were also payments for dependants and widows, and since payments started almost immediately, the Treasury faced an additional lump-sum expenditure to finance payments not 'covered' by past contributions. Thus, in the pay-as-you-go system, contributions were not raised immediately to a scale sufficient to cover all present claimants. Although it was still a flat-rate scheme there was nevertheless some degree of systematic redistribution. In addition, there were elements of forced saving (paternalism), and revenue-raising through the contributory system. It was therefore the inter-war period which saw the evolution of the integrated National Insurance system of flat-rate contributions financing flat-rate unemployment and sickness insurance and at least some pensions.

Two other inter-war amendments were made. In 1929 the Labour government made widows of insurable men eligible for pensions at age 55, and in 1937 a further Act extended pensions to higher-paid workers (the 'black-coated workers' Act). This extension was voluntary and apparently had rather low take-up (Gilbert, 1970). This may have been introduced as a revenue-raising device rather than from any other motive, since it thereby incorporated a greater number of high-earning contributors, although of course contributions were still flat-rate (to merge with the other components of National Insurance). Nevertheless the number of old people on poor relief continued to rise throughout the 1930s, largely, it may be presumed, because they had accumulated insufficient contributions. This led to an important change in 1940 in which the Unemployment Assistance Board was renamed the Assistance Board and took over the task of paying means-tested benefits both to old people as well as to the unemployed who were ineligible for contributory benefits.

State pension provision prior to 1945 had largely been an append-age to the important innovations of contributory state unemployment and sickness insurance. State pensions after 1945 came to dominate state social insurance provision. The 1946 National Insurance Act introduced a flat-rate contributory pension for all men aged 65 and over, and all women aged 60 and over, with receipt of a full pension being conditional on retirement from the active labour force. Since the proportion of the population over retirement age rose by over 45 per cent between 1941 and 1976, while unemployment fell to historically low levels and sickness claims stabilized, the finance of the pension scheme became the major issue of social insurance policy.

It may be asked why after 1945 the commitment was made to a universal pension rather than, say, a means-tested payment to those with insufficient savings. The answer would seem to be that by treating the scheme as a 'quasi-insurance' contributory scheme, larger sums of money could be raised than would have been possible with a non-contributory means-tested scheme financed from general taxation. A paternalist motive plus the possibility of a market failure in the capital market may also be added. Beveridge himself empha-sized the 'subsistence principle'; that it was the duty of the state to provide at least a minimum standard of living through a system of 'social insurance' (George, 1968), but this became eroded as it became increasingly difficult to finance such a costly scheme through flat-rate contributions.

Two other points may be mentioned. First the redistributive motive does not seem to be important: a flat-rate benefit and flat-rate contri-butory system only systematically redistributes due to differential mortality, as shown in Part 2. However some intergenerational redistribution was consequent upon the 'blanketing-in' of people reaching retirement age without sufficient years of contributions under the new scheme. This extra cost was financed by a Treasury subsidy plus a reduction in the level of the flat-rate benefit for all pensioners. But this reduction in National Insurance benefits in turn put the level of the pension just below the official designated poverty level of National Assistance (later Supplementary Benefit) so that many pensioners continued to rely on additional means-tested bene-fits (Atkinson, 1969; Kincaid, 1973). Secondly, people who wished to continue working could defer their pension rights for up to five years, or take their pension and receive the whole or part of it up to a certain level of earnings (the 'earnings rule'), also for five years, after which they received the full pension. Why the state should force individuals to retire from the labour force, or penalize them for not retiring, is difficult to answer. There is in fact a trend in the United States towards retirement becoming an endogenous decision.

The increasing difficulty in financing growing numbers of pensioners without steadily reducing the real value of benefits underlay the next great change in the pension scheme: the move towards earnings-related contributions and benefits. In 1961 graduated contributions related to earnings were introduced. Now, flat-rate benefit combined with earnings-related contributions would be redistributive (see Part 2) but the use of earnings-related benefits and contributions also helped to reinforce the insurance myth. This change is therefore consistent with both the revenue-raising argument and a desire to avoid redistribution.

A further important consideration was the growth of occupational pension schemes in this period, from 5 million covered in 1953 to 12 million in 1965 (George, 1968). This led to demands, especially from the Labour Party, for an earning-related component to the pension for those outside the occupational schemes (consistent with the market failure argument). After several false starts, a 'two-tier' scheme was included in the Social Security Act of 1975, and came into operation in 1978.

2.2 Non-Contributory Transfers

Means-tested benefits

There is now a plethora of means-tested benefits, involving substantial expenditure, as shown in Table 1.1. These may be divided into several categories. Supplementary Benefit guarantees a minimum income while economically inactive, whether through unemployment, sickness, or old age, and is provided either in the absence of or as an addition to National Insurance Benefit. In contrast, Family Income Supplement is paid to those families in work but with insufficient income from earnings. Furthermore, there are local authority means-tested benefits which are primarily concerned with housing costs, and benefits connected to particular disabilities. In historical terms the development of Supplementary Benefit is the most interesting and this is the main benefit discussed here.

The system of relief prior to the developments of this century, known as the old Poor Law, has been much discussed in the literature. It was the fear of indoor relief and a pauper burial that lay behind the growth of Friendly Societies. Parish outdoor relief (subject to 'less eligibility') was permissible for the able-bodied, but as shown above it was only late in the nineteenth century that it became accepted that the demand for relief might be attributable to a deficiency of the economic system rather than of individual 'failure'. Nevertheless the growth of private insurance and provision and later state contributory 'social insurance' encouraged the perception of means-tested 'relief' as a *residual* benefit, even as late as the 1942 Beveridge Report.

The major inter-war problem was unemployment. Given its unequal regional incidence and the limitations on eligibility and duration in the receipt of state contributory benefits, several parishes found themselves with heavy burdens of expenditure on means-tested benefits. Some, such as Poplar in 1921, responded by making large grants of outdoor relief to able-bodied men and reducing support for other services such as the police. The 1929 Local Government Act transferred the function of operating the poor law from parishes to County Borough Councils in an attempt to permit some redistribution, but also to enforce 'less eligibility' and restrict 'Poplarism'. However this did not deter regional differences in generosity of benefit provision, particularly in the treatment of dependants (see Burns, 1941). The Unemployment Act of 1934 therefore instituted state assistance for the unemployed at a national level, superseding both local relief and the transitional payments described above. While the 'work test' was to be conducted at the local employment exchange, the local office of the Unemployment Assistance Board would subject the applicant to a means test. This dual system of administration persisted until 1982. Although there was scope for 'exceptional need' payments, the national scales were less generous than some locally agreed scales and used a wider concept of household income than many local schemes. In the face of bitter hostility in some areas, full implementation did not take place until 1938 and the means test came to have a stigma that persisted for many years.

As mentioned previously, in 1940 the Board was renamed the Assistance Board and took over administration of means-tested relief for the elderly. The Determination of Needs Act of 1941 limited the extent of the means test of household resources to the claimant, his wife, and anyone dependent on him. It was not until 1983 that married women could be claimants for its modern equivalent,

Supplementary Benefit. The final integration of the state means-tested scheme was contained in the 1948 National Assistance Act which established a National Assistance Board to 'assist persons with insufficient resources to meet their requirements'. These now mainly fall into three categories. First, there are the unemployed, a growing proportion of whom have become ineligible or have exhausted their claims on National Insurance benefits (see Chapter 7). Secondly, there are the unemployed, sick, and retired who are reliant on National Insurance benefits which are paid at a slightly lower rate than Supplementary Benefit. The third main group consists of one-parent families. Payment of rent was included in benefit payments but in 1982 this responsibility was transferred to local authorities, while in general the period since 1979 has seen a reduction in the number of discretionary 'exceptional need payments' available through the Supplementary Benefit Office.

The main aim of such state benefits is to redistribute short-term resources in order to deal with poverty. The extent of redistribution that the government is prepared to accept is reflected in the real level at which this minimum income guarantee is set (see Part 4). It is therefore interesting to note that the low-paid poor are excluded. However, since 1970 families with low-income wage-earners have been eligible for a separate means-tested benefit, Family Income Supplement, which is designed to make up half the difference between actual income and the 'scale rate' (depending on family composition). This benefit has been criticized both as encouraging employers to pay lower wages and as a substitute for active labour market intervention such as minimum wage legislation. In addition it is argued that the benefit has worsened the 'poverty trap' and is a poor substitute for a negative income tax. Some of the issues are discussed in Part 4.

Family Benefits

Family benefits were discussed briefly in Chapter 1, where it was suggested that the usual state benefits seem to bear little or no relation to an 'insurance' scheme. Most debate, where explicit, has been in terms of a redistributive motive or a view about population growth. There have been three major innovations in family benefit provision. These are the introduction of tax allowances for children in 1909 (and their later reintroduction in 1957), the introduction of family allowances in 1945, and the replacement of both allowances by Child

Benefits in 1977 under the Child Benefit Act 1975.

One of the key issues identified by studies of the poor in the early part of this century was the correlation between family size and poverty. Two solutions were advocated. The first, supported by trade unions and the Labour Party, was to raise the pay of the family head. The second, supported by some womens' groups in the 1914–21 period, was to provide family benefits to be paid to the woman (Land, 1975). The latter solution proposed family benefits not just for reasons of horizontal equity (concerning the greater perceived needs of large families), but also for vertical equity (because of the relationship between family size and low incomes).

The view which dominated the debate in the 1930s was that without family benefits the rate of population growth in the United Kingdom would decline further, and that ultimately the population would decrease. Subsidies to family support were desirable both on grounds of national prestige and to maintain a lower dependency ratio in the future as the declining population aged. An additional reason for family benefits, argued by Keynes in the 1939–45 war, was that benefits of this type would reduce pressure for higher wages from trade unions which, given the exigencies of war-time finance, would simply lead to a wage–price spiral. Finally, it was argued on efficiency (incentive) grounds that family benefits for those in work would reduce the 'replacement rate' (the ratio of benefits to net income in work) of the unemployed.

The scheme of family allowances introduced in the Act of 1945 therefore gave a weekly payment (plus school milk) for each child, other than the first. Benefits were normally payable to the wife. The small tax allowances for children were removed but family allowances were only occasionally raised and in 1957 child tax allowances were reintroduced. It was argued that tax allowances had smaller disincentive effects than flat-rate benefits, by altering the slope of the budget line facing families rather than its position (see Part 4), although the redistribution engendered by tax allowances would be less than that stemming from flat-rate benefits. The two schemes were merged by the Child Benefit Act of 1975 which introduced a flat-rate benefit payable for each child, and paid at a higher rate for one-parent families. Unlike other social insurance benefits, there is no obligation on the state to index this benefit to the expected rate of prices or earnings increase every year, although there is a statutory duty to consider its real value each year (Ogus and Barendt, 1982). The issue of the optimal provision of dependants' benefits remains a controversial subject.

2.3 Some General Results

What does this brief history of the various parts of the social insurance system suggest? The first conclusion is that the motive of redistribution has played a relatively minor part; indeed, there has been considerable resistance to redistribution. Only means-tested benefits have been extended wholly for reasons of redistribution, suggesting that poverty relief is generally viewed quite differently from general redistribution. Poverty relief has always been carefully circumscribed by considerations of 'less eligibility' or, in modern parlance, disincentive effects. The extensions of unemployment insurance undoubtedly implied some redistribution in effect, but the motives behind these extensions were more often associated with raising revenue and paternalism. The original non-contributory pension was also redistributive but this was soon superseded by the contributory scheme. Finally, family support is mainly associated with horizontal equity (and the frequency with which large families are judged to be in 'poverty').

The basis of social insurance in the three major schemes of unemployment and sickness insurance and pensions has been a contributory system: the National Insurance system. The origin of the National Insurance system lies in the various modes of contributory private provision operating in the early part of the present century. The motives for the gradual take-over of such schemes by the state would seem to be a combination of paternalism (notably in pensions), specific market failures (such as adverse selection and moral hazard problems in the 1930s), and the relative administrative efficiency of state and private provision. A contributory scheme of pseudo-insurance also had advantages over the general tax system for raising revenue, at least in the eyes of the Treasury, and so this motive perhaps also underlies the form of state provision which has developed.

The remainder of the book examines some of the consequences of the system of social insurance that has evolved. Is a separate contributory scheme financed by a payroll tax the optimal means of providing the main social security benefits? Are other social insurance, or tax-transfer systems, superior? Is it possible to make some estimate of the degree of systematic redistribution contained within the various social security components of the overall social insurance system? And does the resurgence of 'partnerships' between the state and private provision, notably in the fields of pensions and sick pay, have any implications for the extent of optimal state intervention?

PART 2

State Pension Schemes

3

Types of State Pension Scheme

Much of the discussion of pensions, towards the end of the nineteenth and beginning of the twentieth century, was motivated by the realization that the aged formed a very large proportion of the increasing number of people in poverty. The system established under the 1834 Poor Law was clearly inappropriate, but it has been seen in Chapter 2 that agreement about a suitable course of action was very difficult to reach. The Royal Commission of the Aged Poor (chaired by Lord Abadare) was set up in 1893 but did not report until 1907, and then did not recommend the adoption of any pension scheme. A separate Committee on Old Age Pensions (chaired by Lord Rothschild) was appointed in 1896, but held that either compulsory or non-contributory schemes were beyond their terms of reference. The Committee reported in 1898 against all the pension schemes which had been submitted, suggesting instead that an increasing number of the 'industrial population' were making adequate provision for old age.

The issue was complicated by the hostility towards state pensions of groups such as the Charity Organisation Society (COS, whose history was described by Bosanquet, 1914), of which Lord Abadare was Vice-President. Furthermore the Friendly Societies, supported by the COS, were strongly against state pensions in defence of their own position. But the Friendly Societies failed to recognize the precarious nature of their resources, caused by the increased payments of sick benefits arising from increased longevity, and poor management. A major difficulty was the 'contribution' issue, as there was considerable opposition to the idea of financing pensions from general tax revenue. In such a difficult situation the establishment of non-contributory pensions in 1908, despite their limited coverage, can be seen as a victory for the highly energetic and well-organized National Pensions Committee (see Stead, 1909).

This situation did not last long, and the famous 1911 National Insurance Act soon introduced the contributory scheme of pseudo-insurance. The *idea* of 'paying for what you get' was an important element of the contributory principle, and this attitude was greatly influenced by the view that such a scheme would remove the 'stigma' associated with means-tested benefits. Stress was therefore laid on a difference between 'assistance' and 'insurance', and from an administrative point of view the use of contributions to determine eligibility was much more convenient than the application of a means test. Despite the fact that no state scheme has reflected insurance principles (indeed most of the arguments for state schemes, discussed in Chapter 1, would explicitly reject the view that they should), the insurance fiction or myth has been highly influential in confusing policy discussion. It is still not difficult to find people who argue, for example, that benefits must be earnings-related if contributions are earnings-related (irrespective of other regulations concerning pension entitlement, including those for dependants and widows), on the argument that people will otherwise be 'unwilling' to pay. The concept of 'willingness' to pay compulsory contributions is of course rather doubtful especially where contracting-out and self-employment opportunities are limited. But the statement that people are unwilling to pay would usually be taken to mean that they would vote for an alternative arrangement, if given the choice.

In the late 1960s and early 1970s, with a revival of interest in general aspects of inequality, a growing amount of evidence of poverty in old age, and high and increasing rates of inflation, further attempts were made to devise new pension plans. Again, agreement was by no means easy to obtain; the six years 1969–74 saw the publication of three White Papers, and a Labour scheme was rejected by the incoming Conservative government of 1970. The Social Security Act of 1975 finally established the new state pension scheme which began to operate in 1978. The plans were unusual in that they were supported by all major political parties, though as a result they inevitably reflect a considerable amount of compromise. Some of the details of this complex scheme are presented in section 3.2 below, and its implications are examined in the following two chapters. However, attention will be given not only to the current.British system but comparisons will be made among alternative types of scheme. Some general aspects of pension plans are first discussed in the following section.

There are of course difficulties in trying to discover which of the criteria discussed in Chapter 1 underlie government policy in the area, and many dangers in trying to find *ex post* rationalizations of government policy. It is extremely rare for policy statements to provide any kind of explanation of the reasons for adopting any particular policy, and even when they do it may not always be appropriate to take such statements at their 'face value'. However, it would be useful if the internal consistency of policy statements could be examined, and their effects assessed using the stated criteria of policy-makers themselves. There is a valuable role for economic analysis, which may perhaps reveal to policy-makers where their recommended policies will not achieve their stated aims. This role is especially useful in such complex areas as pension reform. Once the 'facts' of a situation are agreed, then differences in basic value-judgements become easier to identify.

Although policy statements concerning, for example, the desirability of avoiding poverty in old age and of extending the 'benefits' of membership of occupational pension schemes to a larger number of employees have been made, no justification has been given for any of the specific features of the new British scheme. For example, the choice of an earnings-related pension scheme combined with partial contracting out (explained in detail in section 3.2 and in Chapter 4) inevitably involves significant costs. It is therefore important that the trade-offs involved in that choice should be clearly understood. Value-judgements will ultimately influence the choice made, but as Wilson (1974, p. 22) pointed out before the 1975 Act was passed (completing the movement towards earnings-related benefits)

There is a question of fact that has to be considered. Is there reason to believe that the social choice in favour of graduated pensions has been properly made in the sense that—whatever the value-judgements—the facts of the situation have been sufficiently understood? There is reason to suspect that this condition has not been satisfied.

Some eight years later, Hemming and Kay (1982) referred to the statement by the Secretary of State for Social Services that the cost of commitments had been 'very carefully considered in relation to the capacity of the country to support it', and commented that they 'can find little to indicate that this is a true statement' (1982, p. 300). It will be argued in this Part that the present system does indeed contain an unusually large number of anomalies and inconsistencies.

3.1 Alternative Pension Schemes

The various arguments which are usually put forward to support the use of state schemes, as discussed in Chapter 1, do not of course provide a clear guide to the detailed arrangements of a state pension scheme. In addition to the basic value-judgements, many empirical questions are raised, about which judgements are very difficult. Questions raised earlier in this book and which are particularly relevant here concern the operation of private life insurance markets, markets for financial assets, the extent to which saving and labour supply behaviour are affected by pensions, the extent to which private transfers (through intra-family intergenerational transfers, or charities) would be affected, and the administrative costs associated with various alternatives. Further important questions concern the special needs of the aged (regarding, say, health care which cannot be purchased by individuals), the extent to which individuals can convert capital held in the form of housing into a flow of income, the time preferences of individuals (concerning the extent to which they would choose to shift resources between stages in the life cycle, given adequate information), the likely incidence of taxes, and so on. Many aspects are involved, and they are far from easy to answer. For example, in considering whether individuals are myopic, and would save insufficient amounts to provide for old age (even if fully indexed bonds were available to everyone), the directly relevant data are not available. Observed behaviour has already been affected by the existence of state pensions, and by people's expectations of the future (including expectations about the longevity of the state scheme).

The details of any scheme, if decided in a rational manner, would also depend on the weights attached to particular objectives, and the probabilities attached to different outcomes which cannot be predicted with accuracy. For example, some people believe that a state scheme can be run more efficiently than a large number of private schemes (in terms of efficiency in information collection and decision-taking) and also take a paternalistic view (thinking that people would generally not save enough to provide for a sufficiently high replacement rate during retirement). As a consequence, those people will usually be inclined towards a compulsory state scheme which provides high replacement rates through an earnings-related scheme. But if the same individuals also hold the value-judgement that pensions should be redistributive, there will be some trade-off to be made since a scheme paying a high flat-rate pension involves (other things being equal) a higher amount of redistribution. The difficult issue of redistribution is examined in more detail in Chapter 5, but it is also clear that the method suggested for raising revenue (for example the extent to which the tax structure should be graduated) will also depend on views about the incidence of those taxes.

It would be possible in principle, though quite exhausting, to go through a large taxonomic exercise in order to produce the type of scheme which would be suggested for any combination of views (including value-judgements and judgements about empirical issues). However, it is unlikely that such an exercise would be very profitable for present purposes. Decision-taking in practice will involve a great deal of compromise among conflicting groups, and it should perhaps not be too surprising that new plans are rarely accompanied by an unambiguous statement of principles.

The main contrasts usually made are between schemes which involve a flat-rate payment, and those which pay an earnings-related pension (sometimes, as in the British scheme, as an additional component, or second tier). But many varieties exist, depending on the precise nature of the pension formula, the determination of eligibility, the way in which pensions in payment are adjusted, and the benefits available for dependants, to name only a few factors. Many alternative.methods of financing pensions exist, and the particular method used in Britain, involving a combination of employees' and employers' contributions along with general Exchequer revenue, has already been described. Such a method, with considerable uncertainty about the incidence of contributions, is obviously not supported by those who argue in favour of 'earmarked' taxes, or those who support general fund financing and the integration of taxes and National Insurance contributions. Some aspects of the interaction between income taxation and NI contributions will be examined in Part 4, and these general issues will again be discussed in Part 5. Chapter 4 considers some general comparisons between standard types of scheme, concerning the contribution rates required to finance any specified pension rate. It also examines some features of the British scheme which make its costs very difficult to predict.

Before describing the British scheme, it must be stressed that virtually all state schemes are financed on a pay-as-you-go (PAYG) basis; that is, current pensions are financed from current contributions. While this method of financing is generally regarded as superior to funding for state schemes (and is discussed further in the next chapter), it has the interesting implication that state pensions are often treated as very *short-term* issues. A funded scheme involves, in an obvious sense, a contract between the members and the organizers of the scheme, and it has become customary to treat a PAYG scheme as involving an implicit contract between three 'generations'. Thus the working population agrees to pay the pensions of the retired population, on the understanding that their pensions will subsequently be paid by the next working 'generation'. While this may sound comforting, it is of course entirely fictitious, and there is no general assurance that a scheme which is operated by one generation will be acceptable to subsequent generations. Appeals to the argument that intergenerational redistribution should be viewed as social insurance, against the *risk* of belonging to a particularly large cohort, will not necessarily satisfy members of a working population who *know* that they are supporting a relatively large pensioner population. Pension schemes have had a habit of being very short-lived.

The short-term perspective which is taken in a PAYG scheme can in fact lead to policy measures which a government knows cannot be expected to last long, or indeed must soon be changed. An example, in the context of the British scheme, concerns the regulations for indexation of contributions and pensions, and this is examined more fully in Chapter 4. The insurance myth however works to generate some features which are not entirely consistent with the general approach of PAYG financing. For example the new British state pension was introduced with the claim that it would help to eliminate the widespread poverty in old age (with emphasis on the problems of inflation experienced in the middle 1970s). But the scheme will not be fully 'mature' for many years, and those already retired receive no additional benefits from it. Other forms of transfer payments, such as Supplementary Benefits, must then continue to be made in an inefficient manner, in order to preserve the illusion that people 'get what they pay for'.

3.2 The British Scheme

This section introduces some of the main features of the British state pension scheme. More details are given in Chapters 4 and 5 where the particular feature is examined. The pension is made up of two separate components or 'tiers'. First, a flat-rate pension is paid to all eligible individuals irrespective of their earnings. Secondly, an earnings-related pension or second 'tier' is paid, based partly on the length of time during which individuals have contributed to the scheme. The value of the earnings-related component cannot exceed a maximum or 'upper limit'. For individuals who have contributed to the scheme for at least 20 years the earnings-related pension is one-quarter of the difference between the individual's value of 'pensionable earnings' (up to the limit) and the basic flat-rate pension. Otherwise it is one-eightieth of this difference for each year's contributions.

If for illustrative purposes the basic pension is assumed to be £20 per week and the upper limit £140 per week, then the pension corresponding to any value of pensionable earnings may easily be calculated. All individuals with pensionable earnings greater than or equal to £140 per week would receive a pension of £50 per week, obtained as £20 plus £(140 – 20)/4. Those with pensionable earnings of £100 per week receive a pension of £40, and those with earnings of £60 receive a pension of £30. It can therefore be seen that the ration of the pension to the value of earnings, the 'replacement rate', increases from approximately 0.33 to 0.4, and then to 0.5, as earnings decrease from £140 to £100, and then to £60. This characteristic of the two-tier system—that replacements rates decline as earnings increase—has often been used to suggest that the new state scheme involves a substantial amount of income redistribution from 'rich' to 'poor'. However, the extent of redistribution is much more complex, as will be shown in Chapter 5.

The earnings-related component is based on the individual's average earnings in the best 20 years of working life, after each year's earnings have been adjusted using an index of average earnings. The average earnings of a number of 'best' years must exceed the average earnings of all years, and the extent to which the two averages differ must depend on the degree to which earnings fluctuate over the individual's working life. This aspect is examined in some detail in Chapter 4.

National Insurance contributions are directly proportional to earnings below a maximum weekly value, or 'upper limit', which is the same as that determining the maximum earnings-related pension. There is also an employer's contribution which is directly related to earnings up to the same limit. It was initially envisaged that the limits would be adjusted using either a price or a wage index, whichever turned out to be the larger. However, the regulations require adjustment using at least an index of prices, but in practice the minimum adjustment has been applied. This raises problems over a longer period, if earnings grow faster than prices, as shown in Chapter 4.

A major innovation in the state scheme is the ability to contract out of the earnings-related tier for members of certain occupational pension schemes. Those who are contracted out will continue to receive the basic or flat-rate pension, and must pay contributions to the government scheme at a lower rate than those who are full members. The system is therefore one of 'partial' contracting out. It was not possible to know in advance how many employees would in fact contract out, and the Government Actuary initially underestimated the number. The private scheme must pay what has been called a Guaranteed Minimum Pension (GMP) which is based on average lifetime earnings (rather than the best 20 years) and which is not indexed during retirement. However, the state makes up the difference between the GMP and the pension which would have been received as a full member of the state scheme.

It is almost certain there will be pressure to change the state scheme, especially when National Insurance contributions rates increase with the increasing 'maturity' of the scheme. The pressure for change will depend partly on what happens to unemployment rates, real earnings growth, labour force participation, and demographic trends. All of these are extremely difficult to predict. Indeed, the complexities of the scheme have contributed to the enormous difficulties in pension planning; many of the orders of magnitude can only be guessed on the basis of little information.

Within the general framework of two-tier pensions with earnings-related contributions and earnings limits, the most obvious change would be to break the link between the earnings limits for contributions and those for pensions. The pension formula could then be quite different from the contributions schedule. A possibility would then be to raise the upper limit for contributions (thereby increasing total revenue using the same proportional rate) while not raising the pensions limits by the same extent. How the basic pension and maximum pension are changed will depend on the extent to which either 'income replacement' or the provision of pensions at an 'adequate' level is regarded as the main objective of the scheme. It is difficult to pursue both objectives consistently, as shown in the next chapter.

4

Contributions and Pensionable Earnings

It has been seen in Chapter 3 that the new British state pension scheme introduced in 1978, as a result of the 1975 Social Security Act, is not only very complex but involved many entirely new elements. There was thus little experience, either in Britain or the rest of the world, on which to base any detailed analysis of the scheme's implications. When estimates were required for the 1911 National Insurance Act, the difficult job was given to Alfred Flux, who later stated, 'The basis of ascertained fact upon which it was necessary to build at that time was no means as broad or as solid as could have been desired' (1934, p. 105). The task facing the Government Actuary's Department in 1975 could have been no easier than that facing Flux 64 years earlier.

It is perhaps even more alarming that the problem seems to have been given fairly low priority. A report on the financial provisions of the Pensions Bill was rather hastily produced (DHSS, 1975, Cmnd.5928), containing short-run estimates until just after the end of the present century. Only in 1982 was a brief and long awaited *Quinquennial Review* published, covering the period 1975–80 and providing revised estimates of longer-term implications. Furthermore, there has been very little public debate on the state pension scheme. Despite the fact that the initial estimates of the Government Actuary were rather optimistic (in terms of assumptions used about growth, unemployment, and demographic trends), it was nevertheless quite clear from the beginning that the new scheme would involve substantial increases in the rates of National Insurance contributions. Yet only the regulations concerning job mobility, and issues of 'pension portability' have been widely debated. Even the huge growth of the funds of private pensions, stimulated by the new scheme, have received surprisingly little attention. The lack of public debate has been accompanied by relatively little academic analysis, although the studies which have been made are all critical of the scheme or the official estimates, or both. This curious lack of attention contrasts strongly with the experience of other countries, especially the United States where pensions have been a prominent 'live' issue for some time.

Short and long views

As argued in the previous chapter, there is one feature of the scheme which to some extent militates against pensions being regarded as an urgent issue. This arises from the fact that the new scheme contains substantial promises relating to an uncertain and distant future. The full costs of the scheme will not be fully apparent until well into the next century, and there is perhaps a general impression that marginal adjustments to benefits and contributions can be made over a long period. However, the pay-as-you-go (PAYG) nature of financing means that future generations of workers are 'committed' to paying uncertain, but without doubt high, contributions to finance the earnings-related pensions of the current working population. The idea of a social contract between generations may be a convenient device for pedagogic purposes, but no actual binding agreement has been made. There is no assurance that the fictitious 'promises' will be met, although there has been an understandable reluctance to take this possibility seriously, and to comtemplate anything other than minor adjustments. Recent governments seem to have had few qualms about using retrospective legislation, however, even where expectations have been formed over a long period. Previous state pension schemes have not been noted for their longevity.

A clear indication of this tendency to take a myopic view of what is essentially a long-term issue is provided by the current regulations concerning indexation (mentioned at the end of Chapter 3). The initial proposal to index the earnings limits, and consequently the basic pension, to either average earnings or prices (whichever turns out to be greater), was soon abandoned in favour of adjustment using 'at least' an index of prices. In fact pension adjustments have kept strictly to the lower limit of policy options, although the use of an earnings index in the calculation of pensionable earnings (with more remote implications) has been retained. This policy has been adopted for short-run purposes, although it is widely recognized that allowing the earnings limits to fall relative to average earnings would, as explained in Section 4.2, 'change the shape of the scheme beyond all recognition' (Government Actuary, 1982, p. 24).

The rational discussion of policy requires a clear appreciation of the costs involved, and therefore of the opportunities forgone. The purpose of this chapter is therefore to consider some aspects of the trade-offs and costs involved. The relationship between flat rate and earnings-related schemes is first briefly described in section 4.1, using a simple framework of analysis. Section 4.2 then examines some details of the British scheme, in particular the '20 best years' rule used in calculating pensionable earnings. Finally section 4.3 considers the nature of the contracting-out facility in the new scheme.

4.1 Earnings-related Pensions in a Simple Framework

It is possible to obtain some idea of the 'trade-offs' involved in policy choices by first considering a very simple framework of analysis, developed in Creedy (1980b, 1982a). Very briefly, the framework is concerned only with a single cohort of individuals, and each member begins work at the same age and retires at the same age. There is no differential mortality and no variability in earnings over life (that is, no *relative* income movements). Where there are earnings limits relating to contributions, these are assumed to remain constant in real terms, so that contributions are the same in each period over the working life. For convenience, funded pension schemes are examined. Thus each individual pays contributions into a fund at regular intervals, and the fund accumulates, earning interest, until the cohort retires. The fund is then shared among the members of the cohort, who receive a pension from the fund at regular intervals. Because of these simplifying assumptions, it is possible to carry out the analysis *as if* there were just two periods; the working period is consolidated into one period and the retirement period is consolidated into the second period. The amount available for redistribution can thus be expressed as a single contribution figure multiplied by $(1 + r)$, where r is the 'effective' rate of interest. The important comparisons are however independent of the rate of interest used. This framework allows the contributions rate needed in any type of scheme, in order to finance pensions according to the specified pension formula, to be calculated.

It may perhaps be thought that the analysis of a funded scheme has little relevance to state schemes which are run on a pay-as-you-go (PAYG) basis. However, the concern here is with comparisons among different types of scheme, not with the absolute levels of the contribution rates in each case. In a PAYG analysis, the effect of the interest rate would be replaced by that of population growth. The levels may be different, but the relevant trade-offs are unchanged when comparing alternative schemes.

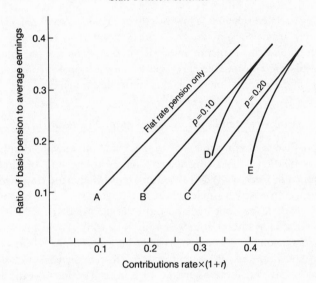

Fig. 4.1   *Benefits and contributions with flat-rate and earnings-related pensions*

Diagrammatic comparisons

The case of flat-rate pensions only, financed from earnings-related contributions, may be used as a 'bench-mark'. This is shown in Fig. 4.1 as the line marked A, where there is no difficulty in calculating the contributions rate needed to finance any given pension. If an earnings-related second tier is then added to the basic pension, it is clear that the contributions rate must be increased. The extent of this increase will depend partly on the form of the distribution of income. In fact the total amount needed is equal to the basic pension multiplied by the number of people with income less than or equal to the flat-rate pension, *plus* the proportional pension rate multiplied by the total income of those with income above the flat-rate pension. Examples are given in Fig. 4.1 for a lognormal distribution of income with coefficient of variation of 0.471 (similar to that in the UK) but again the comparisons are not sensitive to this assumption. The line marked B is for a two-tier scheme which has a proportional pension rate , p, of 0.10, and line C is for a scheme with a rate of 0.20. It can be seen that the contribution rate, needed to finance any given flat-rate pension, has to be substantially increased as the second-tier pension rate is increased.

In the British two-tier scheme there is an upper earnings limit which restricts both the base on which contributions are levied and the total amount of pension payments. Comparisons are shown in lines D and E for the pension rates corresponding to line B and C respectively, where the upper limit is maintained at seven times the basic pension. It can be seen that this type of scheme requires higher contribution *rates*, for a given basic pension, than the simple two-tier schemes. However, as the flat-rate pension increases, the upper earnings limit increases to such an extent that the total amount of income above the limit is negligible, and lines B and D converge, as do C and E. Figure 4.1 clearly shows that for the low basic pension, as in the British system, the upper earnings limit has a greater effect in reducing the contributions base than in reducing pension payments. The additional costs of having a two-tier scheme along the lines of the new British state pension, in terms of the higher contribution rates needed to finance any given basic pension, are therefore well illustrated in Fig. 4.1.

But the contrasts shown in the simple framework actually understate the costs of the British scheme, because of the fact that the contributions base is quite different from the earnings base on which pensions are based. These differences arise from the awkward indexation regulations and the '20 best years' rule for calculating pensionable earnings. Extra costs are also imposed by the generous treatment of women. These aspects are therefore examined in the following section.

4.2 The British State Scheme

It has already been stressed that the problems of estimating the financial implications of the new state pension scheme are formidable, and it would be impossible to examine them all in this book. While the previous section has shown in a simple form the nature of the policy choice in moving from a flat-rate to a two-tier pension scheme, this section concentrates on a particular feature which further increases costs, namely the '20 best years' rule, and then briefly discusses some wider aspects. All estimates of future pension costs must be based on an explicit set of assumptions about earnings and price changes, and changes in the earnings limits and basic pension. However, one response to increasing costs is actually to fall short of the previously stated pension commitment. A recent example of this type of policy—the reduction in the basic pension relative to average earnings by maintaining only the real value of the earnings limits—has already been mentioned. The implications of this policy, which also has the unwelcome effect of reducing the contributions base, must therefore first be examined in more detail.

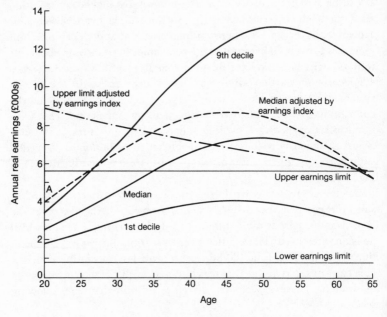

Fig. 4.2   *Age–Earnings profiles*

Indexation problems

The features of the British scheme can be illustrated conveniently by considering the possible experience of a single cohort of male employees. On the assumption that changes taking place over time (such as productivity and technical change) have a similar effect on the rate of growth in the earnings of all age-groups, and that the same general price index can be applied to all age-groups, steady growth in real earnings simply increases the rate of growth of real earnings of all individuals in the cohort by the same proportionate amount each year.

Some age–income profiles, for employees between the ages of 20 and 65, are shown in Fig. 4.2. This shows the first and ninth deciles and the median earnings of a cohort at each age. The general shape of the profiles are based on estimates taken from Creedy and Hart (1979), using genuine longitudinal earnings data. The figure assumes that there is general growth in real earnings of 1 per cent per year; for higher rates of growth the profiles would of course become steeper, and earnings would on average reach a maximum later in life. Individuals obviously experience relative earnings mobility, moving between the deciles of the distribution, but Fig. 4.2 conveniently illustrates the pattern of the age–earnings profile for the cohort.

Now assume that the cohort begins work at age 20 in the same year in which the state pension scheme begins. The average earnings of the cohort in the first year are £2644. Cross-sectional evidence shows that average earnings in that age-group are about 70 per cent of the average of all age-groups combined, so that an appropriate value of the latter would be £3780. In the new pension scheme the upper earnings limit was initially set at about one and a half times average male earnings, implying that a suitable value for the upper limit is £5670. Consequently the lower limit is about £810 (one-seventh of the upper limit).

Where the earnings limits are adjusted in line with prices, they can be shown as horizontal lines, since the vertical axis of Fig. 4.2 represents real earnings. This means that a large proportion of individuals in the cohort would exceed the upper earnings limit in most years of working life.

Consider the hypothetical example of an individual who receives the median earnings of his cohort in each year of working life. This is of course extremely unrealistic, but serves to illustrate the character of earnings indexation. The individual's eligible earnings will follow the profile of median earnings until the upper earnings limit is exceeded, after which eligible earnings remain at the constant limit until the last few years of working life. Before calculating the individual's pensionable earnings it is necessary to adjust each year's earnings using an index of *earnings* rather than prices. Thus the eligible earnings shown in Fig. 4.2 must be increased by the extent to which average earnings growth exceeds the growth of prices. Two additional lines are shown in Fig. 4.2. The first (indicated by ----) shows the profile of median earnings adjusted for real earnings growth. Not only does the individual share in real earnings growth, but at retirement his eligible

earnings are raised yet again. The second line (–·–·–) shows the effect
of adjusting the upper earnings limit, at retirement, for real earnings
growth over previous years. Pensionable earnings in the state scheme
are therefore the 'best 20 years' earnings, following the line from A to
B (---), then moving along the line –·–·–. It is difficult to justify these
awkward features of using two different methods of indexation and it
is most unlikely that they could continue to be used for long, although
it is not of course possible to predict exactly how the scheme will be
adapted. Results using alternative methods, described in the following subsection, are therefore shown below.

The twenty best years' earnings

The initial report of the Government Actuary's Department (1975)
made no explicit reference to the problem of estimating pension
liabilities when pensionable earnings are based on only the best 20
years' (adjusted) earnings. Nevertheless it was assumed that, for those
under 16 years in 1978, the average would be 10 per cent higher than if
it had been based on all the years from age 16 to 65. Much lower
percentage were added for the older age groups, on the grounds that
no attempt was being made to examine the mature scheme. This is a
further example of the myopic planning mentioned earlier in this
chapter. In the *Quinquennial Review*, a summary of the procedure used
was given (1982, pp. 35–7), and further details were later provided in
Stewart and Young (1982), although insufficient information was
given in order to allow their method to be replicated. The task is of
course necessarily very complicated. The calculation must allow not
only for variations in earnings over the working life but also for
unemployment, labour force participation, migration, and periods of
self-employment. It was estimated that selective averaging would
eventually increase the 'career earnings' of men by 35 per cent, and of
women by an average of 65 per cent (made up of 30 per cent for single
and divorced women and 75 per cent for married women and
widows). A fairly high level of aggregation seems to have been used on
the assumption that the occupational structure of earnings will remain
unchanged. The basis of the calculations in the *Quinquennial Review* is
the result that, from a cross-sectional profile of average earnings over
age, the 20 best years' earnings are obtained between the ages of 30
and 50. However, there is no indication that any adjustment was
made for the difference between cohort and cross-sectional age-

earnings profiles. Furthermore, there is no acknowledgement of the important point that the average value of the set of individuals' averages of their best 20 years' earnings is *not* the same as the average of the highest 20 years' annual averages. The former is the relevant variable, but only the latter has been calculated.

In estimating the costs of the state earnings-related pension, Hemming and Kay (1982) obtained overall results which were broadly similar to those of the Government Actuary's Department (1975), but they argued that the adjustment for the 'best 20 years' rule would need to be higher (although their estimates, of about 20 per cent, were still lower than the *Review* figures quoted above). Hemming and Kay based their estimates on average age–earnings profiles for a variety of occupations (using cross-sectional data). But they did acknowledge (1982, p. 303) that these would give 'conservative' estimates because of the relative earnings variability which was being ignored.

The recognition of the importance of earnings variability requires the use of a simulation analysis, since complete longitudinal data are not available. Simulation analyses have been carried out by Creedy (1980a, 1982c) using a model of age–earnings profiles. The model was estimated using the longitudinal data for male employees, mentioned earlier in this section, in Creedy and Hart (1979). The data provided information about the process of year-to-year changes of *individuals*, as well as information about the form of the age–earnings profile. Some results are shown in Table 4.1, for two different types of indexation, both of which are more consistent than the actual scheme described earlier. The schemes examined are referred to as A and B, and are described as follows:

Scheme A In this case the earnings limits, pensionable earnings, and pensions during the period of retirement are all calculated using earnings indices.

Scheme B In this case pensionable earnings are based on real earnings in each year, but the earnings limits and pensions in retirement are adjusted using earnings indices.

Furthermore the two schemes are examined using two different ratios of upper to lower-earnings limits. The ratios used are seven (as in the current legislation) and ten. Schemes A and B are of course equivalent when there is no general growth in real earnings. Earnings were simulated between the ages of 20 and 65, and the proportionate growth in general real earnings is denoted g.

TABLE 4.1   *Average pensionable earnings*

General growth of real earnings	Type of scheme	Ratio of upper to lower earnings limit	Average lifetime (between limits)	Average best 20 years (between limits)
0	A and B	7	4113	4765
		10	4454	5390
0.01	A	7	6378	7387
		10	7073	8702
	B	7	5188	6260
		10	5774	7290
0.02	A	7	9859	11414
		10	10973	13526
	B	7	6633	8487
		10	7431	9823

Earnings basis (£) [spanning the last two columns]

Notes: In scheme A everything is adjusted in line with the growth of average earnings. In scheme B pensionable earnings are based on real earnings but the earnings limits are adjusted using an earnings index. Where $g = 0$ the two schemes are equivalent.

Source: Creedy (1982b, p. 104).

The effects of using selective averaging, and alternative indexing methods, can be seen from the last two columns of Table 4.1. With $g = 0$, average pensionable earnings, when based on each individual's best 20 years' earnings, are 16 per cent greater than when based on average lifetime earnings. This percentage increases to 21 for the higher earnings limit of ten times the lower limit. The existence of general growth in real earnings (in which the cohort shares) can be seen to have little effect on this comparison for Scheme A. For both $g = 0.01$ and $g = 0.02$ the differences between the averages are 16 per cent and 23 per cent, for ratios of upper to lower limits of seven and ten respectively. However, this result does not hold for the alternative system B which bases pensions on real earnings but adjusts the earnings limits in line with the general growth of average earnings. For $g = 0.01$ selective averaging leads to average pensionable earnings of 20 per cent and 28 per cent higher than when using lifetime averaging, for ratios of earnings limits of 7 and 10 respectively. These percentages can be seen to rise to 28 and 32 respectively, when the value of g increases to 0.02. It has already been noted that the calculations do not allow for factors such as large amounts of unemployment, sickness, migration, or self-employment. These factors would obviously increase the difference between the results of using different averaging procedures. It is however difficult to compare these results with those of Stewart and Young (1982), who do not discuss the effects of real earnings growth, examine only one method of indexation, and do not refer to any earlier studies with which they are familiar.

Wider aspects of pension costs

Despite differences in some of the details of the estimation exercise (including different assumptions about future trends in unemployment, growth, and demographic changes) there is no disagreement in general terms. It is widely recognized that the British scheme will eventually provide fairly high replacement rates by historical standards, financed from very high rates of National Insurance contributions. However, it is important to examine pension arrangements using a wider perspective. For example, the estimation of the likely future resources of the elderly must take into consideration not only pensions but other factors such as wealth accumulation and various other sources of income (in addition to, say, the public provision of special health services). Similarly the 'cost' of pensions is not measured only by the total value of pension transfer payments in the PAYG scheme. The pension scheme also interacts with both the system of income taxation and the Supplementary Benefit system.

If pensions raise more people above the level at which means-tested benefits are available, then expenditure on the latter will obviously fall. The extent of the net change in expenditure depends partly on the extent to which Supplementary Benefits are actually taken up by those entitled to them. The interaction with the income tax system largely arises through the effect of the age allowance; that is, the higher personal allowance given when either the taxpayer or his wife is 65 years or over. If the age allowance is seen as part of the system of 'tax expenditures', then as pensions increase, so the effective cost of the allowance is increased, although some pensioners will have higher taxable incomes. A framework within which some of the relevant interdependencies can be examined, including induced changes in retirement behaviour, has been suggested by Altmann and Atkinson (1982), who provide estimates for a range of policies. Their analysis helps to illustrate the conceptual difficulties of examining pension costs, and also clearly indicates those many aspects where empirical information is desperately required; that is, where the results are most sensitive to the assumptions which have to be made in the absence of better data. One aspect of pension costs which causes special difficulties is that of contracting out, and this feature is examined in the following section.

4.3 Contracting Out of the State Scheme

The difficulty of forming consistent rationalizations of many of the features of the British state pension scheme has already been mentioned. It is likely that they represent a considerable amount of compromise in order to obtain agreement from all major political parties, after a number of schemes had been aborted following general elections. But the contracting-out arrangements, which can be seen as representing a negotiating victory for the private pension industry, present the greatest challenge. Before considering the details of these arrangements (described briefly in Chapter 3 above) it is therefore worth discussing some of the relevant basic arguments relating to private and state pension provision.

Some basic issues

The state provision of an 'adequate' flat-rate pension is often thought to be justified by most of the four criteria suggested by Diamond (1977), and discussed in Chapter 1. These are mainly market failure (private arrangements are not available to all individuals on reasonable terms), and paternalism (many individuals will take too optimistic a view of the future, and will make inadequate plans for retirement). There is little evidence to suggest that a desire for redistribution has played a significant role in pension arrangements. Nevertheless it may be argued that a state pension scheme is a more efficient mechanism for dealing with poverty in old age than other forms of income support (such as the administratively costly means-tested benefits, whose coverage may also be less than adequate because of low take-up rates).

It is possible that these arguments could be extended to support a state second tier of earnings-related pensions, designed to achieve minimum levels of income replacement in addition to providing an adequate pension. The private pension industry is largely based on 'group schemes', organised on a company basis, and there is much lower access to these schemes for the lower-paid and manual workers. Furthermore, the company schemes penalize those who are more highly mobile. Although this aspect has often been mentioned (and has received some attention in the media), the effects are difficult to assess, since movers may negotiate wage increases to allow for pension effects, and many larger companies operate internal labour markets where there is little external mobility and the pension is just one element of the long-term pay structure.

The information requirements and decision-taking processes in making pension plans are extremely complex, so that it may be thought that there is an efficiency gain from the state organization of earnings-related pensions. Another, market-failure-related, argument concerns the general lack of private index linking (of pensions in payment, since the indexation of earnings is often thought to be implicit in the use of 'final salary' schemes). This point must be treated with caution, since it has sometimes been claimed that it is impossible for private schemes to include indexation of pensions. This view was certainly expressed by the Second Permanent Secretary in the DHSS when the new scheme was introduced (see Atkinson, 1977, p. 218). But with the use of properly hedged funds (made easier by the introduction of special index-linked securities), and with lower initial benefits, indexation is possible although a *guarantee* does involve additional costs (see, for example, Hemming and Kay, 1982). Indeed, under present arrangements where schemes have no obligation to provide indexation the existence of inflation confers significant benefits on those operating the private funds. The liabilities, especially of early leavers, can be met more easily.

Although the arguments of the previous paragraphs may support some kind of state earnings-related pension on top of a flat-rate scheme, it may nevertheless be thought that there are some individuals who feel that they are being forced to save too much, thereby leading to efficiency losses. If the paternalistic argument is not dominant here, then policy-makers may agree to relax the compulsory element in the second tier, and allow partial contracting out of the state scheme. However, and as Diamond (1977, p. 298) noted, the arrangements must be carefully planned if the scheme contains an element of redistribution, otherwise those who remain will be worse off. This aspect is considered again in Chapter 5, section 3. It may perhaps be argued that private schemes offer more variety and flexibility than a state scheme could possibly offer, and therefore that contracting out would allow wider 'consumer' choice in this respect also. This position was indeed taken by Atkinson (1977, p. 217), although it is open to question in view of the group nature of most private schemes which now exists. In judging the role of private schemes there is the further argument that private schemes may help to stimulate growth because they are funded.

The preceding arguments suggest rationalizations for either a flat-rate pension only (set at a fairly high level); a combination of a compulsory earnings-related pension with a necessarily lower flat-rate pension; or a second tier from which individuals may contract out, leaving the state with the obligation to pay only the flat rate. Nothing in the discussion of basic issues suggests that those contracting out should receive favourable income tax treatment. Indeed they would need to pay higher contributions for their flat-rate pension (relative to those remaining in the scheme), otherwise a redistributive scheme could not exist.

The private and public sector partnership

The partnership between the state and private schemes in Britain does not fit any of the 'models' discussed above. The decision of whether or not to contract out is taken by the employer, whose employees would then belong to the same group scheme. Problems for early leavers therefore still remain, although these are reduced as the scheme approaches maturity. A scheme which is contracted out must pay each individual what is referred to as a Guaranteed Minimum Pension (GMP). This is based on the average of the individual's 'lifetime' qualifying earnings; that is, of the earnings measured above the lower earnings limit and below the upper limit. The contracted-out scheme has no indexation of pensions in payment after retirement, and has less generous indexation of earnings than in the state scheme; for early leavers this is fixed at 8½ per cent per year. Furthermore, the provisions in the contracted-out scheme for widows, whereby a widow can receive one-half of her husband's GMP, is much less generous than in the state scheme, where a widow can inherit her husband's pension and continue to receive any pension of her own, up to a maximum. The important feature of the British scheme is that the state then ensures that the individual receives the same pension as if he or she had not been contracted out. Thus the state pays the difference between the GMP and the amount which an individual with the same earnings history would receive in the state scheme. This of course includes the indexation of pensions in retirement.

The nature of the contract between the state and the private scheme is therefore rather uncertain, at least from the point of view of the state. In return for the agreement to pay an unspecified proportion of each individual's pension (a proportion which falls as inflation rises), the private scheme receives a National Insurance *rebate*, equal to a proportion of contributions paid on earnings measured above the lower earnings limit. From 6 April 1984, the employee and employer National Insurance rates for contracted-in members are 9 and 11.45 per cent respectively of gross earning up to £250 per week, where earnings exceed £34 per week. Contracted-out contributions are the same as above, as proportions of earning below £34, but are reduced to 6.85 and 7.35 per cent of earnings measured above £34 (up to £250 as before). The rebate is therefore equal to 6.25 per cent of earnings measured above £34.

The rebate can then of course be used to help pay for contributions to the contracted-out scheme. The anomaly here is that employees can deduct the contributions to the private scheme from their taxable income, and the contracted-out scheme also receives very favourable tax concessions. Creedy and Gemmell (1984, p. 57) have shown that this tax concession for contracted-out employees is equivalent to a reduction of more than one percentage point in the standard rate of income tax. No official reasons for this feature seem to have been given, however.

It has been suggested by Hemming and Kay (1982, p. 305) that the contracting-out arrangements are equivalent to an investment by the state in certain private sector pension funds. The usefulness of this investment thus depends on the real rate of return obtained. Hemming and Kay suggest that this rate will probably be slightly negative and that little more than a quarter of the pension entitlements of contracted-out employees will be met by GMPs (1982, p. 207). The Government Actuary anticipates that the number contracted out will remain steady at about 11 millions, but that the unexpected large amount of contracting out at the start of the scheme meant that the contributions of those remaining in the state scheme had to be increased to make up for the high total value of rebates (1982, p. 17). The rebate is expected to fall steadily until early in the next century, as the scheme matures.

Contracting out under the present arrangements therefore leads to further elements of unpredictability, and makes the achievement of a reasonable basic pension more difficult to achieve. Not only did the government accept the false claim that it is impossible for private schemes to provide indexation, but they then provided special index-linked securities (offering a fairly attractive real rate of return) which could only be purchased by the private funds. Looked at from the point of view of financing government expenditure in a way which does not involve an increase in the money supply, the sales of such bonds may even seem attractive to governments in the short run. However, without further analysis of the long-run implications of increasing this form of government debt, it is not obvious that this is the most appropriate method of pension provision. It is too simplistic to argue, for example, that a large amount of index-linked debt provides a strong incentive for governments to pursue policies which restrain inflation.

The difficulties inherent in the British scheme are not however only a reflection of the unique form of pension partnership which has been adopted. An analysis of contracting out of the earnings-related component of a two tier scheme, using the simple framework described in section 4.1 and without the awkward complications arising from the use of GMPs, shows that there are also severe administrative complexities in addition to the greater difficulty of financing the flat-rate component (see Creedy, 1982a, pp. 65–70). The effects on redistribution of contracting out will also be discussed in the next chapter.

5

Lifetime Redistribution

A state pension scheme provides probably the clearest example of a government policy whose redistributive impact can only be assessed on the basis of comparisons over a very long period of time. For example, in a pay-as-you-go scheme the contributions (whether in the form of an hypothecated tax or as part of an income tax) of each member of the working population are used to pay the pensions of the current 'stock' of pensioners. But those contributions provide the individual with a qualifying 'right' to receive a pension at a later stage in his life cycle (or perhaps for dependants to receive a pension if he does not survive beyond retirement age). This is of course the basis of Samuelson's (1958) well-known demonstration that a metaphorical social contract between three generations can increase welfare. Samuelson's result applied to a simple growth model in which contributions and benefits were directly proportional to earnings, and the results were extended by Aaron (1966) to show that, 'social insurance can increase the welfare of each person if the sum of the rates of growth of population and real wages exceeds the rate of interest' (1966, p. 372).

The problem with these simple results, whereby income transfers between generations can improve welfare, but where no effective redistribution takes place either within or between generations (so long as the appropriate rates of growth are constant) is that they do not describe any *actual* pension schemes. In practice there are usually complex eligibility requirements, earnings limits, and other complications already discussed in earlier chapters. These imply that there is a wide dispersion in individual rates of return from membership of the state scheme. Some basic analytical problems are discussed in section 5.1, which is followed by an analysis of the redistributive aspects of the British state scheme. Section 5.3 then considers the possible 'limits' to redistribution, in the context of the simple two-period model presented in Chapter 4.

5.1 Some Analytical Problems

It should first be noted that, even in the case of an 'actuarially fair' funded pension scheme for a homogeneous and 'risk-pooling' group of individuals who face the same probabilities of unemployment and earnings changes, and the same mortality rates, there will be some *ex post* redistribution within the group. The fact that some individuals die before retirement age, and that some receive pensions over a long period while others benefit for only a short period, means that the *actual* rates of return will differ from the *ex ante* rates. The conceptual difficulties of dealing with lifetime inequality when there are differences in the length of life, combined with a reluctance to regard purely 'random' redistributions as significant for policy purposes, have led some people to criticize the use of *ex post* measures of redistribution. However, the approach taken here is to investigate the *systematic* redistribution which arises because in practice some risks are associated with income. In view of the complexity of the processes involved, and the difficulty in separating the various components or 'causes' of income inequality, it is argued that an analysis of the implications of any policy for *ex post* redistribution is indeed vital for a rational analysis of policy choices.

One problem (discussed again in Chapter eleven) is that the measurement of redistribution is complicated by the need for a basis of comparison. Whether pensions are examined using measures of individuals' lifetime contributions and benefits (in relation to a measure of earnings), by calculating rates of return, or by the use of explicit measures of dispersion, a statement of the 'redistributive effects' necessarily involves comparison. It is of course extremely difficult to estimate the implications (for saving, retirement behaviour, intra-family income sharing, and labour supply) of not having a state pension scheme. Most studies take the admittedly unsatisfactory position of making comparisons with a distribution of lifetime earnings; that is, with an unspecified distributionally 'neutral' scheme. This approach is also taken below.

Forms of redistribution

It is usual to distinguish between *inter*generational and *intra*generational redistribution. The former contrasts the average circumstances of groups who become members of a state scheme at different points in time, while the latter contrasts the circumstances of different individuals who enter the scheme at the same date. The earlier studies, especially in the United States, concentrated on the question of whether compulsory membership of a state pay-as-you-go scheme provided a reasonable rate of return for the younger cohorts, compared with the older age groups. The latter usually gain on the introduction of a new scheme by being 'blanketed in'; that is, by being given higher benefits than their earlier contributions would normally warrant in insurance terms. It was also feared that the younger groups would obtain a raw deal because of various provisions in the US scheme for relative indexation of contributions and benefits. One implication of compulsory intergenerational transfers through a state pension scheme is of course that voluntary intra-family and other charitable transfers may fall, or be 'crowded out', and there is evidence to suggest that this may be significant (see Cullis and Jones, 1983, for discussion and further references).

Intra-generational redistribution may take a number of forms arising largely because of the differential treatment of demographic groups in most state pension schemes. For example, a single man who has exactly the same age–earnings profile as a married man (whose wife does not work or has contracted out of the state scheme) and who lives for the same number of years after retirement, will obtain a much lower rate of return on his contributions. Pension schemes usually treat men and women quite differently; women often obtain full benefits after a much shorter amount of time in the labour force, and have a lower retirement age and longer life expectancy than men. For simplicity the following analysis is restricted only to the single pension received by men. Some of the *ex post* redistribution (among those with equal annual average lifetime earnings), is 'random' to the extent that the pension formula does not usually take into account the time profile of contributions, and there is a dispersion in the age at death. But there may also be systematic influences at work, particularly if there is a tendency for those with relatively high lifetime earnings to pay the bulk of their contributions later in a shorter working life, and to live longer after retirement. These systematic factors may outweigh any 'progressivity' which might be implied by the benefit formula, as discussed further in section 5.2 below.

An alternative approach to examining the distributive implications of pensions may be briefly mentioned here. This involves the estimation of non-marketable pension rights of individuals, in order to include them as a component of human capital in the analysis of the dispersion of wealth. Even if a pension scheme were entirely distributionally neutral, pension wealth (the present value of expected pension benefits) would form a much higher proportion of total wealth for those with relatively lower values of non-human capital. Thus their inclusion in the distribution of wealth would have the effect of reducing a measure of relative dispersion (even after allowing for the higher contractual savings in private pension schemes of the higher wealth holders). These aspects will not however be examined below, but for a recent analysis see Dunn and Hoffman (1983).

Some earlier studies

The financial and redistributive effects of state pension schemes have attracted considerably more attention in the United States than in Britain. As indicated above, earlier American studies were concerned initially with the question of whether the state scheme gave 'value for money'; examples include Harvey (1965) and Deran (1966). The method used in virtually all the studies has been to compare the accumulated value of contributions (from membership of the scheme up to retirement), with the discounted value of pensions (from retirement to death). Alternatively the same basic approach can be used to calculate a rate of return from the pension scheme; that is, the rate of interest for which the accumulated contributions are equal to the discounted value of benefits. Lifetime benefit–contribution ratios, or internal rates of return, were then obtained for different income, occupational, or demographic groups. The most comprehensive early analysis was by Brittain (1967, reprinted in 1972), who showed that, so long as benefits are adjusted in line with earnings, the average yields varied from 2.78 to 6.28 per cent (1972, p. 168). The lowest was better than that previously obtained from private savings, while the highest value was low compared with long-run equity yields. Brittain also found that the yields were systematically higher for the relatively low earners, although his estimates made no allowance for differential mortality (see Brittain, 1972, p. 170). At about the same time Aaron (1967) examined similar issues, paying particular attention to occupational differences in age–earnings profiles. He showed that members of the US scheme received 'value for money', that there was a certain amount of systematic redistribution from high to low lifetime earners, but that substantial inequities occurred because benefits were related only to the last few years of earnings before retirement.

Aaron (1977) later carried out a much more extensive analysis of the redistributive effects of the US state pension scheme. This valuable study allowed for differential mortality (using the results of Kitagawa and Hauser (1973) for different income, race, education, sex, and marital status groups), different earnings profiles of occupation and education groups, and different ages of entry into the labour force. Aaron showed that the apparent progressivity of the benefit formula was fully offset by the effect of differential mortality, which in turn was reinforced by variations in age at entry and educational attainment: 'In short, retirement benefits are regressive, not progressive' (Aaron, 1977, p. 157).

The main comparable, but far less detailed, studies of British schemes were made by Atkinson (1970) and Prest (1970). Both investigated the likely impact of the 1969 proposals of the Labour Party, which were subsequently scrapped following the Conservative Party victory of 1970. Similar results were obtained by each study, although only Atkinson made any allowance for differential mortality (using results of Revell (1967) for top wealth holders), and he calculated rates of return in addition to benefit–contribution ratios at different rates of interest. The proposals seemed to favour older cohorts (who would have been 'blanketed' into the scheme), married couples and single women compared with single men, and gave a higher rate of return to the lower paid.

Later British studies were made in connection with the new state scheme introduced in 1978, and these are discussed in the following section. But several features of the earlier studies may be mentioned here. First, in any examination of pension plans it is necessary to make explicit assumptions about changes in average real earnings, and sometimes also about changes in an index of prices. The results may depend on those assumptions, and on corresponding assumptions made about the indexation of, say, contribution and benefit ceilings. It has been shown in Chapter 3 that the British legislation has indexation regulations which cannot be expected to last very long, so that some sensible choice must be made. Secondly, even in the case of Aaron's later study which allowed for occupational and other differences in average age–earnings profiles, the models allowed no *individual* relative earnings changes from year to year. In view of the special averaging procedure used in the new British scheme, such changes must be explicitly taken into account. Thirdly, Aaron's (1977) work clearly shows the importance of allowing for differential mortality when examining intra-generational redistribution. A fourth characteristic of these studies (*and* those discussed in the next section) is that in considering differences between generations they are essentially partial equilibrium analyses. In particular, they do not allow for the possible effects on future growth rates of alternative methods of financing the pensions of a series of cohorts. Such wider effects may introduce additional intergenerational redistribution, where current pensioners are benefited at the expense of slower growth, especially if aggregate savings are reduced (in the context of a life-cycle saving approach). A more general analysis of the US system, concentrating only on intergenerational redistribution, has more recently been made by Leimer and Petri (1981). They considered the effects of alternative policies (including partial funding, which provides an earlier stimulus to investment) and showed that the differences between cohorts are much greater than indicated by the usual rate of return calculations. No comparable studies seem to be available for Britain, however.

5.2 The British State Scheme

Despite the point made at the beginning of this chapter that a lifetime perspective must be taken in considering pension redistribution, it was often claimed at the time the scheme was introduced that the pension formula is progressive. The two-tier formula, described in Chapter 3, does indeed give a lower ratio of annual pension to pensionable earnings, for higher values of the latter. For example, in the fully mature scheme with a basic pension of £810, an individual with pensionable earnings of £5000 would receive an annual pension of 37 per cent of pensionable earnings; since $(810 + 0.25 (5000 - 810))/5000 = 0.37$. On the other hand, someone with pensionable earnings of £2000 would receive an annual pension of 55 per cent of pensionable earnings.

Despite this feature of the pension formula, the scheme is not necessarily redistributive. Many other factors have to be taken into account. Ignoring for the moment the differences between arrangements for men and women, and between single and married persons, it is necessary to allow for (at least) the following complications. First, National Insurance contributions are obviously regressive because of the upper earnings limit. Secondly, there are differences in the time-period during which individuals contribute to the scheme (since full entitlement does not require participation over the whole of the 'working life'). Thirdly, different age–earnings profiles imply a different timing of contributions. In the current British scheme this is complicated by the fact that the earnings limits are adjusted using a price index, but at retirement all previous qualifying earnings are revalued using an index of average earnings, so that higher earnings in earlier years may turn out to be more important in affecting pensionable earnings. But as explained in Chapter 3 this type of arrangement may perhaps be expected to be short-lived. Fourthly, the averaging procedure means that there is no simple relationship between, say, annual average lifetime earnings and the average of the 20 best (inflation adjusted) years' earnings. Fifthly, there is the important role played by differential mortality.

Some simulation results

Given these complications it seems that the most appropriate method of examining the intra-generational redistribution implied by the British state pension involves the use of simulation techniques. Allowing for the varying experiences of men, women (including widows, and in each case considering single and married persons separately) for experience of sickness and unemployment, and non-participation in the labour force (including differences in age at entry) over the life cycle, and in each case for different general earnings profiles associated with different occupation and education groups, would present formidable difficulties. However, more narrowly based simulations have been carried out by Creedy (1980a, 1982c), as discussed in the previous chapter. These simulations, which allow for differential mortality, were also used to examine the possible extent of *ex post* redistribution of lifetime earnings among a group of men who were 'almost fully employed' over the whole of their working life, and were fully contracted into the state scheme. In the first study, ratios of accumulated contributions to discounted pensions (at retirement) were compared with annual average lifetime earnings. The results showed a very small amount of redistribution, with considerable variation in the ratios (Creedy, 1980a, pp. 60–1). In the second study the approach taken was to compare the present values at age 20 of alternative income streams. The dispersion of net lifetime income (that is, income after the payment of contributions and the receipt of pensions over the period of retirement) was compared with the dispersion of gross earnings over the working life. Furthermore, employers' contributions were ignored.

TABLE 5.1 *Dispersion of alternative distributions (no general growth in real earnings)*

Distribution		Rate of interest	Measure of dispersion		
			η	σ^2	$I(1.6)$
Lifetime earnings		0.02	0.342	0.132	0.090
		0.04	0.324	0.123	0.082
Post contribution earnings		0.02	0.348	0.135	0.092
		0.04	0.330	0.124	0.084
Net lifetime income	(i)	0.02	0.339	0.129	0.088
		0.04	0.325	0.121	0.082
	(ii)	0.02	0.337	0.128	0.088
		0.04	0.324	0.120	0.081
Post contribution earnings		0.02	0.345	0.132	0.091
		0.04	0.326	0.122	0.082
Net lifetime income	(i)	0.02	0.339	0.129	0.088
		0.04	0.323	0.120	0.081
	(ii)	0.02	0.339	0.129	0.088
		0.04	0.323	0.120	0.081

$m/b = 7$ brackets the first Net lifetime income block; $m/b = 10$ brackets the second Net lifetime income block.

Note: Case (i) is for pensions based on average lifetime earnings and Case (ii) is for pensions based on the best 20 years' earnings (in each case between earnings limits). Contributions rate = 0.05.

Source: Creedy (1982c, p. 106).

A number of comparisons are presented in Table 5.1, for the situation in which there is no general growth in real earnings over the period. Here the schemes described in Chapter 4, and referred to as schemes A and B, are equivalent. In each case the contributions rate is set at 5 per cent of gross earnings below the upper limit in each year, and results are given for two annual real rates of interest (0.02 and 0.04). Three measures of dispersion are used; the coefficient of variation η, the variance of logarithms σ^2, and Atkinson's measure $I(1.6)$, based on an 'inequality aversion' parameter of 1.6. It can be seen that there is a negligible difference between results using a ratio of upper to lower earnings limits of ten and those for a ratio of seven. Table 5.1 clearly shows that contributions are slightly 'regressive', since they raise the measures of dispersion of past contribution earnings relative to lifetime earnings. However, inclusion of the receipt of pensions shows that the system as a whole results in very little redistribution of lifetime income from the relatively high to the relatively low earners.

TABLE 5.2 *Dispersion of alternative distributions (with general growth in real earnings)*

Distribution	Pension scheme	Rate of interest	Measure of dispersion		
			η	σ^2	$I(1.6)$
Lifetime earnings	—	0.02	0.352	0.139	0.095
		0.04	0.333	0.125	0.085
Net lifetime income	A	0.02	0.346	0.135	0.092
		0.04	0.332	0.125	0.085
	B	0.02	0.344	0.134	0.091
		0.04	0.331	0.124	0.085
Lifetime earnings	—	0.02	0.362	0.146	0.100
		0.04	0.343	0.133	0.090
Net lifetime income	A	0.02	0.355	0.139	0.096
		0.04	0.341	0.030	0.089
	B	0.02	0.350	0.138	0.094
		0.04	0.338	0.130	0.088

(The first four rows correspond to $g = 0.01$; the last four rows correspond to $g = 0.02$.)

Notes: In scheme A everything is adjusted in line with the growth of average earnings. In scheme B pensionable earnings are based on real earnings but the earnings limits are adjusted using an earnings index. The ratio of the upper to the lower earnings limit is 7 in every case. Pensionable earnings are based on earnings in the best 20 years, and the contributions rate is 0.05 of earnings up to the upper limit.

Source: Creedy (1982c, p. 107).

Comparable results for the situation in which real earnings grow at a steady rate are shown in Table 5.2. As before, contributions are assumed to be 5 per cent of gross earnings below the upper limit. Results are shown only for the situation in which pensionable earnings are based on earnings in the best 20 years, and where the ratio of upper to lower earnings limits is seven. The existence of steady growth in real earnings, in which all members of the cohort share, implies that the dispersion of discounted lifetime earnings is higher than in Table 5.1. Nevertheless neither variant of the new British scheme implies a significant amount of *ex post* intra-generational redistribution.

Flat-rate pensions

An alternative to the two-tier scheme has often been suggested is the use of a flat-rate pension financed from earnings-related contributions (no upper earnings limit). The use of a fixed pension set in relation to average earnings involves a saving in administrative costs. There would be no need to maintain records of complete earnings histories, though records relating to eligibility would need to be maintained. The absence of earnings-related benefits would make it possible, with the same contributions rates, to pay a higher basic pension than otherwise. Simulations were therefore carried out for a pension of one half of the average earnings of all age-groups combined. In the case where there is no general growth in real earnings, average earnings remain at the real value of £3780 (as discussed on page 61) so that the appropriate value for the basic pension is £1890. This is significantly higher than the basic pension in the two-tier scheme.

TABLE 5.3   *Dispersion of net lifetime income (flat-rate pension, no general growth of average real earnings)*

	Measure of dispersion		
Rate of interest	η	σ^2	$I(1.6)$
0.02	0.325	0.119	0.081
0.04	0.315	0.114	0.077

Notes: Contributions rate = 0.05 in each case. The pension is a half of average real earnings in each year.

Source: Creedy (1982c, p. 109).

It is clear that a flat-rate scheme will involve some redistribution of lifetime earnings. Since contributions are assumed to be directly proportional to earnings the relative dispersion of pre- and post-contribution earnings are equal. Redistribution occurs because of the equalizing effect of the fixed pension. However, this is offset to some extent by differential mortality. The *ex post* redistributive effect may be seen from Table 5.3, which shows alternative measures of the distribution of net lifetime income for a contributions rate of 0.05, and with no general growth in real earnings (there was little difference between values for different rates of growth). The values in Table 5.3 must be compared with the dispersion of discounted lifetime earnings given in Table 5.1.

In contrast to results for the new state scheme, Table 5.3 shows that a flat-rate scheme would involve noticeably more *ex post* redistribution. The extent of the reduction in the dispersion of net lifetime income compared with that of gross lifetime earnings depends to some extent on the measure of dispersion used. The coefficient of variation is reduced by about 5 per cent, and the other two measures reduced by about 10 per cent, when the rate of interest is 2 per cent per year. The reduction is slightly less when the annual rate of interest is higher.

Other forms of redistribution

In their study of the wider costs of some alternative pension arrangements, which allowed for interdependencies between pensions, the tax system and the Supplementary Benefit system, Altmann and Atkinson (1982) present provisional estimates of the 'average lifetime earnings' of a number of cohorts. Although they acknowledge that their calculations are 'extremely crude' (1982, p. 92), substantial differences between cohorts were revealed. For example, in the case of married couples, average lifetime incomes were estimated to be considerably larger in the year 2031 than in 1986; these differences ranged from 60 per cent (for the age-group 60–4) to 130 per cent (age-group 80 and older). Those retired or close to retirement at the introduction of the scheme in 1978 are much worse off than the younger cohorts can expect to be, so long as the metaphorical social contract is not broken. Despite the many conceptual and technical problems in measuring lifetime earnings and intergenerational redistribution, there seems little doubt that the latter aspect is more significant than intragenerational redistribution. More research needs to be carried out on this question.

On the basis of the provisions for women in the new British pension scheme (rather than a full-scale study of redistribution), it seems that they obtain a much 'better deal' than men. Women have a lower retirement age than men (60 rather than 65, and their average length of life is longer), and a widow can inherit her husband's pension if she is over 50 when he dies (and a proportion of the pension if she is over

40), irrespective of the age of the husband. However, a widower can inherit his wife's pension only if they are both over retirement age when she dies. Inherited pensions are paid in addition to the individual's own pension, subject to a maximum. Bearing in mind the further point that wives are on average younger than their husbands, and spend less time at work, Hemming (1984, p. 136) has argued that 'women get four times as much benefit per pound of contribution as men'. While acknowledging that previous British pension schemes have placed women at a disadvantage relative to men, Hemming suggests that more equal treatment would produce considerable reductions in the long-term costs of the new scheme.

It has been suggested above that the British pension seems to imply very little intra-generational redistribution among income groups, but that intergenerational effects are perhaps more important. It is therefore worth asking whether a pension scheme, which is designed primarily to shift income between the working life and retirement period of individuals, could *in principle* be expected also to provide an instrument for the redistribution of lifetime income among individuals. This is examined in the following section.

5.3 Redistribution in the Simple Framework

In Chapter 4 a very basic framework of analysis was used to examine the relationship between pensions and contributions in alternative schemes. The two-period approach may also be used to examine 'lifetime' redistribution within a single cohort. This is achieved by comparing present values of gross earnings with those of net earnings; that is, earnings after the payment of contributions and receipt of pensions. The approach, set out in Creedy (1980b, 1982a), has also been adopted by Shimono and Tachibanaki (1982) to examine the implications of the Japanese pension scheme. The basic framework does not (unlike the simulations) allow for differential mortality, or relative changes in earnings over working life, or possible labour supply responses. Thus the results can to some extent be regarded as showing the 'limits' to redistribution through pensions. Some results, taken from Creedy (1982a, p. 51) are shown in Fig. 5.1 for different types of pension scheme. The coefficient of variation of the distribution of gross earnings used in the calculations was 0.471 (as in Chapter 4 above).

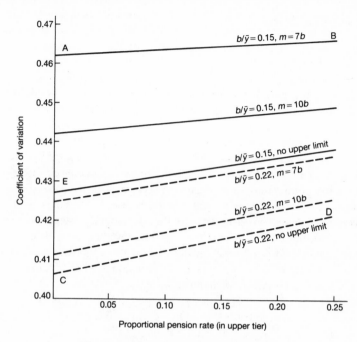

Fig. 5.1 *Dispersion of discounted net income*

Notes: Interest rate = 0.6; b = basic minimum pension; $\bar{y}$ = arithmetic mean earnings (£5431); m = upper earnings limit.

Figure 5.1 shows the relationship between the coefficient of variation of discounted net income and the proportional pension rate used in the upper tier. Examples are given for two different values of the basic pension, for a system without upper earnings limits, and for two different values of the ratio of the upper earnings limit to the basic pension. For example the line marked AB in Fig. 5.1 represents a two-tier scheme with a basic pension of 15 per cent of average earnings and an upper earnings limit of seven times the basic pension (which is the ratio used in the British scheme). The bottom line of Fig. 5.1 marked CD, illustrates the case of a two-tier scheme with no upper earnings limits and a higher basic pension of 22 per cent of average earnings. It is worth noting that the relationship between the coefficient of variation of discounted net income and the proportional pension rate is linear, although it is by no means obvious that this should turn out to be the case. The intercept on the vertical axis, where the proportional pension rate is zero, gives the relative dispersion for a system with only a flat-rate pension. The earnings limit, where appropriate, must therefore be regarded as applying only to earnings-related contributions.

In interpreting these results it is important to stress that variations in the policy parameters (the proportional pension rate and basic minimum pension) are being considered in the context of a self-financing scheme in which any increase in the proportional pension rate must be matched by an appropriate increase in the contributions rate (see Chapter 4 for further details). Increases in the proportional pension rate would otherwise result in larger increases in the coefficient of variation of discounted net income. As the proportional pension rate in the upper tier increases, substantial increases in the contributions rate are required in order to ensure that the scheme is self-financing. Since the burden of the higher contributions falls proportionately more heavily on those with earnings below the upper limit, the dispersion of discounted net income is less unequal than it would be if contributions remained unchanged.

The values in Fig. 5.1 may be compared with the coefficient of variation of discounted net income resulting from a system which combines earnings-related contributions (with no upper limit) with a flat-rate pension only. Using the same rate of interest it is found that the coefficient of variation is equal to 0.404 and 0.375 respectively, for a flat-rate pension of 15 and 22 per cent of average earnings. These values are substantially below points E and C respectively in Fig. 5.1, demonstrating the extent to which an upper earnings limit on contributions (even without earnings-related pensions) reduce the redistributive potential of pensions.

These results show that the dispersion of discounted net income is very sensitive to two ratios. First, relative dispersion is reduced substantially as the ratio of the basic pension to arithmetic mean earnings is increased; compare the continuous lines of Fig. 5.1 with the lower dashed lines for higher basic pensions. In the new British scheme the basic pension is only about one-fifth of average earnings. Secondly, relative dispersion is reduced as the ratio of the upper earnings limit to the basic pension is increased. It is very important to stress that these comparisons are not sensitive to the rate of interest used in the calculations.

The extent of redistribution in the above examples is much less than indicated in the comparisons of annual earnings, which will be reported in chapter eleven below. In the latter case a much larger proportion of the tax revenue is used for distribution to low-income groups. In the former case much of the redistribution is of income between time-periods rather than among persons. Furthermore, the basic framework set out in Chapter 4 can be used to show that partial contracting out of two-tier schemes (and complete contracting out of flat-rate schemes) considerably reduces their redistributive ability (see Creedy, 1982a, pp. 70–4). This contradicts the confident statement of the Second Permanent Secretary in the DHSS that, 'it proved possible to devise contracting-out systems which left the redistributive and subsidy element of the state scheme more or less intact' (Atkinson, 1977, p. 216).

The main result of this chapter is therefore that two-tier pension schemes allow little intra-generational redistribution of life earnings, when the higher contribution costs are properly taken into account. This result occurs despite the nature of the pension formula which seems to give a lower replacement rate to higher earners. The existence of the earnings-related component also means that the basic pension must be lower than otherwise for any given level of contributions. This feature makes the maintenance of an adequate minimum pension more difficult to achieve. Both points are reinforced when contracting out of the state pension is allowed.

PART 3

Unemployment and Sickness

6
Labour Market Dynamics and Social Insurance

It has been seen that one of the implications of increasing longevity towards the end of the last century was to increase significantly the number of aged people who were nevertheless unable to work because of sickness or disability. This placed great strain on the sickness schemes run by Friendly Societies, and on the system of poverty relief under the old Poor Law. The 'solution' to this problem took the form of a state pension payable on reaching a set age, so that the qualifying condition, other than the contribution record, could easily be checked (thereby bypassing the moral hazard problem). Although individuals could remain in employment above the 'pensionable age', most people moved into the 'permanent' state of retirement when eligible for a pension.

Unemployment and sickness therefore present quite distinct issues, since they are usually *interruptions* to employment. Some form of insurance must be devised to cover these types of temporary experience. Chapter 7 considers unemployment, and Chapter 8 then examines sickness insurance. Disability and invalidity benefits are also included in Chapter 8, although these interruptions to employment may turn out to be permanent. Before discussing these schemes, however, it is useful to consider in some detail the processes which govern the movement of individuals among the labour market 'states' of employment, unemployment, and sickness. This is the object of the present chapter.

Stocks and flows

These movements or transitions of individuals among states are important for a number of reasons, not least because they have implications for the possibilities of private insurance and the design of social security systems. The figure for the *stock* in a particular state, at a point in time, provides only one dimension of the problem. One issue concerns the incidence of unemployment and sickness across the working population. For example, the number of people unemployed each month receives wide media coverage, but provides little information about the character of the stock. Are the unemployed that are counted the same people each month, or is there rapid turnover of the unemployment register? Do people leaving the register re-enter it frequently, and when they leave the register do they all return to employment or enter other labour market states, such as sickness, or even leave the labour force completely?

These questions are crucial in the evaluation of state schemes, since schemes usually have a number of provisions relating to the duration of spells of sickness and unemployment, and to past employment history. For example, the British scheme has a 'linked-spells' rule, whereby spells not separated by a minimum number of weeks are grouped as a single spell for determining benefit exhaustion. These aspects will be examined in the next two chapters.

The general discussion in Chapter 1 of economic arguments concerning state and private insurance also emphasized the relevance of population heterogeneity with regard to the risks faced by individuals. If the experience of unemployment and sickness is highly concentrated among a small proportion of the working population then Chapter 1 suggested that there was a greater likelihood of private market failure. Depending on the 'causes' to which the high risks are attributed, then views concerning redistribution are also relevant. An important point concerning population heterogeneity in the risks faced by individuals is that the optimal provision of social insurance may require quite distinct modes of treatment for different types of person. The appropriate policy for someone who suffers very infrequent short spells of unemployment may be completely inappropriate for someone who suffers long spells, often separated by only a few weeks of employment. It will be argued that the extent of population heterogeneity has too often been neglected in social insurance planning.

Finally, another crucial issue is whether individual risks are constant, irrespective of past history or the current labour market state occupied. Does past unemployment increase the likelihood of present unemployment? Does the probability of leaving the unemployment register depend on the duration of the current spell of unemployment? Unfortunately, as shown later, it is not possible to answer this question unequivocally when using aggregative data. But this issue is important in designing social security systems. Suppose, for example, that the long-duration unemployed have such low (constant) probabilities of moving into employment that the degree of generosity of unemployment benefits has an insignificant impact on their exit probability, through possible incentive effects. Then the redistributive case for generosity would seem to outweigh the incentive case against generosity. However, if the length of time already spent in unemployment affects an individual's chances of gaining employment (for example because 'discouraged' people reduce their intensity of job search, or because employers use simple rules of thumb in screening candidates) a different policy would be recommended.

The process by which individuals move among states is therefore considered here in some detail. Section 6.1 examines a simple framework for describing transitions and relationships between stocks and flows. Section 6.2 deals with the important question of 'state dependence', and whether individual heterogeneity, as opposed to state dependence, explains declining aggregate exit probabilities from particular states. The implications for social insurance are considered briefly in section 6.3, and these issues prove to be crucial in the ensuing examination of the unemployment insurance and sickness insurance schemes in Chapters 7 and 8.

6.1 Simple Models of Labour Market Transitions

Virtually all the UK data relating to unemployment and sickness experience are collected as part of the administration of social insurance. Yet the kind of data which are required, for a thorough examination of those aspects of labour market dynamics which are relevant for evaluating the system, are not available. Only information about incompleted, rather than completed spells, is published; there are few data relating to flows; and steps have only recently been taken to collect longitudinal data tracing the work experience of individuals over a long period of time.

In the absence of such data it is first worth examining some aggregate relationships, under very simple assumptions about labour market dynamics. Given the total number of spells recorded per year, and the size of the working population, the ratio of the former to the latter gives the aggregate (average) frequency of spells per year. Since there are roughly 4 million spells of unemployment and 10 million spells of notified sickness each year in the United Kingdom, it can be found (given the size of the working population) that the average annual number of spells of unemployment is roughly 0.14, and for spells of sickness it is roughly 0.35.

The unemployment rate, that is the ratio of the number unemployed to the working population, is determined jointly by the average frequency of spells of unemployment and the average duration of unemployment (although reference is usually made to a *rate*, it is of course strictly a ratio of two *stock* magnitudes). In fact if s, u, and d denote the average spell frequency, the unemployment rate, and the average duration of unemployment respectively, then the simple relationship holds that

$$u = sd \qquad (6.1)$$

With a total number in unemployment of about 3 million, the average duration of unemployment is therefore $(3/4) \times 52$ weeks; that is, about 39 weeks. With about 1.1 million sick, the average length of a spell of sickness is $(1.1/10) \times 52$ or about 5.7 weeks. These figures approximate those for the United Kingdom during 1983.

If, furthermore, it is assumed that all individuals have the same exit probability, and that this probability is constant irrespective of spell length (i.e. no duration dependence) then this exit probability is equal to $1/d$. So under this assumption in 1983 in the United Kingdom the average weekly exit probability from unemployment was 0.025 and from sickness it was 0.18. These results are obtained on the assumption that the distribution of completed spell durations is generated by what is known as a first-order Markov process, in which the constant exit probability is dependent solely on the labour market state currently occupied.

The Markov process is usually used in the context of a simple 'transition matrix' approach. Few suitable data have been available for the UK (though see Creedy and Disney, 1981b), but the approach has been used in the United States for some time. The simple formulae above apply to specified moves from each defined state in the labour market, and a set of transition rates can be obtained from observations on individuals at discrete points in time. Each transition rate measures the proportion of individuals in one state at the first point in time who are observed to be in another specified state at the second point in time. The longer the time-period between observations, the greater the probability of multiple state changes within the period. Furthermore external conditions may affect the probabilities during the period, if it is long enough; for example the level of labour demand may change. Therefore it is desirable to look at short-period transitions such as the monthly or even weekly exit probabilities described above. Some examples of transition rates are shown in Table 6.1, and are taken from Marston (1976, p. 175). The table omits the proportions of 'stayers', although these can easily be calculated. For example, the first row shows that over 35 per cent of whites aged 25–59 who are unemployed one month are back in employment in the next month while a further 10 per cent leave the labour force, so the remaining 54 per cent (the stayers, or flow 'uu') are still unemployed in the next month. These data have clear implications for the working of the social security system, indicating those age, sex, or racial groups which suffer more employment instability and thereby have inadequate contribution records, and which, on average, suffer longer durations of unemployment and sickness.

TABLE 6.1 *Gross transition rates between labour market states, US aged 25–59, monthly average 1967–73*

Race and sex	eu	en	ue	un	ne	nu
White males	0.009	0.004	0.355	0.102	0.080	0.038
White females	0.009	0.048	0.273	0.294	0.043	0.012
Non-white males	0.015	0.011	0.316	0.126	0.109	0.034
Non-white females	0.012	0.043	0.226	0.337	0.054	0.031

Notes: eu = from employment to unemployment
en = from employment to not in the labour force
ue = from unemployment to employment
un = from unemployment to not in the labour force
ne = from not in the labour force to employment
nu = from not in the labour force to unemployment.

Source: Marston (1976), p. 175.

This approach unfortunately has several limitations. The first drawback, already mentioned briefly, is that even if the underlying model is correct, taking transitions over a discrete interval will ignore multiple moves within the period. Creedy and Disney (1981b) show, using the data in Marston (1976), that the discrete time assumption leads to a large overestimate of the average duration in any particular state. For example the average duration of unemployment spells for white males aged 16–19 (from Marston, p. 177) is found to be 6.81 weeks. When the same data are used to estimate a continuous time Markov model, which explicitly allows for moves made between observation dates, it was found that the average duration fell to 3.77 weeks.

The other crucial assumptions underlying the Markov model of transitions are that the exit probability is constant and dependent solely on the current state occupied. One test of the validity of the first assumption is to look at moves over two or more discrete periods, and to compare this with transitions over the whole period. In the example of all white males in Table 6.1, the probability of exit from unemployment between one month and the next is (ue + un), or just under 0.46, since individuals can move into employment or out of the labour force. Therefore the number of those who were unemployed at the beginning of the first month who remain in unemployment for *two* months is calculated as $(1 - 0.46)^2$, plus the few who have made the moves ue with eu and un with nu in the two months. Given the probabilities in Table 6.1, this gives a proportion of stayers for white males, for two months, of just under 0.3. For longer time-periods the proportion staying in any state for any given 'cohort' declines over time at a constant rate. However most evidence shows that the proportion of stayers does not decline as rapidly as suggested by this model of constant probabilities (see, for example, Clark and Summers, 1979, p. 24). This suggests that the aggregate probability of exit from any labour market state even for a sub-group, defined by age, sex, or race, is not constant and so invalidates one of the assumptions of the first-order Markovian process. Section 6.2 considers why this probability might decline.

TABLE 6.2   *Proportions of three cohorts of men by date of birth experiencing unemployment in 1972 in Britain*

Weeks of sickness 1971	Proportion unemployed in 1972		
	Cohort born 1943	Cohort born 1933	Cohort born 1923
None	0.057	0.037	0.044
⩾ 1	0.124	0.116	0.096
⩾ 3	0.169	0.119	0.119
⩾ 5	0.186	0.141	0.127
⩾ 7	0.207	0.173	0.170
⩾ 9	0.250	0.171	0.130
⩾ 13	0.263	0.227	0.143

Source: Creedy and Disney (1981b), p. 84.

The third underlying assumption mentioned above was that the exit probability was dependent solely on the current state occupied. Table 6.2 gives some data from Creedy and Disney (1981b) for three sample cohorts of men in Britain which casts doubt on this assumption also.

This table suggests that previous spells of sickness increase the probability of current spells of unemployment. This occurs not simply because there is a high transition rate from sickness to unemployment (which is not directly relevant here), but because even the preponderant small spells of sickness appear to increase the probability. This evidence has important implications for social security and it may explain the result (discussed further in Chapter 7) that for the period before 1980, when the 'linked-spells' rule operated over 13 weeks, around 17 per cent of newly unemployed claimants had experienced a spell of sickness within the previous 13 weeks compared with roughly 6 per cent of the population as a whole. Further longitudinal evidence relating to individuals over three successive years, reported in Creedy and Disney (1981b, p. 81), shows clearly that the proportion of individuals making specified moves between the last two years depends on the labour market state occupied in the first year, and that successive changes are not independent.

The conclusion to be drawn from this is that a simple model of labour market flows, in which there are constant probabilities and past history does not matter, does not explain the actual transitions between labour market states. In particular it does not describe fully the close connection between present and past spells of unemployment and sickness. It will be argued below that these interrelationships have implications for the operation of the social security system in Britain that were not originally foreseen. One important feature is the high proportion of the unemployed dependent on Supplementary Benefits even in periods of high employment. The tests described above all relate to fairly broad aggregates, or widely defined groups of individuals. The main classifications used are sex and age, and it is not clear that some of the assumptions of the Markov model are inappropriate to much more narrowly defined groups. Thus population heterogeneity must be considered, and this is the emphasis of the next section. Prior to this, however, it is useful to refer briefly to a problem raised by the failure of those who collect the data to record the durations of completed spells of unemployment.

Completed and uncompleted spell durations

Data are usually available for the distribution of uncompleted spells. Unfortunately there is no simple relation between these distributions and those of completed spells although on occasions mistaken interpretations have been drawn from uncompleted durations. On the one hand, in a constant economic environment, the point at which a spell is observed will on average be its midpoint. Salant (1977) calls this phenomenon 'interruption bias' and it suggests that the duration of completed spells will on average be twice that of uncompleted spells. On the other hand, repeated censuses such as the monthly count of the unemployed will on average observe longer spells more frequently than shorter spells. Indeed short spells which start and finish between two successive monthly counts will never be observed at all. This second aspect, called 'length bias' by Salant, forestalls any simple relationship between completed and uncompleted durations. The frequency of observing spells will depend on the distribution of completed spells. If the variance of this distribution is low, then 'interruption bias' will dominate. But the variances of the distributions of durations in labour market states such as employment, unemployment, and sickness are not in general low. In these cases there is 'length bias' in observing uncompleted durations. Available evidence suggests that the average durations of completed spells of unemployment and sickness in most countries are much lower than the average duration of uncompleted spells, suggesting that 'length bias' outweighs 'interruption bias'. Marston (1976) illustrates the point for spells of unemployment in the United States, and an example for the case of sickness spells in Britain is provided in Chapter 8 of the present book.

This point might at first sight seem merely technical, but data interpretation has had important implications for social security policy. Once techniques and data became available for studying spell durations in Britain and the United States, it was apparent that the average completed spell durations of unemployment and sickness were much shorter than had been thought from the observed uncompleted spells. If spell lengths were short, the redistributive case for state intervention to provide insurance appeared to be weaker. However, such a line of argument takes no account of 'dependence on the past', and population heterogeneity.

6.2 Further Analysis of Exit Rates

Section 6.1 showed that transition rates between labour market states for broadly defined groups of individuals were neither constant nor independent of past history. Aggregate data usually show declining probabilities of exit from states such as unemployment and sickness. This is also the reason, as Salant (1977) shows, why 'length bias' outweighs 'interruption bias', as described in the previous section. It is necessary to consider why the observed exit rates are not constant. In fact there are two quite distinct but not incompatible reasons for this.

Consider two types of individual: 'A-type' individuals with a fixed and high probability of exit from a particular state, and 'B-type' individuals with a fixed and low probability of exit. If a cohort consisting of equal numbers of A and B individuals are traced, it is generally found that, as time passes, a greater proportion of the B-type individuals are left in that state. Obviously those individuals who have low exit probability will on average remain longer in the state. The composition of the group in the state changes. This is sufficient to generate an observed declining aggregate exit probability for A and B individuals together. What is observed is a declining proportion of individuals with the greater probability of exit. Now suppose that all individuals have constant exit probabilities but there is a wide variety of types of person, with characteristics which cause their exit probabilities to differ also. It may only be possible to observe some of these characteristics (age, race, or sex), but some others (such as aptitude or laziness) will not be observable, at least in survey data. If these last characteristics, which generate 'unobserved heterogeneity', are important in determining individual exit rates, for example from unemployment to employment, then what may appear to be declining exit probabilities will actually be a 'sorting' process by which individuals with 'inferior' characteristics will remain unemployed.

This 'unobserved heterogeneity' model of exit probabilities suggests that the hypothesis of constant probabilities can be maintained, but at a much more disaggregated level. The important conclusion for policy is that it is not the experience of a particular state which affects exit probabilities but the underlying characteristics of the individuals. There is a certain amount of evidence which is consistent with this model. Lancaster (1979) showed that as more characteristics are introduced into an analysis of a sample of unemployed, the role of declining exit probabilities in explaining the outflow rate lessens. Cripps and Tarling (1974) used a model with a distribution of constant exit probabilities to generate the distribution of durations of male unemployment in Britain from 1932 to 1973. They argued that for much of the period nearly all long-term unemployment was attributable to a small proportion of those entering unemployment (1974, p. 310). While this conclusion seems less plausible for recent years, it seems appropriate for sickness experience. Similarly Creedy and Disney (1981a) found that a simple model, with four groups of individuals with constant probabilities, could generate distributions reflecting many aspects of the unemployment insurance regime in the United Kingdom. These aspects included the proportions exhausting their claim on Unemployment Benefit through remaining on the register for 52 weeks, and through the operation of the 'linked-spells' rule. The important conclusion of all this for labour market policy is that resources should be put into identifying 'negative' characteristics of the sick and unemployed in order to forestall long durations, rather than using labour market policies where eligibility is conditional on the attainment of long durations. An example of the latter type of policy is the use of training schemes limited to those who have been unemployed over 12 months.

Alternatively, it has been argued that the observed decline in exit probabilities does in fact stem from some form of state dependence. It seems undesirable to explain the decline *wholly* in terms of unobserved phenomena, particularly as most studies such as Lancaster (1979) and Nickell (1979), show declining probabilities even when account is taken of a large number of variables. In addition there are good reasons for believing that the employability of an individual will indeed decline the longer the experience of unemployment or sickness. This may occur as a result of loss of skills, although this decline may be offset by the individual reducing the wage for which he or she is willing to work (the 'reservation wage') as duration lengthens. It is most likely that there is both unobserved heterogeneity and declining individual exit probabilities.

Heckman and Borjas (1981) identify several types of state dependence; that is, ways in which current spell duration and previous labour market history affect current exit probabilities. These include what they term 'occurrence dependence' (called 'spell dependence' above) by which the number of previous spells affects the current exit probability. Disney (1979) provides evidence for Britain that the probability of present unemployment is related to the history of previous spells, which is compatible with this type of state dependence. A second type of state dependence is 'duration dependence', which is more familiar and links the current exit probability to the length of the current spell. Unfortunately it is extremely difficult, without a great deal of individual longitudinal data, to separate state dependence from unobserved heterogeneity. Finally, Heckman and Borjas refer to 'lagged duration dependence' as existing when the current exit probability depends on the duration of previous spells. Narendranathan, Nickell, and Metcalf (1982) provide evidence that a history of long-duration unemployment and sickness forces individuals into lower paid jobs and greater risk of future unemployment, which may provide support for this third type of state dependence. However, careful tests by Heckman and Borjas (1981) on US data fail to find any clear-cut evidence for state dependence in the case of unemployment experience, while regression analysis to determine the impact of measured characteristics on the probability of unemployment and duration of unemployment do not predict the high degree of concentration of unemployment experience which is actually observed.

Although the causes are very difficult to isolate, there is no doubt that experience of unemployment and sickness is highly concentrated among a small proportion of the work-force. For example Disney (1979) found that 5 per cent of three cohorts of men accounted for 80 per cent of the unemployment experienced by those cohorts in Britain over the three-year period 1971–3. Similarly Clark and Summers (1979) found that 2.4 per cent of the unemployed accounted for 41 per cent of all unemployment in the United States in 1974. Similar evidence for the incidence of sickness in both Britain and France is contained in Chapter 8. Further evidence suggests that, at least since the inter-war depression and prior to the mid-1970s, a large proportion of the work-force did not experience any unemployment.

6.3 Implications for Social Insurance

The preceding analysis has several implications for the provision of social insurance, some of which have been mentioned during the course of the chapter. It remains therefore to identify the major issues for social insurance policy. The first stems from the evidence, described above, that the labour market is characterized by considerable heterogeneity of individual experience of employment, unemployment, and sickness. One important conclusion stems from this. For unless there is an efficient system of risk-rating (that is, a scheme by which individual contributions are closely related to individual risks) there will necessarily be cross-subsidization among individuals in the long run and therefore redistribution. The nature of the redistribution depends on the way in which risks are associated with earnings while in employment, and this will be examined in the next two chapters. Some of these issues have been discussed in Chapter 1, and of course this element of risk-sharing explains why the unemployment insurance and sickness insurance schemes may be called 'social insurance' as opposed to conventional risk-rated insurance. The likelihood of adverse selection problems (when individuals know their own risks) further suggests that state social insurance must be compulsory for all. It may be mentioned here that the heterogeneity of labour force experience also implies that models of optimal social security provision for short-term interruption which treat individuals as homogeneous, such as those of Baily (1978) and Flemming (1978), may give misleading results.

A second theme stemming from the preceding analysis concerns the concentration of unemployment and sickness among a small proportion of the work-force. This concentration can arise from heterogeneity and from state dependence. A theme of Chapter 7 will be the failure of the National Insurance scheme to have provided adequate earnings replacement for the unemployed because of its eligibility conditions. Chapter 8 suggests that the long-term sick have faced similar problems. Inevitably, perhaps, a scheme of social insurance provision which implicitly assumes that interruptions to employment are widely spaced, of short duration, and random in their incidence, as opposed to frequent, long duration, and concentrated among a proportion of the population at risk, will fail to provide adequate insurance cover for those primarily at risk. In turn this raises the important question of whether a 'quasi-insurance' system is the best method of providing income maintenance for the unemployed and sick. As shown in Chapters 7 and 8, there has been a general drift towards means-tested benefits for these groups, and the use of selective labour market policies for the long-term unemployed and sick. This has been combined with a simultaneous erosion of National Insurance benefits for a short-term claimants. This trend may call into question the rationale for using the National Insurance scheme of benefits and contributions as a way of dealing with temporary interruptions to employment.

Finally recent research, some of which has been described here, gives a better picture of those most at risk of unemployment and sickness, and how this concentration of experience has come about. Such data allow more effective direct use of labour market policies, both 'active' such as retraining and subsidies and 'passive', namely social security payments, aimed at particular groups. They also help to establish the likely consequences of such policies. Some such targeting already exists, for example in specific disablement benefits, but the point is more general. As an illustration, the next chapters consider in more detail the thorny question of whether social insurance provision induces changes in individual behaviour: for example whether individuals prolong spells of unemployment or sickness as a result of the existence of state social insurance benefits. Better knowledge of the actual experience of individuals with particular characteristics, for example the change, if any, in their exit probability over the spell, gives a better guide to the impact of social insurance than more aggregative analyses.

7
Unemployment Benefits

Unemployment in the United Kingdom rose from 5.7 per cent of the labour force in 1978 to 13.2 per cent at the beginning of 1984. Concurrently, transfer payments to the unemployed rose from £1.4 billion in 1978–9 to £6.5 billion for 1984–5 (from 8.5 to 17.2 per cent, respectively, of social security expenditure; HMSO, 1984). Not surprisingly this increase in expenditure on unemployment benefits, over a period when the government has imposed tight overall constraints on public expenditure, has generated much controversy. Much of the discussion concerns the extent to which the potential moral hazard problems of state unemployment insurance have contributed to the rise in unemployment. One response of the government was to abolish the Earnings Related Supplement to Unemployment Benefit, starting with the 5 per cent 'abatement' in 1980. Many comparisons can be made with the experience of the 1930s, described in Chapter 2.

It is obviously not possible to examine all aspects of unemployment insurance here. Section 7.1 continues the theme of the previous chapter by showing how eligibility for unemployment benefits depends on both the nature of the rules governing eligibility *and* the structure of labour market flows. Section 7.2 then considers some market failure aspects of unemployment insurance, and finally section 7.3 provides some evidence about the redistributive effects of the UK system, using longitudinal evidence. However, some important features of the system are first described.

Unemployment benefits in the UK

Unemployed people in the United Kingdom may be eligible for two kinds of benefits. These are as follows:

(i) *National Insurance Unemployment Benefits.* Since 1982 these are flat-rate, and may be received for up to a year in a single or linked spell of unemployment. Eligibility is dependent on having paid a sufficient value of National Insurance contributions over a specified period, called the 'contribution year'.

(ii) *Supplementary Benefit*, with, since 1983, related housing benefit. These benefits are means-tested, and are payable to households with no income from employment whose income from other sources falls below a designated minimum level. Unemployed households are entitled to Supplementary Benefit at the (lower) short-term rate, and may receive it either as a supplement to Unemployment Benefit, or as a substitute for National Insurance benefit when claimants are ineligible for Unemployment Benefit, for example having exhausted their claim by virtue of the spell duration exceeding a year. In the late 1970s, when unemployment was lower than current levels, Clark (1978) found that 38 per cent of male unemployed recipients of Supplementary Benefit had insufficient contributions to be eligible for Unemployment Benefit; 3 per cent and 1 per cent respectively had their claim for Unemployment Benefit disallowed for leaving a job voluntarily and for industrial misconduct. The remainder had exhausted their entitlement to Unemployment Benefit or were supplementing it with the means-tested benefits.

The proportion of households receiving Supplementary Benefit in these last categories has increased substantially in recent years. This has resulted from an increasing number of the unemployed having spells (or linked spells) in excess of one year, and from the phasing out of Earnings Related Supplement. Table 7.1 gives the number of unemployed in selected years, the proportions of the unemployed in various benefit categories, and total expenditure on the various benefits. These data show that in recent years the proportion of unemployed in receipt of Unemployment Benefit has declined sharply. The treatment of the short-term unemployed has been less generous since the abolition of the Earnings Related Supplement, the 5 per cent 'abatement' of Unemployment Benefit in 1980, and the subsequent decision to tax Unemployment Benefit. The result is that in a period of rising unemployment, Unemployment Benefit is the only major social security benefit, other than Sickness Benefit, for which the level of nominal expenditure has actually declined.

7.1 Eligibility for Unemployment Benefits

This section examines benefit eligibility using a model of flows between employment and unemployment. The most important element of Table 7.1 is the substantial and increasing role of means-tested benefits in the provision of unemployment insurance.

TABLE 7.1 *Unemployment Benefits: some aggregate statistics*

Year	Number of unemployed (million)	Unemployed receiving UB only (%)	Unemployed receiving UB and SB (%)	Unemployed receiving SB only (%)	Expenditure on Unemployment Benefit (UB) (£ billion)	Expenditure on Supplementary Benefit (SB) for the unemployed (£ billion)
1	2	3	4	5	6	7
1975–6	1.20	37.6	11.1	33.3	0.55	0.55
1978–9	1.36	31.5	7.1	39.5	0.67	0.71
1981–2	2.76	35.7	8.5	39.3	1.80	2.30
1983–4	3.08	25.6	7.8	52.6	1.67	4.50

Notes: Columns 1, 6, and 7 are for financial years. Column 2 is for December. Columns 3, 4, and 5 are for November (1975–6 and 1978–9) and December (1981–2 and 1983–4).

Sources: Department of Employment *Gazette*, HMSO *Social Trends* (various issues) and HMSO (1984).

However, in planning the system it was envisaged that only 'residual categories' of the population would be forced to rely on means-tested benefits. This raises a number of important issues relating to the motives for state provision of unemployment insurance and the manner in which it is provided, discussed in later sections of this chapter.

At first sight it appears that the substantial reliance of the unemployed on means-tested benefits stems largely from the rule by which Unemployment Benefit is only payable, in a single spell of unemployment, for a maximum of 52 weeks. Now when unemployment rises, the average duration of spells of unemployment increases, so that an increased proportion of the unemployed exhaust their entitlement to National Insurance benefit. As described in Chapter 6, section 6.1, the average weekly probability of leaving the unemployment register, compatible with the stock and flow characteristics of the register in 1983, was approximately 0.025. It can be shown that if this 'exit' probability were constant and independent of spell duration, 26.8 per cent of a cohort of entrants to the unemployment register would still be unemployed 52 weeks later, so becoming wholly reliant on means-tested benefits (assuming they were eligible on grounds of family income deficiency). However, in 1983 the actual proportion with durations exceeding 52 weeks was 41 per cent and rising. Furthermore, as Table 7.1 suggests, the proportion of the unemployed reliant solely on Supplementary Benefit was well over 50 per cent. Clearly the presumption that eligibility can be explained in such a manner is too simplistic.

There are two reasons for the disparity described in the previous paragraph. The first is the existence of the 'linked-spells' rule, by which spells of National Insurance benefit separated by a period of employment of eight weeks or less are treated as a single spell. This means that some individuals will exhaust their Unemployment Benefit well before a year of the current spell has elapsed. However it is difficult to ascertain the impact of this rule without examining the outflow from employment as well as from unemployment.

A second possible reason for the disparity is that the aggregate exit probability from unemployment is not constant. If it declines with duration, then the proportion of the stock of unemployed experiencing durations greater than 52 weeks will be higher than in the constant probability case. As described in Chapter 6, however, the aggregate declining exit probability may stem from declining individual exit probabilities, from population heterogeneity, or from a combination of both. Heterogeneity seems the more plausible reason for the large disparity. For example, Nickell (1979) found that individual probabilities only declined after 26 weeks. This is not enough to have a large effect on the proportion with durations over 52 weeks: for example if the exit probability were 0.03 for the first 26 weeks and then halved, the proportion with durations exceeding 52 weeks would only rise to 30 per cent.

A simple model of labour market flows

A model is therefore needed which incorporates both flows out of employment *and* unemployment, and population heterogeneity. A model of this type, following Creedy and Disney (1981a), can be constructed as follows. Assume that each individual has a constant probability of obtaining employment if unemployed, say θ, and of becoming unemployed if employed, say λ. These probabilities differ among individuals, but four main groups may usefully be distinguished. Individuals with high θ and low λ will on average experience few and short spells of unemployment. Individuals with high θ and high λ will suffer more frequent but on average short spells of unemployment. Young people will come into this category whereas older workers, characterized by low θ and low λ, will tend to experience less frequent but prolonged spells of unemployment. Finally, there is a group with low θ and high λ who suffer frequent and prolonged spells of unemployment. Each of these groups poses distinct policy problems and it is apparent that the unemployment insurance regime will affect each group differently. For example, those with high λ will tend to be affected by the 'linked-spells' rule while those with low θ will be affected by the 52-week duration rule.

Before proceeding with the analysis, it is important to understand the meaning of these constant probabilities. External changes, such as changes in the level of aggregate demand for labour, or a change in the tax and benefit regime for those both in and out of work, may be expected to change these probabilities. The crucial assumption is that the probabilities are 'state independent'; in the context of Chapter 6, a pure sorting model is being used. It might be argued that such a model ignores considerations such as variations in the exit probability stemming from changes in benefit eligibility at different parts of the spell of unemployment. However the model used here is compatible with many behavioural models. At one extreme are models in which individuals have full knowledge of the regime of taxes and benefits and behave 'rationally' throughout the spell of employment or unemployment. At the other extreme are models in which it is assumed that the regulations governing eligibility are so complex, or individuals so myopic, that exit probabilities from unemployment and employment are independent of the tax and benefit regime and wholly dependent on personal characteristics (such as perceived skills) and job characteristics (such as working conditions in different firms). These important issues are considered further in the next section.

Although there may in practice be a wide range of values of θ and λ distributed among individuals, the restriction of the analysis to the four groups described above is facilitated by assuming that there are only two values of each probability. Low values are denoted by the subscript 1 and high values by the subscript 2; thus θ_1 is the probability of leaving the unemployment register by those with a low chance of gaining employment. A proportion $P(\theta_1)$ of the labour force has this low probability. The following values, and proportions are taken from Creedy and Disney (1981a):

$\theta_1 = 0.013$ per week, with $P(\theta_1) = 0.1$
θ_2 is allowed to vary, depending on aggregate demand, with $P(\theta_2) = 0.9$
$\lambda_1 = 0.0006$ per week, with $P(\lambda_1) = 0.85$
$\lambda_2 = 0.036$ per week, with $P(\lambda_2) = 0.15$

A change in the aggregate demand for labour is assumed to affect the outflow probability θ_2 for the majority of the unemployed, $P(\theta_2)$. Changes in the aggregate unemployment rate therefore stem from changes in the average duration of unemployment spells for this group, and a change in the composition of the unemployment register, rather than from changes in the inflow rate. Evidence in support of this assumption may be obtained from statistics of aggregate inflow and exit rates for the unemployment register, which show that in general the outflows fluctuate considerably more than inflow numbers, which are relatively stable except for 1980.

The final component of the model concerns the joint probabilities $P(\lambda_i, \theta_j)$ where $(i, j = 1, 2)$. These may be obtained as follows. Denote the conditional probability of having a low value of θ, given that one has a high value of λ, by $P(\theta_1|\lambda_2)$. Then the joint probability may be obtained, following standard rules, as $P(\theta_1,\lambda_2) = P(\theta_1|\lambda_2) P(\lambda_2)$. The other joint probabilities can then be calculated by subtraction from the marginal proportions. There is a certain amount of evidence, quoted in Creedy and Disney (1981a), that many of those with a high probability of becoming unemployed also have a low chance of gaining employment. The conditional proportion $P(\theta_1|\lambda_2)$ is therefore expected to be *higher* than the aggregate (marginal) proportion of the labour force having the value θ_1. Since there is no direct evidence concerning the likely values of this conditional proportion, a range of values is used in the following analysis.

Benefit exhaustion: the 52-week duration rule

The framwork described above may now be used to investigate various aspects of the unemployment insurance regime, in particular the causes of the high proportion of the unemployed in means-tested benefits. First, the proportion of the unemployed with durations of 52 weeks or more gives a guide to the impact of the benefit exhaustion rule. The equilibrium outcomes for various values of θ_2 and $P(\theta_1|\lambda_2)$ are shown in Fig. 7.1. It is convenient to present 'equilibrium' proportions; that is, the proportions which apply when the aggregate unemployment rate is stable and outflows from the register are exactly matched by inflows.

There are two interesting features of the relationships depicted in Fig. 7.1. First, the proportions of the unemployed with durations of 52 weeks or more at high rates of unemployment are compatible with the evidence. This contrasts with the simple constant probability and homogeneous population case discussed at the beginning of this section. Secondly, the relationship between the proportion experiencing long durations and the aggregate unemployment rate is non-linear. The reason for this is simple. At low rates of unemployment the stock is dominated by the group with low exit probability, θ_1. As aggregate demand for labour falls, the exit probability, θ_2, falls, the unemployment rate rises, and ultimately the stock comes to be dominated by the group with the value θ_2. At the extreme, when $\theta_1 = \theta_2$, and the unemployment rate is 14.8 per cent, the proportion of the labour force experiencing durations over 52 weeks is over 50 per cent.

One difficulty in making comparisons with experience in the UK is that the actual stock is not generally observed in equilibrium. Nevertheless there is some evidence supporting the relationship depicted in Fig. 7.1; for example in the mid-1960s the unemployment rate rose from 2½ per cent to a stable 3 to 4 per cent for several years. At the

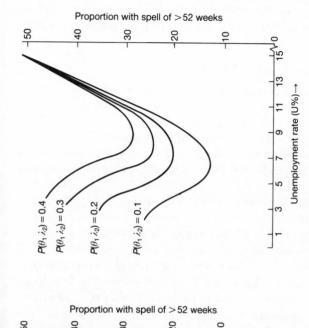

Fig. 7.1 *Proportion of unemployed with a spell of unemployment exceeding 52 weeks*

Source: Creedy and Disney (1981a) extended to higher unemployment rates.

higher rate, the long-duration proportions were nevertheless lower. However once the unemployment rate began to rise beyond 6 per cent from the beginning of the 1970s, the positive relationship between the rate and the proportion experiencing long durations was established.

Benefit exhaustion: the linked-spells rule

Appraisals of the unemployment insurance regime have generally ignored the impact of the linked-spells rule. However the present framework may be used to calculate the proportion of any cohort of the unemployed with a previous spell of employment of less than a specified number of weeks. Not all of these will of course go on to experience durations long enough to be affected by the spell-linking procedure.

Again a simple linear relationship between the effect of the rule and the unemployment rate need not be expected. As the unemployment rate rises, the likelihood of experiencing consecutive spells of unemployment increases, but the lengthening durations of spells of unemployment will reduce the probability of multiple spells of unemployment in a given period. Creedy and Disney (1981a) found that on balance the proportion affected by the rule is hardly affected by the value of θ_2, and therefore the aggregate unemployment rate. However, the value of the conditional proportion $P(\theta_1 | \lambda_2)$ does have some effect. Figure 7.2 shows the relation between different periods of linking and the proportion of the unemployed affected by the linking rule for a single value of the conditional probability. Prior to 1980 a third and, since 1980, over a fifth of the unemployed are potentially affected. Again this result is confirmed by DHSS data which record 30–5 per cent of those entering the register before 1980 as having a linked spell of unemployment, and one-half of all entrants having a linked spell of unemployment or sickness. These surprisingly high proportions therefore reinforce the importance of the linked-spells rule in determining why reliance on means-tested benefits is more extensive than even the prediction of the impact of the 52-week rule with a heterogeneous population.

It therefore appears that even a rather simple model of flows between employment and unemployment, using a heterogeneous population with only four groups, is able to predict with greater accuracy the proportion of the unemployed reliant solely on means-tested benefits. The extent to which the high proportion stems from the

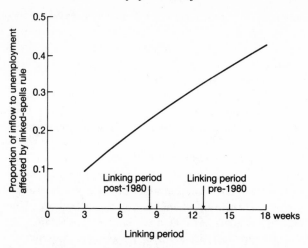

Fig. 7.2 *Effect of the linked-spells rule*

Note: Value of $P(\theta_1 | \lambda_2) = 0.2$. The proportions are almost invariant with respect to the value of θ_2.

impact of the 52-week rule and from that of the linked-spells rule can be clearly seen. An immediate question is whether the characteristics of the system were foreseen when these particular regulations were designed. It would appear that the architects of the 1946 National Insurance scheme believed that a commitment to full employment would preclude a large number of long-duration unemployed claimants. However this view seems to have taken little account of the heterogeneity of the population at risk. The linked-spells rule gives rise to problems even with low unemployment. It seems that the introduction of the linked-spells rule was related to the operation of the scheme of sickness insurance described in more detail in the next chapter, and its impact on eligibility among the unemployed was largely an unanticipated by-product of this scheme.

The question of whether it is an undesirable outcome, for such a high proportion of the unemployed to be partially or wholly dependent on means-tested benefits, raises several issues. For many claimants, the financial implications of relying on Supplementary Benefit rather than Unemployment Benefit are small. However, those who exhaust their claim on Unemployment Benefit but are barred from obtaining

Supplementary Benefit because their assets or other family income are above the threshold will suffer. Furthermore, the discretionary nature of means-tested benefits may induce a preference for National Insurance benefits over Supplementary Benefits among claimants, even where there is financial equality of treatment.

From the point of view of administration there would appear to be a serious disadvantage of this trend, since means-tested benefits are generally more costly to administer than National Insurance benefits. A witness to the Social Services Committee of the House of Commons 1981–2 (HC306) estimated that the cost of administering Supplementary Benefit, as a proportion of benefits paid, had fallen from 18 per cent in 1979 to 11 per cent at that time. The latter figure was still above that for National Insurance benefits which, in the case of Unemployment Benefit, has been estimated to be 8 per cent (Dilnot, Kay, and Morris, 1984). In fact, since 1979 the greater administrative costs stemming from the increased proportion of means-tested benefits in the social security budget have more than outweighed the savings obtained from measures to increase administrative efficiency (Disney, 1984b). However, the frequently expressed view that means-tested benefits have the advantage over universal or contributory benefits of concentrating resources on the most needy, poses the question of what rationale there is for a separate, contributory 'quasi-insurance' scheme of unemployment insurance. This is considered in the next section.

7.2 Market Failure and Unemployment Insurance

The present UK system of unemployment insurance, as with other parts of the social insurance system, combines a quasi-insurance scheme, where eligibility depends partly on contributions, with a pure transfer scheme financed out of general taxation. This juxtaposition of two distinct transfer schemes raises several issues. First, the question was raised at the end of the previous section of whether there is any rationale for this division. Secondly, to what extent does the system actually contain elements of a genuine 'insurance' scheme and, if so, is the degree of 'insurance' provision optimal?

The use of two different types of arrangement might be justified if a division could be established between the 'insurable' population and those who, at least in relation to unemployment, might be regarded as 'uninsurable'. The latter category might include those who, in the notation of the last section, have a high value of λ (probability of losing a job) and a low value of θ (probability of finding a job). At the beginning of the state scheme of unemployment insurance, this division was held to be clear-cut, as in the following remarks of Llewellyn Smith in 1910: 'The scheme must be contributory, for only by exacting rigorously as a necessary qualification for benefit that a sufficient number of weeks' contributions shall have been paid by each recipient can we possibly hope to put limits on the exceptionally bad risks . . .' (quoted by Beveridge (1930), p. 265).

Although this might offer a justification for incorporating a part of the population in a quasi-insurance scheme and compensating the remainder through an orthodox transfer scheme (assuming there are no adverse selection problems involved in identifying the two groups), it is apparent that in periods of high unemployment, such as the 1930s and the 1980s, no clear-cut division can be made. Many unemployed now find themselves wholly dependent on means-tested benefits because of the dynamics of a depressed labour market.

The insurance component of the UK system

Although the provision of means-tested benefits for the unemployed must be regarded as a pure transfer scheme, it is also true that Unemployment 'Insurance' Benefit contains pure transfer and redistributive components. Four major reasons are the following.

(i) There is no link between the *level* of contributions paid and the *level* of benefits received since the abolition of Earnings Related Supplement. It must be stressed that such a link does not depend on the use of, for example, earnings-related contributions combined with earnings-related benefits. Even before the abolition of earnings-related benefits, the link was very tenuous because of the way in which benefits were calculated (depending on contributions in a single 'contribution year').

(ii) There has been a payment of dependant's allowances for Unemployment Benefit since 1922, so the value of benefits paid to a claimant bears no relation to previous contributions.

(iii) There is no explicit risk-rating in determining payment of contributions. In fact the insurance component was to be one of the cornerstones of Beveridge's proposals. It was hoped that the redistribution stemming from the pooling of risks (as discussed in Chapter 1) would be limited by the various 'quasi-insurance' provisions: the limits on benefit duration, the linked-spells rule, and the provision of 'waiting days' (in insurance terms, a 'deductible'), by which benefit is not available for the first three days of a spell of unemployment (this does not apply to a linked spell). Nevertheless there are other eligibility conditions, which may be regarded as responses to the moral hazard problem of the unemployment insurance scheme. These include the rules by which, notwithstanding the value of contributions accumulated, the claimant must satisfy the benefit office that he or she is available for work, has a reasonable prospect of a job on the stated terms of availability, and is willing and prepared to accept a job on those terms (see Ogus and Barendt, 1982). Furthermore a claimant may be disqualified from receiving Unemployment Benefit for up to six weeks through leaving employment voluntarily, losing a job through misconduct, or refusing to take an employment opportunity offered to him or her. All of these exclusions have a clear insurance rationale, although they have sometimes raised contentious legal points. However it might be argued that these are *sufficient* grounds for exclusion from Unemployment Benefit. They are all intended to establish whether unemployment is involuntary and whether the claimant is actively seeking work. The various exclusions concerned with such matters as the value of contributions attained, and duration limits on benefit, are in contrast not concerned to establish the claimant's position *vis-à-vis* the labour market but are components of a concept of 'social insurance' which has increasingly served to relegate a majority of claimants to the means-tested sector. The unemployment insurance system therefore intermingles eligibility conditions based on social insurance provisions with those based on labour market conditions, in an arbitrary and unsatisfactory manner (see Disney, 1981, for further discussion of this issue).

(iv) There is no explicit experience-rating in determining payment of contributions by the employer. Although (as mentioned in Chapter 2) a refund to employers, conditional on their lack of claims on the unemployment fund, was originally proposed in Britain, it was dropped in 1920. The Redundancy Fund in Britain only partially compensates for Redundancy Payments, and thereby incorporates some experience-rating, but no such provisions exit for the payment of National Insurance contributions. In the United States, where there is a degree of experience-rating in the unemployment insurance scheme, the impact has been to change the method of reducing labour input. In particular there has been a much greater emphasis on the use of temporary lay-offs (Hamermesh and Rees, 1984). In the United Kingdom, in contrast, schemes which have been designed to avoid redundancies, such as the Temporary Short Time Working Compensation Scheme, from 1979 to 1984, have been introduced separately from the unemployment insurance scheme and interact with it in a complex manner. An important issue in this context is whether short-time working and related provisions should be compensated through the National Insurance Fund or through separate arrangements between individual employers and their work-force. There is as yet little evidence on the redistributive and other implications (Ogus, 1975; Richards, 1984).

Moral hazard

Of all the issues concerning unemployment insurance, the moral harzard question—the extent to which the insurance system discourages the claimant from remaining in employment or seeking employment when out of work—has generated the most heat. Although the concern with incentives is not surprising, particularly in periods of high unemployment, there are two reasons for thinking that the issue has received excessive discussion, at least relative to other important issues such as eligibility for the various benefits. The first reason is that a moral hazard problem did not appear to be the cause of the supersession of private unemployment insurance schemes by public provision. Trade unions which paid unemployment insurance often provided generous replacement rates, but minimized moral hazard problems because of the relative homogeneity of claimants, the use of short durations of benefits, and the tying of the insurance system closely to available job opportunities by providing information about vacancies and by subsidizing travel for job search. The second reason is that the present state system of unemployment insurance has a number of regulations, described above, which make initial benefit receipt conditional on involuntary unemployment and continued receipt dependent on availability for work. The strict enforcement of eligibility conditions would seem to reduce the importance of moral hazard for policy purposes, although there are major issues of legal interpretation (see Ogus and Barendt, 1982).

The subject of labour supply will be examined in Chapter 12, though it is worth discussing here some of the special issues relating to unemployment. In summarizing the current state of research three issues stand out as worthy of mention. The first highlights the contrast between studies using time-series and cross-sectional data. The former studies generally investigate the relationship over time between the unemployment rate and some average measure of the ratio of benefits to net income at work. There is vast scope for different assumptions regarding the trending of time-series, the degree of disaggregation of the labour force, the measures of average benefits and income, and the specification of an underlying structural model to describe the operation of the labour market during the period in question. The studies generally attempt to estimate an elasticity of the unemployment rate with respect to changes in the ratio of benefits to net incomes over time, and values of this elasticity (usually assumed to be constant) are found to be well over 1 (unity).

Cross-sectional studies, in contrast, generally use survey data in order to estimate the relation between individual replacement rates and individual exit probabilities from unemployment. Given the probabilities, the expected durations of spells of unemployment can easily be derived. These studies calculate elasticities which give the average change in the expected duration of unemployment spells resulting from changes in the replacement rate. Most elasticities calculated by this method lie in the range 0.4 to 0.6.

Time-series and cross-sectional studies give quite different elasticities since they are measuring different things. For example, lengthening durations cannot be equated with rising unemployment rates, unless the change in average duration translates into a similar net effect on the unemployment rate (that is, there is no substitution among applicants for given vacancies) and that other things remain constant, notably the inflow rate into unemployment. Furthermore, there are the well-known problems (as in consumption function estimates) of translating cross-sectional differences in individual behaviour into aggregate behaviour over time. Nevertheless, it is perhaps surprising that the cross-sectional elasticities always appear to be lower. Atkinson (1981) summarizes these and other related methodological issues.

The second problem, peculiar to time-series studies, lies in the problem of separating cause and effect. There were several years in Britain, especially in the inter-war period, in which a rapid rise in unemployment actually *led* to an increase in the generosity of benefit provision. Although this may have induced subsequent incentive effects, a positive statistical correlation gives a spurious indication.

This issue separates Benjamin and Kochin (1979), who argue that much of inter-war unemployment in Britain was voluntary, from their many critics, such as Metcalf, Nickell, and Floros (1982).

A third crucial issue concerns the way in which the benefit regime is modelled. Many estimates of the incentive effect are based on the simplistic assumption that all claimants are eligible for, and receive all available benefits. Generally, the more stylized the benefit regime assumed, the greater the incentive effect found. For example, many studies of the impact of the introduction of the Earnings Related Supplement in 1966 paid no attention to actual eligibility for, and receipt of, the Supplement. They thereby obtain quite implausible implicit elasticities of duration stemming far beyond the period for which the Supplement was actually paid (the 28th week of a spell). More recently, Atkinson *et al.* (1984) have argued that once actual benefit profiles are specified in some detail, little econometric evidence can be found for any incentive effects on duration (this result is admittedly at variance with almost every other study). Similar problems exist in modelling the denominator of the replacement rate. Many simply use the average income at work of those currently unemployed. But alternative estimates exists, and it is not clear how past or projected (hypothetical) earnings in work should be used. The replacement rate will again be discussed in Chapter 12.

There is furthermore the fundamental question of whether rational behaviour is a plausible assumption to make in the context of unemployment in a complex benefit regime, quite apart from the question of whether the researcher is able to identify and then model the variations in individual circumstances implied by the regime. Minford (1983) believes that both are possible and that there have been large disincentive effects, only ameliorated by the sharp cuts in short-run Unemployment Benefits in 1980. His critics divide into those who are clearly sceptical about the whole exercise and those, such as Dilnot and Morris (1983), who, having calculated hypothetical average and marginal replacement rates at various points of a spell of unemployment, find little evidence of high marginal rates. It seems, therefore, that while the discussion of the moral hazard aspect of unemployment insurance will not abate, a definite answer as to its significance will remain unresolved.

7.3 Redistribution and Unemployment Insurance

Chapter 6 pointed to the consequences, for an insurance system without efficient risk-rating, of population heterogeneity and 'state dependence'. In such circumstances there would inevitably be some degree of systematic redistribution among individuals. Thus there would be not simply the redistribution from the employed to the unemployed at a point in time (which would occur even with a homogeneous population and no 'state dependence') but certain groups of individuals would gain a higher effective rate of return on their contributions. Section 7.2 pointed out that quite apart from the Supplementary Benefit scheme, which is explicitly redistributive, the rules governing payment of National Insurance benefits to the unemployed also departed from strict risk-rating and so might lead to systematic redistribution. The object of this section is to gain some estimate of its magnitude.

Previous studies of the characteristics of the unemployed, such as Disney (1981) and Nickell (1980), have drawn attention to the differential incidence of unemployment across groups according to characteristics such as age, sex, skill, and occupation. This section focuses on two main issues. There is the relation between individual incidence of unemployment and individual position in the earnings distribution, which gives one measure of the extent of systematic redistribution for the unemployment insurance system as a whole in the absence of risk-rating. The second issue concerns the extent of redistribution, within the two unemployment insurance schemes, among the regions of the United Kingdom. This latter calculation reveals one dimension of the magnitude of transfers from net contributors to net recipients for each part of the two unemployment insurance schemes at a point in time.

The degree of vertical redistribution within the unemployment insurance system will depend on the interaction between benefit and contribution conditions on the one hand and the incidence of unemployment on the other. The actual extent of redistribution depends on the relation between unemployment incidence and gross income level when each is measured over a reasonably long period of time; for example, the degree of redistribution would be considerably reduced if relative earnings levels compensated for differential risk of unemployment, just as relative occupational earnings levels may compensate for differential risk of industrial injury (see Chapter 8).

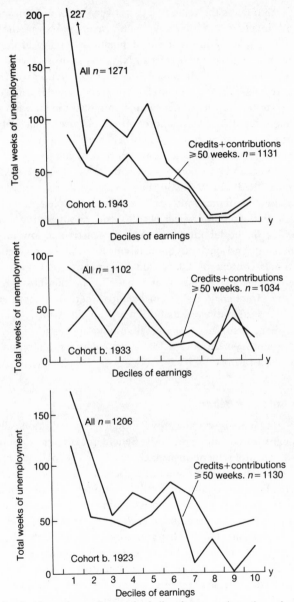

Fig. 7.3 *Incidence of unemployment by deciles of gross earnings; three cohorts of men, average 1971–3*

Note: Data supplied by DHSS © Crown Copyright 1984.

Figure 7.3 depicts the relationship between income from employment and incidence of unemployment, averaged over the years 1971–3, for samples of three cohorts of men born at ten-year intervals. The weeks of unemployment refer to National Insurance credits and the income deciles are annualized measures of notified individual earnings. In each case the relation between credits and income deciles is given separately for the whole sample and for those for whom there are complete or almost complete earnings histories. The data give clear negative relationships for the cohorts born in 1923 and 1943, showing that low-income earners have a higher incidence of unemployment, and a weaker relationship for the middle cohort. The cohorts born 1923 and 1943 also show evidence that the incidence of unemployment is higher among those with incomplete labour force histories, with the missing weeks of contributions suggesting exit from and re-entry to the labour force. This interaction of low incomes, unemployment, and spells out of the labour force has been noted in the United States context by Clark and Summers (1979), and similar evidence concerning earnings and benefits in the US has been reported by Hutchens (1981). On balance, therefore, there is clear evidence for systematic redistribution within the United Kingdom unemployment insurance system, stemming from the higher incidence of unemployment among low-income earners in a regime with no explicit risk-rating.

Redistribution among regions

An interesting issue is whether this systematic redistribution is limited to the means-tested Supplementary Benefit scheme or encompasses the whole unemployment insurance system. The data in Fig. 7.3 describe credited weeks of unemployment and do not distinguish between the benefits, if any, received. So a quite different approach is used here to examine this issue, in which the net redistributive effect among the geographical regions of each of the unemployment insurance schemes is calculated. This gives one measure of the degree of redistribution within each scheme, and it will contain a systematic component given the persistence of regional disparities in unemployment rates. The analysis, described in more detail in Disney (1984a), estimates payments of Unemployment Benefit, including Earnings Related Supplement, and Supplementary Benefit to the unemployed, for each region. It then calculates the implicit contribution rate and

TABLE 7.2 *Net regional transfers of the Unemployment Insurance (UI) system in the UK 1982*

Region	Net injection (outflow) of the National Insurance UI scheme (£ million)	Ratio of benefits to contributions (National Insurance UI scheme)	Net injection (outflow) of the Supplementary Benefit UI scheme (£ million)	Ratio of benefits to contributions (Supplementary Benefit UI scheme)
1	2	3	4	5
Great Britain	(30.6)	0.979	(75.5)	0.969
England	(81.0)	0.937	(193.1)	0.910
South East	(198.6)	0.639	(461.6)	0.530
East Anglia	(8.9)	0.801	(22.1)	0.721
South West	(3.4)	0.964	(12.5)	0.921
West Midlands	36.3	1.273	80.3	1.381
East Midlands	(6.4)	0.933	(14.9)	0.902
Yorkshire and Humberside	19.0	1.155	70.0	1.415
North West	41.3	1.249	99.4	1.358
North	32.3	1.421	65.6	1.509
Wales	18.9	1.298	28.5	1.242
Scotland	32.3	1.233	86.9	1.428
Northern Ireland	30.0	1.984	75.3	3.035
United Kingdom	0.0	1.0	0.0	1.0

Note: Totals may not add up due to rounding.

Source: See Disney (1984a) for methodology.

proportion of tax receipts necessary to finance aggregate national expenditure on each of these benefits. The contribution rate is then applied to each region's wage bill and the proportion of tax receipts is applied to a simple regional tax function in order to calculate contribution and tax receipts for each region.

Table 7.2 gives the net receipts and the ratio of receipts to payments of each region for the two unemployment insurance schemes. It is apparent from columns 2 and 4 that both schemes involve some net regional redistribution. Although a comparison of columns 3 and 5 suggests that the relative redistribution associated with the means-tested benefit (column 5) is the greater, the results support the argument of section 7.2, that the 'quasi-insurance' elements in the regime governing payments of Unemployment Benefit are unable to preclude significant systematic redistribution within the National Insurance scheme as well as within the means-tested sector.

In a more detailed study of the redistributive aspects of unemployment insurance it would of course be necessary to extend the time-period of analysis to longer than the three consecutive years of the cohort data mentioned above. It would, for example, be of interest to have information for separate cohorts about the life cycle of unemployment experience. This may then usefully be combined with an analysis of pension entitlement, thus extending the analysis of Part 2. A yet more ambitious approach would also include the wider range of taxes, such as income and VAT, which are considered later, in Part 4. But this must await further evidence and research.

8

Sickness Benefits

8.1 Sickness Insurance in Britain

Types of sickness benefit

There are three main types of benefit in Britain, which can be described as follows.

(i) *Contributory benefits*, like Unemployment Benefit and pensions, where eligibility depends on achieving a certain value of contributions. The major benefits here are *Sickness Benefit* and *Invalidity Benefit*.

(ii) *Employment-related benefits*, which require the individual to be an employed contributor at the commencement of the spell, but which do not require the claimant to have attained a certain value of contributions. The major benefits of this kind until 1983 were the industrial injury benefits: short-term *Industrial Injury Benefit* and the long-term *Industrial Disablement Benefit*. In 1983 the short-term injury benefit was abolished. Furthermore responsibility for the first eight weeks of all spells of sickness or injury was transferred to the employer under a new scheme called *Employer's Statutory Sick Pay* (SSP).

(iii) *Non-contributory benefits*, which are dependent only on the medical status of the claimant or the person for whom the claimant is responsible. These include the *Attendance Allowance* and the *Invalid Care Allowance* for cases where the claimant needs constant attention, the *Mobility Allowance*, and the *Non-Contributory Invalidity Pension* (NCIP). The last is essentially an invalidity benefit for non-contributors but is paid at a lower rate. A majority of NCIP claimants are women.

Table 8.1 gives a breakdown of expenditure on state sickness insurance benefits in 1984–5 and the average daily number of recipients. The figure of £3.7 billion spent on state sickness benefits can be contrasted with the £15.3 billion spent on retirement pensions and the £2 billion on Unemployment Benefit during the period. As with both the retired and the unemployed, some sick people are also eligible for Supplementary Benefits. However the amount of Supplementary Benefits received by the sick, both in addition to National Insurance benefits and as a substitute for those benefits for which the claimant is ineligible, is much less than that paid to the unemployed. This is because Invalidity Benefit may be paid for an unlimited duration, and there are the non-contributory benefits mentioned above. In 1984–5 only £375 million of the £9 billion total expenditure on Supplementary Benefits was spent on the sick.

TABLE 8.1   *Sickness Insurance: expenditure and recipients 1984–5 (Great Britain)*

Type of Benefit	Expenditure (£ millions)	Average daily recipients (1000s)
Pension benefits: National Insurance		
Invalidity Benefit	1,928	740
Industrial Injuries Benefits	439	180
Pension benefits: Other		
Attendance Allowance and Invalid Care Allowance	581	500
Non-Contributory Invalidity Pension	201	215
Mobility Allowance	356	350
Short-term benefits		
Sickness benefit*	246	150
TOTAL	3,751	2,135

* This excludes short-term sick covered under the Statutory Sick Pay scheme. Refunds to employers of SSP are estimated to total £597 million in 1984–5.

Source: HMSO (1984).

Stocks and Flows

Table 8.1 shows the characteristics of the average stock of sick, with Invalidity Benefit being the largest benefit both in terms of expenditure and average daily number of recipients. Since Invalidity Benefit is paid to those on a spell or linked spell of sickness of over 26 weeks, the stock figure suggests a relative preponderance of medium- to long-term claimants. Although the stock figures are useful when considering public expenditure, it is also important when designing a social security system to have knowledge of the characteristics of the *flow* of individuals through labour market states. When examining the nature of the flows of sickness claimants, a very different picture emerges.

In most years between 1963 and 1983 the annual number of claims for sickness benefits averaged over 10 million. As described in Chapter 6, the average duration of a completed spell can be approximated by the average stock at successive points in the period divided by the flow of new entrants over that period. Such a calculation gives an average duration of a sickness spell of about five and a half weeks. But there is a very wide dispersion; indeed over 60 per cent of claimants for sickness benefits are usually back at work after a fortnight and 90 per cent within six weeks. At the other extreme those who become disabled, invalids, or severely handicapped, are likely to remain in receipt of sickness benefits for a very long period. In Britain from 1971–3, for example, 5 per cent of each of three cohorts of men born in 1923, 1933, and 1943 accounted for almost 60 per cent of total weeks of registered sickness (Disney, 1976). Similarly, in France from 1978 to 1980, 4 per cent of the insured population accounted for 50 per cent of payments of sickness benefit and other health expenditures. This extreme bimodality in the distribution of exit probabilities from the sickness register between short-term and long-term claimants suggests that a scheme of state sickness insurance might usefully contain quite distinct provisions for the two main kinds of potential claimants. Recognition of this point led to a radical amendment of state provision of earnings replacement for short-term sickness in the UK in 1983.

The introduction of Statutory Sick Pay

In 1983 an important change occurred in the provision of short-term sickness benefits through the National Insurance scheme. The new scheme, initiated in the 1982 Social Security and Housing Benefits Act, transferred the administration of claims for sick pay lasting less than eight weeks to employers, who were then under an obligation to pay Statutory Sick Pay (SSP). They would then recover payments by deduction from their monthly payment of National Insurance contributions. The scheme contained many radical departures from existing provisions, including the abolition of the contributions requirement for short-term claimants, and dependants' allowances. The government justified this transfer of responsibility on the following three grounds:

(i) The administrative cost to the DHSS of processing 10 million claims was 'considerable', given the low average expected duration of sickness claims.

(ii) The state scheme of short-term benefits duplicated existing occupational sick-pay schemes, which covered 80 per cent of full-time male and 78 per cent of full-time female employees (DHSS, 1977), and

(iii) The transfer of responsibility to employers would eliminate the anomaly by which the statutory part of sick pay was untaxed, whereas the part added by the employers' sick-pay scheme was taxed. Anyone receiving full pay while sick would therefore have been better off sick than in health at work; see the Green Paper (HMSO, 1980, pp. 1–3).

It is worth noting that the original proposal suggested that SSP claims on employers should be financed by an across-the-board reduction in the rate of National Insurance contribution, rather than compensation to particular employers on the basis of actual claims. In consequence, the introduction of SSP raised a number of interesting issues in relation to sickness insurance: the existence or otherwise of market failure (point (ii) above); the question of moral hazard (point (iii) above); and the problems of adverse selection (the method of financing) and the weight to be attached to redistribution among the healthy and the short-term and long-term sick. The description of SSP as 'privatization of sickness benefit' (by Lewis, 1982; and suggested by the Green Paper, p. 2) is, however, overdramatic.

Eligibility for benefits

The role of eligibility requirements for unemployment benefit has been examined in Chapter 7. There is a wide range of conditions applying to the receipt of the various sickness benefits described earlier, and some of the benefits are non-contributory. Coupled with the introduction of the various non-contributory benefits, the trend in the 1970s was towards more generous treatment of long-term incapacity relative to the short-term sick (the latter being reduced in real terms). This trend was highlighted by the introduction of SSP, but also by the abolition of Earnings Related Supplement for short-term benefits and a change in the linked-spells rule in 1980, by which the linking rule was shortened from 13 to eight weeks. For Unemployment Benefit, as described in Chapter 7, the shortening of the linking period had the effect of reducing the number of claims to Unemployment Benefit terminating before 52 weeks was reached in the current spell. For Sickness Benefit, however, the result was different for it is possible, by judicious use of absences, for the claimant to link up spells of sickness in such a way as to attain the long-term rate of benefit quicker. Reducing the linking period made this possibility more difficult.

The onus is on the claimant to prove initial incapacity, normally by medical certificate, but since 1982, for a spell of seven days or less, the claimant now merely signs a declaration that he or she is incapable of work. It is up to the employer to decide what extra evidence, if any, is necessary in order to claim SSP. The analogy with the 'misconduct' clauses in Unemployment Benefit are that claims are precluded where the cause of the incapacity is wilful (e.g. an extended hangover), where there is a failure to attend for medical examination, or refusal to submit to medical treatment.

Unlike Sickness and Invalidity Benefits, entitlement to SSP merely depends on being a contributor, rather than on a value of individual contributions. The self-employed continue to rely on Sickness Benefit. The waiting-day provisions remain the same but the 'linked-spells' period is reduced to two weeks, not eight as with Sickness Benefit. After eight weeks of sickness the orthodox scheme of Sickness Benefit comes into operation and Invalidity Benefit, as before, after 26 weeks. There are three rates of benefit, according to earnings, for SSP, and there are no dependants' allowances. Originally the Green Paper advocated that a 'cap' of 75 per cent of earnings should be put on SSP, but this was subsequently amended to a lowest SSP rate of £25 weekly (approximately equal to the current short-term National Insurance scale rate for a single person). However, there is no statutory requirement to uprate the SSP scale rates in line with prices. The redistributive impact of replacing Sickness Benefit by SSP for short spells is clearly to benefit high-income single earners, whereas low earners and families will suffer. Finally short-term Industrial Injury Benefit is also replaced from 1983 by SSP and Sickness Benefit.

The self-certification provisions have, not surprisingly, been criticized (see for example Lewis, 1983). Self-certification, with full compensation to employers for claims, does not appear in principle to offer any means of monitoring whether absence is generally due to sickness or, say, to firms encouraging absences and claiming the SSP payments when order books are low. In practice the method of control chosen was through DHSS inspectors monitoring absentee records. It has, however, been argued that this procedure will induce employers to screen out the potentially sick applicants more carefully, so allowing them more flexibility in presenting their absence records if required at a later stage. In fact evidence suggests that SSP claims have considerably raised expenditures on short-term sickness benefits by the government. Although the introduction of SSP had the notional effect of reducing public expenditure by refunding SSP payments at source by deduction from employers' NI contributions, these deductions have grown faster since 1983 than expenditures on either Sickness Benefit or Invalidity Benefit (Disney, 1984a). There must be some concern about the combination of self-certification and the method of monitoring records that the government has chosen and indeed it has since had second thoughts on at least the first of these issues.

8.2 Paternalism and Sickness Insurance

The paternalist case

The paternalist motive for state intervention, as discussed in Chapter 1, stems from the case where individuals left to their own devices do not make enough provision against undesirable outcomes occurring, although insurance markets exist. This failure of provision may stem from ignorance of the relevant probability distributions or myopia. In the present context it might seem that the likelihood of underinsurance would be greatest for relatively catastrophic changes in health (stemming, for example, from a serious accident) because individuals have difficulty in assessing the probability of such events and their costs. But ignorance may lead to overinsurance as much as underinsurance. A counter-argument might suggest that a general run-down in health status, stemming from frequent and increasingly prolonged spells of sickness, is more likely to result in underinsurance.

Evidence as to how individuals insure against different types of event supports the proposition that some risks are underinsured relative to others. For example Kunreuther (1976), from actual evidence of insurance against flood and earthquake damage, and Slovic *et al.* (1977), from experimental data, argue that individuals tend to insure against high-risk small losses but underinsure against low-risk large losses. Clearly this suggests that individuals find difficulties in attaching probabilities to low-risk but calamitous outcomes. Although these results, in the context of sickness, suggest that underinsurance would be prevalent primarily among long-term claimants, such generalizations must however be qualified if medical and media information give greater predominance to long-term illness (serious accidents, heart disease, or cancer) and less to repetitive illness (influenza, respiratory problems, or backache, for example).

The only conclusion to be drawn from this is that there may be a case for compulsory insurance provision to offset both short- and long-term income loss from sickness. Nevertheless the argument does not necessarily justify *state provision* of sickness insurance. As with motor insurance, it may be compulsory but privately provided. It must not be confused with the redistributive arguments. However, the insistence on individuals taking out sickness insurance with full earnings replacement raises a further welfare problem. It cannot be assumed that the satisfaction gained by an individual from a given level of income will remain constant before and after the illness or accident occurring. Sickness or incapacity may impair the ability of the individual to derive benefit from a given level of income, or may result in special needs which require a different level of income for the same level of welfare to be attained.

If compulsory insurance suffers from this difficulty, the optimal level of earnings replacement in a full state scheme of sickness benefit poses equally fundamental problems. However, these seem largely irrelevant in practice in Britain given that the average replacement of earnings in the state sickness scheme is well below full replacement for SSP, and only slightly more generous for National Insurance benefits.

Industrial risks and labour market compensation

The state scheme of sickness and invalidity benefits in the UK makes a distinction between disability and ill-health stemming from accidents at work and industrial diseases on the one hand, and from other causes outside work on the other. In general industrial injury benefits have been contributory benefits while other benefits such as the NCIP and the various allowances for the disabled, many of which were introduced in the late 1970s, have been financed from the central Exchequer. This illustrates the tradition of 'industrial preference' in UK social insurance, since the less generous provision of non-contributory invalidity benefits was justified by the belief that contributors should receive more generous provision as a result of their payments into the NI Fund. Nevertheless the labour market may offer at least partial compensation for industrial risk if more risky jobs are compensated by higher pay; an example of the theory of 'compensating differentials' which can be traced back to Adam Smith.

One way of assessing how individuals value undesirable outcomes is by using labour market data in order to assess what compensation in the form of higher earnings is required by individuals in order to engage in occupations which bear greater than normal risks. Given that those who are willing to work in these occupations are the least averse to bearing those extra risks, this sum is essentially the minimum compensation which the labour market provides for risk. Obviously at first sight the distribution of earnings bears little relation to the distribution of risk across industries or occupations, so it is important to standardize these earnings to account for other productive characteristics such as skill, education, and training. Marin and Psacharopoulos (1982) derive occupational earnings functions for the UK in just such a manner in order to obtain the *ex ante* 'value of life'. This is calculated from the extra earnings obtained in incurring an extra risk of a fatal accident, evaluated at the mean earnings for the occupation.

An identical approach can be used to see whether extra risk of severe accident, as defined by the Factory Inspectorate, is compensated by extra earnings. Table 8.2 contains some evidence on individual earnings and risk in Great Britain using *New Earnings Survey* data for 1970, the last year for which comparable data on accidents and occupational sick-pay schemes (used in a later section) are available. Some extra data were obtained using *Health and Safety Statistics*, and only two other variables were included, the proportion covered by collective agreement and the percentage skilled. The results are straightforward. In both equations, manual earnings are positively related to risk although the coefficient is not significant for women. However, few women work in seven of the most risky industries. Using these coefficients to estimate the compensatory value attached to risk of severe injury (multiplying the coefficient on risk by mean income times 100,000) gives no evidence of underinsurance; indeed the values derived are so large as to suggest that the risk variable is picking up the return attributable to other, omitted, variables. It does however seem that women are less likely to obtain compensation than men and this possibility of underinsurance may extend into other, more direct, forms of insurance against earnings loss due to sickness or invalidity. However in so far as the results suggest at least partial compensation for risk in the labour market, the case for 'industrial preference' is thereby weakened.

TABLE 8.2   *Risk and industrial earnings*

Dependent variable	n	Equation				R^2
$\ln w_m$	27	2.89+ (25.9)	0.068 $\ln r$ + (4.0)	0.125 $\ln U_m$ + (1.53)	0.024 $\ln SK_m$ (2.23)	0.6320
$\ln w_f$	20	2.41+ (14.1)	0.045 $\ln r$ + (1.7)	0.267 $\ln U_f$ − (3.0)	0.174 $\ln SK_f$ (0.15)	0.3790

Notes

1. All variables in logarithms (ln). t statistics in brackets: 95% confidence level statistic: 1.71 for male equations, 1.75 for female equations.
2. Observations are for manual workers across 27 industries. Seven industries have too few female manual workers to obtain a sample; regressions on a dummy variable for these seven industries (not shown here) show a significantly higher risk of severe injury in these industries (some 30–40% higher).
3. w is median manual annual wage, m and f subscripts are male and female.
   r is severe injuries per year per 100,000 at risk.
   U is manual percentage covered by collective agreement.
   SK is manual percentage skilled.

Source: *New Earnings Survey*, 1970.

8.3 Market Failure and Occupational Schemes

The market failure issues concerning state insurance have been discussed in Chapter 1. In the context of sickness insurance, it is useful to distinguish between individual and occupational risks (such as those discussed in the previous section). In the case of individual risks, if the insurer is able to risk-rate individuals, even by some approximation such as experience-rating, there will be high-risk but risk-averse individuals who will nevertheless be unable to afford the premia. This is more likely if low income is associated with sickness, which will apply particularly to people with long-run invalidity or disability. The use of a state scheme is largely a redistributive argument for state intervention. If on the other hand risks cannot be assessed and behaviour cannot be monitored effectively, then a sickness insurance scheme will attract high-risk individuals and so raise the premium above the 'fair' rate. This problem of adverse selection will also affect firms which offer sickness insurance schemes.

Current provisions of state sickness insurance

The main provisions of the present state sickness insurance scheme were described in section 8.1, and it was suggested in Chapter 2 that market failure played a minor part in its inception, although the administrative costs of arrangements prior to 1946 may have been excessive. The present state scheme of sickness insurance, as with other state schemes, cannot be regarded as 'classical' insurance at all. There is not explicit risk-rating, and although entitlement is dependent on the value of contributions paid, the state provides various non-contributory benefits for those ineligible for National Insurance benefits.

Unlike unemployment insurance, the question of moral hazard has not been a central and controversial issue until recently for state sickness insurance, although the existence of sickness insurance may induce individuals to claim benefit more frequently or to prolong their periods of recovery. A time series study by Doherty (1979) showed a rather large implicit elasticity of days lost through sickness, with respect to the level of Sickness Benefit. However, Fenn (1981), in a cross-section analysis of individual sickness spell durations, found a significant but small elasticity of duration with respect to the replacement rate. Since Fenn's elasticity of 0.06 is about a tenth of that obtained from similar studies for unemployment insurance, this suggests that moral hazard problems in practice are unlikely to be significant given that earnings replacement is only partial. Nevertheless there are provisions in the scheme which are clearly designed with incentive problems in mind, such as the 'waiting days' rule, the introduction of the lowest rate of SSP, and the abolition of Earnings Related Supplement. On the other hand, unlike unemployment insurance, the long-term sick are in general treated more generously than the short-term sick (comparing the rate of Invalidity Benefit with that of Sickness Benefit).

Although the absence of individual risk-rating implies some redistribution via cross-subsidization, one controversial proposal in the Green Paper (HMSO, 1980) did raise this issue at the industrial level. The government originally proposed that claims paid by individual employers would not be fully recovered, and that employers as a whole would be compensated by an overall reduction in the rate of National Insurance contributions. Such a proposal would penalize employers who, through the characteristics of their workers or their industries, bore a relatively higher incidence of sickness claims. This in turn might have induced these employers to screen new entrants more carefully, as with self-certification. Therefore both the CBI and the trade unions were united in opposition to this proposal, and there is now full compensation. As argued in section 8.2 however, this may have exacerbated the problems of controlling SSP claims by employers.

Occupational sick-pay schemes

Private sickness insurance, through occupational sick-pay schemes, is extensive throughout industry in the United Kingdom. Their existence was used as a justification by the state for reducing state involvement in the provision of short-term earnings replacement for the sick in 1983. Two questions arise: firstly, is sick-pay coverage positively correlated with risk across industries? Secondly, is the behaviour of individuals affected by the existence of occupational sick-pay schemes, for example, in prolonging spells of sickness? A negative answer to the first question, in conjunction with a positive answer to the second, might suggest a rationalization for current state intervention: the market failure argument suggesting compulsion, the moral hazard suggesting low earnings replacement.

The DHSS survey of 1974 contains a wealth of information, much of it reprinted in the Green Paper (HMSO, 1980), concerning occupational sick-pay schemes. The proportion of men covered varies from a maximum of 95 per cent, in the public sector and food, drink, and tobacco, to a minimum of 50· per cent, in shipbuilding and vehicles. The proportion of married women covered varied from 90 per cent, in the public sector, professional and scientific services, and chemical and allied industries, to less than 40 per cent in agriculture, and clothing, and footwear. Most employees could obtain sick pay within six months of starting employment with the firm. Further details are shown in Tables 8.3 and 8.4 which give the duration of benefits and levels of earnings replacement found in the survey. Table 8.3 suggests that most employees obtain sick pay during the whole duration of state-financed SSP and indeed some are still in receipt even when they become eligible for Invalidity Benefit. Table 8.4 shows that a majority of non-manual workers can obtain full earnings replacement at the start of the spell of sickness. Indeed prior to 1983 they might have been better off sick than working, given that Sickness Benefit was not then treated as taxable income. Manual workers fare slightly worse but taken together these tables suggest that, subject to obtaining coverage under such schemes, full earnings replacement of short-term sickness by private schemes is extensive.

TABLE 8.3   *Occupational sick-pay schemes: average maximum durations of payment, 1974 (Per cent)*

	Up to 8 weeks	9 to 26 weeks	27 or more weeks	At employers' discretion
All men	30.4	32.6	26.6	10.2
Manual	37.2	34.9	21.2	6.4
Non-Manual	18.0	28.6	36.4	16.9
All women	35.0	29.7	25.5	9.6
Manual	45.7	28.7	19.4	6.3
Non-Manual	30.2	30.2	28.3	11.2

Source: HMSO (1980), p. 21.

TABLE 8.4   *Occupational sick-pay schemes: average amounts of sick pay at commencement of spell, 1974 (Per cent)*

	Full pay		Other
	without deductions	less NI benefit	
All men	11.5	55.0	33.2
Manual	7.7	42.3	49.9
Non-manual	17.7	75.3	7.0
All women	19.3	66.6	14.0
Manual	13.0	54.2	32.9
Non-manual	21.7	71.5	6.9

Source: HMSO (1980), p. 22.

The coverage of industrial sickness insurance can be investigated using the following simple model. Assume that there are two types of job: 'safe' and 'risky'—the latter bearing a fixed risk of accidental death or injury across industries. However, industries will differ in their proportions of 'safe' and 'risky' jobs with average risk in each industry (the r in Table 8.2) derived from the proportion of 'risky' jobs in that industry. On the assumption that workers are offered insurance in 'risky' jobs, there should be a positive correlation between average industrial risk and industrial coverage by occupational sick-pay schemes. A negative correlation would suggest the possibility of market failure. Of course in practice jobs differ in their degree of riskiness, and industrial average risk is not a weighted average of two kinds of jobs. In additional, women are excluded from some of the most 'risky' jobs, such as those in underground coal-mining, and this will reduce the value of the results for women.

TABLE 8.5 *Risk and sick-pay coverage*

Dependent variable	n	Equation	R^2
COV_m	27	$0.644 - 0.004r$ $(9.2) \quad (0.42)$	0.0071
COV_f	27	$0.478 - 0.004r + 0.227D$ $(6.0) \quad (0.35) \quad (1.84)$	0.1244

Notes
1. t statistics in brackets; 95% confidence level is 1.71.
2. *COV* is the proportion of an industry's manual work-force covered by an occupational sick-pay scheme, m and f subscripts are male and female.
   r is severe injuries per year per 100,000 at risk.
   D is a dummy (= 1) for the seven industries for which there is an insignificantly small number of female manual workers.

Source: *New Earnings Survey*, 1970.

Table 8.5 presents simple regressions of the proportions covered by an occupational sick-pay scheme, related to the risk of severe injury. It is apparent that for both men and women, sick-pay coverage is negatively, but insignificantly, correlated with risk. Occupational sick-pay coverage therefore seems to bear little relation to risk for manual workers but there is no clear evidence either of significant market failure. Indeed attempts to explain proportionate industrial sick-pay coverage find quite arbitrary differences. For example, Nickell (1977), using the same data, found that male coverage was positively related to the proportion aged 25-54, and negatively related to the proportions aged 21-4 and skilled. All except the last seem plausible, but for women the results suggested a positive relation to the proportion aged 21-4 and covered by a local union agreement, while the coefficient on the skilled proportion was negative, and the R^2 value was low.

To test whether occupational sick-pay coverage has an effect on sick-pay claims, a further model may be developed. Suppose

$$P_i = P_i(b_i, w_i, r_i) \tag{8.1}$$

where P_i = the proportion of industry i claiming sickness benefit in any given period;

b_i = the average level of benefits paid in industry i in that period.

Generally, a positive correlation between the level of benefits and the proportion claiming might be expected, along with a positive correlation with the risk measures. The relation between the wage and the proportion claiming is less clear. For while one might expect the basic relation to be negative, it has already been shown that the wage partially compensates for risk and is thus correlated with that term. Furthermore, given that most benefits are earnings-related, a correlation between b and w might be anticipated. Thus the sign on w is uncertain.

A further problem is that there are no data on benefit levels in sick-pay schemes across industries. The following procedure is therefore adopted. Average benefits in an industry are a weighted average of those paid to individuals covered by sick-pay schemes and those not covered:

$$b_i = S_i b_i^s + (1 - S_i) b_i^{ns} \qquad (8.2)$$

where S_i is the proportion of industry i covered by a sick-pay scheme and superscripts s and ns refer to total benefits of those covered by a scheme and not covered respectively. Rearranging (8.2) gives

$$b_i = (b_i^s - b_i^{ns}) S_i + b_i^{ns}$$
$$= \Delta b S_i + b_i^{ns} \qquad (8.3)$$

where Δb is the extra benefit received by being covered by a sick-pay scheme. Now,

$$b_i^{ns} = SB = a_0 + a_1 w_i \qquad (8.4)$$

where SB is the level of state Sickness Benefit, which, it is assumed, is composed of a flat-rate and an earnings-related component. It is also assumed that occupational scheme benefits are a constant proportion of earnings across industries. Thus

$$\Delta b = c w_i \qquad (8.5)$$

Therefore, equation (8.3) may be rewritten as

$$b_i = c w_i S_i + a_0 + a_1 w_i \qquad (8.6)$$

Having eliminated b and inserted S, equation (8.1) can be examined, bearing in mind that the sign on w is uncertain. S, of course, should be positively correlated with P. The results are given in Table 8.6. The dependent variables are the proportion of an industry's manual workforce making a certificated sickness claim in 1970 and absent from work. For men, it is apparent that certificated sickness is positively related to the risk of severe injury and to coverage by a sickness insurance scheme. Given that there is no correlation between risk and coverage, this suggests that the existence of sick-pay cover induces more claims. On the face of it, this might suggest a moral hazard problem and a justification for the lower replacement rate of the state scheme. However, when uncertificated absence from work is added to certificated sickness, no significant correlation is found with sick-pay coverage. This suggests that the existence of a sick-pay scheme raises the proportion of absence due to sickness that is certificated rather than causing a severe problem of moral hazard. This assertion is supported by the evidence for women, where no relationship between coverage by sick-pay schemes and sickness claims is revealed in Table 8.6.

TABLE 8.6 *Sickness, Risk, and Sick Pay*

Dependent variable	n	Equation				R_2
$P_{c,m}$	27	-0.020 (0.8)	$+0.003r$ (7.5)	$+ 0.021S_m$ (2.5)	$+ 0.004w_m$ (0.1)	0.7361
$P_{c+nc, m}$	27	1.26 (0.6)	$+0.003r$ (6.4)	$+ 0.005S_m$ (0.6)	$+ 0.088w_m$ (1.1)	0.7014
$P_{c,f}$	20	-0.025 (1.4)	$+0.002r$ (2.0)	$+ 0.012S_f$ (1.0)	$+ 0.415w_f$ (3.2)	0.4735
$P_{c+nc, f}$	20	-3.97 (1.7)	$+0.067r$ (0.4)	$- 0.119S_f$ (0.4)	$+ 2.28w_f$ (2.3)	0.2523

Notes
1. t statistics in brackets; 95% confidence level is 1.72 male and 1.75 female.
2. S, r, w as Tables 8.2, 8.5; m and f are male and female. P is proportion of industry work-force which registered a spell of absence; c and nc indicate certificated sickness and uncertificated absence.

The current state scheme contains no explicit risk-rating provision and benefits are well below full income-replacement, especially for short-term sickness under the new SSP scheme. In planning SSP it was assumed that occupational sick-pay schemes provide adequate benefits in supplementing or indeed replacing the state scheme.

However, there is no evidence of occupational sick-pay coverage correlating with the incidence of industrial risk, although the probability of sickness is significantly correlated with that risk. In examining certificated sickness there is some evidence of moral hazard problems but this is reduced when all absences from work are considered. Thus under the present combination of state and private provision, there seem to be arbitrary differences in the treatment of individuals in respect of income replacement and in relation to risk of sickness.

8.4 Redistribution and Sickness Insurance

For those with no work histories, long-term and disability benefits may be seen as direct redistributive transfers. But those who have some labour market experience are nevertheless likely to benefit from systematic redistribution arising from the state insurance scheme, if sickness is generally concentrated in lower-paying and part-time jobs. Indeed given 'industrial preference' in benefit provision, the net redistribution to those with work histories may be even greater. It was shown earlier that 'industrial preference' was initially justified on quasi-insurance grounds. Such a preference was also thought to be necessary in order to encourage people to work in dangerous industries. However, as section 8.3 argued, there is some evidence of compensation through higher wages in such industries.

There has nevertheless been criticism of the level of sickness benefits, especially for those without a work history. But evidence suggests that expenditure on the disabled and long-term sick has, after the unemployed, been one of the fastest-growing components of social security expenditure: for example from 1978 to 1984 expenditure on this group grew faster than total benefit expenditure, even including the unemployed (HMSO, 1984). Part of this rise must however be attributed to the dwindling job opportunities for 'marginal' workers such as the disabled, in the face of the rise in unemployment during the period.

For the sick as a whole, and the short-term sick in particular, the case for and extent of systematic redistribution is less clear. The introduction of SSP in 1983 was based explicitly on the idea that state intervention, on either market failure or redistributive grounds, was less justifiable for the short-term sick. The structure of earnings-related contributions and flat-rate benefits (except for the small earnings-related component, phased out in 1982) suggests a degree of systematic redistribution, but its extent depends crucially on the *incidence* of sickness. Redistribution is increased if sickness is negatively related to earnings, and vice versa.

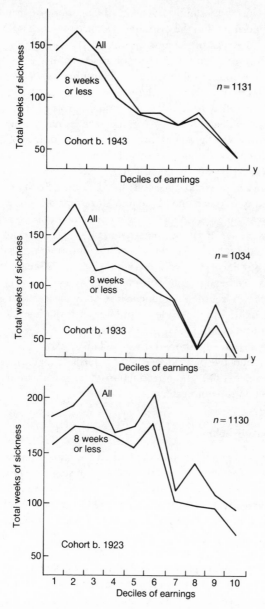

Fig. 8.1 *Incidence of sickness by deciles of gross earnings: three cohorts of men, 1971–3*
Source: Data supplied by DHSS © Crown Copyright 1984.

Figure 8.1 provides some evidence of the relation between the relative income position and the average incidence of sickness (defined as the number of weeks of sickness credits) in the period 1971–3. The data refer to samples of three male cohorts born in 1923, 1933, and 1943, and information about the total number of sickness credits received in each year was available. Since the income deciles are annualized measures of notified individual earnings, the gradients provide clear evidence that low-income earners have a higher incidence of sickness. The gradients are slightly flatter for the cohorts born in 1933 and 1943, when only those experiencing eight or less weeks of sickness in any one year are taken into account. These are mostly the short-term sick who would since 1983 be receiving SSP. There is however a difficulty in that some of the total durations of eight weeks in a particular year might simply be longer spells overlapping two years, while several longer durations in a single year might in fact encompass several unlinked spells of eight weeks or less. It is interesting therefore to note that SSP incorporates three rates of benefit delineated by earnings level, so reducing quite considerably the degree of systematic redistribution. A reasonable conclusion from the relation between taxes and benefits and the evidence in Fig. 8.1 is that there is systematic redistribution within the overall state sickness scheme but that it is considerably less for the short-term sick. This is partly because of the weaker relation between incidence of short-term sickness and earnings levels and, since 1983, the introduction of SSP with three rates of benefit linked to previous earnings.

8.5 Alternative Schemes

The variety of state provision in the United Kingdom and the shifts in emphasis over the years suggest that there is no single optimal form of state sickness insurance. The appropriate scheme varies according to existing private arrangements and financial conditions. It is therefore not surprising to find different forms of provision among the richer Western countries. In part, these differences stem from the early form of intervention and existing private arrangements at that time. For example, Germany adopted a paternalist view of state intervention in the late nineteenth century and implemented an early integrated form of social insurance to forestall a more active role for trade unions and other mutual forms of insurance (Rimlinger, 1971). In contrast, Chapter 2 showed that state provision in the UK reflected a tradition of voluntarism and decentralized provision.

Present arrangements concerning the degree of integration of the various programmes also differ among countries. It has been seen that in the UK, the National Insurance scheme covers payment of pensions, unemployment, and sickness insurance. However in Austria and Germany sickness insurance and the health services are covered by a single, separate, contribution; in Denmark sickness benefits are financed by a special tax on incomes; and in Australia they are financed from general taxation. Sickness and unemployment insurance benefits in Canada are financed separately from pensions. Most countries do not risk-rate, suggesting that a market failure in private provision has not led to the substitution of government-run conventional insurance. In the context of the previous section, it is interesting that in the Netherlands the employers' contribution varies across industries according to differences in industry-specific risk of illness and injury (Kaim-Caudle, 1973).

On the benefit side, most countries pay earnings-related benefits to the sick, with the UK being a notable exception. Average real replacement rates are therefore generally higher in other countries, and there is consequently less redistribution. Most countries provide unlimited duration for disability and invalidity benefits and these, unlike short-term benefits, are often financed out of general taxation. In the UK there is no such distinction, although as shown earlier, there are a number of non-contributory invalidity pensions.

No other country, therefore, has devised a scheme like SSP, although the period 1978–83 saw reductions in sickness and invalidity benefits in numerous countries including Belgium, France, Norway, and the United States. The nearest parallel to SSP is perhaps in West Germany which, in 1969, introduced the Wage Payment Continuation Act. This entitled claimants to full gross pay from the employer during the first six weeks of the spell of sickness, with the conventional state scheme of sickness insurance coming into operation thereafter. The German scheme offers the administrative benefit of decentralizing payments of sickness benefit for the many short-term spells without having a reduction in earnings replacement for the short-term sick (unlike the UK scheme). In the UK those in the fortunate position of being covered by an occupational scheme may well receive full earnings replacement whereas others may receive considerably less under SSP provisions. A problem with full replacement of earnings is that it encourages firms to select applicants more carefully in order to avoid potential costly claimants. Furthermore, it penalizes firms in high-risk industries. As argued earlier, however, this seems less of a problem for short-term claimants.

This brief international comparison therefore points to some of the more puzzling anomalies in the present state scheme of sickness insurance in the UK. As described in section 8.1, claimants clearly divide into the short-term and the long-term, the latter experiencing either continued invalidity or recurrent serious spells of labour market absence. The UK scheme provides SSP for the short-term claimants, supplemented by occupational sick-pay schemes. SSP was introduced to reduce administrative costs to the government and to increase reliance on occupational provision, but is less than generous to those without occupational sick-pay coverage. One possibility would be to follow West Germany in enforcing compulsory provision by employers of sick pay, at a generous level, for short spells. Many sick in the UK are already covered by such arrangements anyway, and such a scheme would render SSP unnecessary (saving further administrative costs). Problems arising from adverse selection and screening nevertheless remain.

At the other end of the spectrum of claimants, the UK offers a plethora of contributory and non-contributory benefits for the long-term sick, handicapped, and invalids. Most countries other than the UK have realized that enforcing eligibility requirements for contributory benefits is extremely difficult for those with prolonged labour market absence, so that long-term invalidity benefits are now non-contributory. A shift in this direction would also save administrative costs in the UK and avoid the need to pay different rates of benefit to individuals according to whether the benefit is contributory or non-contributory. Removing the short-term sick and Invalidity Benefit from the National Insurance scheme leaves a remnant of claimants experiencing, say, spells of between eight and 26 weeks, for whom contributory benefits seem justifiable. But many of those whose uncompleted duration lies in that range will remain to become long-term claimants and even those who complete durations of that length will be experiencing recurrent problems of illness and disability. The role for contributory sickness insurance therefore seems limited.

PART 4

Tax-and-Transfer Schemes

9

Alternative Social Security Systems

Part 1 of this book has examined the arguments which have been used to justify some form of state system of compulsory insurance providing income transfers to certain groups of individuals, such as the unemployed, sick and disabled, and aged. It also examined the extent to which these arguments have played a part in the historical development of social insurance provision in the United Kingdom. Part 2 then examined pensions, while Part 3 considered schemes of unemployment and sickness insurance. An attempt was made to assess the UK schemes, using the economic criteria set out in Chapter 1. Many problems and inconsistencies were discussed, and indeed (as noted in the Introduction) there has in recent years been much general criticism of the idea of social insurance. The complex eligibility conditions operating in the pseudo-insurance system have served to eliminate large numbers of individuals from receipt of benefits, and have placed stress on the system of Supplementary Benefits.

Even if some type of state system is justified, there remains the important question of exactly what form this intervention should take. Critics have often argued, by implication, that an insurance system is insufficiently redistributive because benefits are paid subject to the eligibility conditions being satisfied, irrespective of perceived needs. Their emphasis has usually been on poverty relief, rather than other criteria by which to judge social insurance (discussed in Chapter 1). A number of proposals for reforming the social security system therefore involve the use of some type of much more fully integrated tax-and-transfer system. These contrast with those proposals which have recommended a strengthening of the insurance aspects, whereby higher benefits would more readily be paid to those suffering prescribed contingencies. Nevertheless, those in favour of a scheme based mainly on contingency benefits usually recommend that benefits should be included in the usual definition of income for tax purposes.

It is therefore necessary to examine alternative social security systems in the context of tax-and-transfer schemes as a whole. The policy choice among different types of tax-and-transfer system

presents severe difficulties, especially where questions of the extent to
which the state *should*, and *does*, redistribute resources are concerned.
The aim of this Part of the book is to compare alternative tax-and-
transfer systems, and in particular their redistributive implications.
The present chapter describes a simple taxonomy of schemes and
outlines a method by which a comparison of the redistributive impact
of such schemes is facilitated. More complex comparisons are developed in later chapters. One of the important components of this analysis is a comparative analysis in order to show the relationships among
variables such as benefit levels, cut-off points, and tax rates. The
detailed analyses do not allow for possible variations in the labour
supply behaviour of those in or out of work, and they do not allow for
possible effects of the tax system on the demand for labour by employers. The special question of labour supply, which has received much
attention in recent years, is, however, examined in Chapter 12, also in
the context of complete tax-and-transfer schemes.

The point of departure in what follows is that any social security
system is faced with a *budget constraint*, under which the benefits paid to
specified groups must be financed, either by general taxes or special
earmarked taxes, such as the National Insurance contribution in the
United Kingdom. The concept of the budget constraint has both a
practical and an analytical application. In practice, the state can be
observed to implement this budget constraint in varying ways and
with varying degrees of success. It may, for example, require that
receipts from an earmarked tax should roughly balance outgoings on
an annual basis, on the particular social security expenditures for
which the tax is earmarked. This type of pay-as-you-go scheme is
roughly typified by the National Insurance 'Fund' in the United
Kingdom. In addition, the state may control public expenditure
directly; for example, by using cash limits (although in general these
are not applied to social security expenditure) or attempting to limit
social security expenditure within an overall budget constraint such as
the Public Sector Borrowing Requirement (PSBR). In addition to its
obvious practical relevance, the concept of the budget constraint is
essential in order to derive the comparisons of various tax-and-transfer
schemes that follow. Although the idea of a budget constraint is basic to
economic analysis, surveys have nevertheless shown that many people
simultaneously vote for higher benefits and lower or unchanged tax
rates; see for example Sandford (1980, pp. 1–2), and the models of
positive public choice outlined by Mueller (1979). For a recent

questionnaire of public sector choice, see Hockley and Harbour (1983), which shows more promising results.

The assumptions used in this chapter produce what may be termed 'static' comparisons; that is, alternative tax-and-transfer schemes are compared given a fixed total income and a fixed distribution of income, both measured within a single period. The restriction imposed by these assumptions may be seen by considering, for example, what would happen if a state pension were introduced suddenly for all those over a certain age. Within the relevant age-group, the pension would be expected to affect work effort; in particular, with normal preferences for goods and leisure, it would make it more attractive for people in that age-group to become economically inactive. For persons of lower age, the expected future pension would affect current work effort, both by raising expected income and by lowering current disposable income (since the pension is assumed to be financed by extra taxation). It would also affect saving behaviour and therefore the ratio of unearned to earned income in present and future periods. Extending the analysis from this example to a comparison of many kinds of tax-and-transfer systems, it is possible that there are some systems for which these effects are substantial. Indeed, some 'supply-side' economists have asserted that the disincentive effects of current tax-and-transfer systems are so substantial that, paradoxically, higher tax revenues can be generated by lower tax rates. While remaining sceptical on this point, it is apparent that the 'static' comparison, while a useful first approximation, ignores some vital issues. A 'dynamic' comparison must therefore take account of both the impact of alternative tax-and-transfer systems on total income and also extend the analysis to a multi-period world. Chapter 12 considers the first point in greater detail, and of course a longer-term perspective has been used in Parts 2 and 3.

9.1 The Negative Income Tax and Social Dividend

The Negative Income Tax (NIT) and Social Dividend (SD) schemes can be examined together because the main distinction between them is administrative. The basic NIT scheme proposed by Friedman (1962) was supposed to replace all means-tested and contingency benefits, and was to be administered through the tax system. It involves a simple linear tax schedule, shown in Fig. 9.1, whereby those with gross income, y, above a certain level, a, *pay* tax at a constant marginal rate, *t*, say. Those below the gross income, *a*, *receive* a payment through the tax system which brings their 'after tax' income, *z*, up to the appropriate point on the line TT.

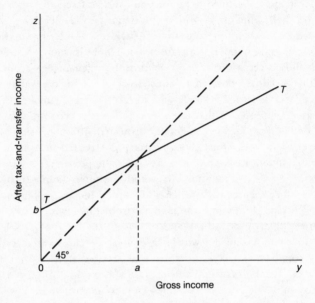

Fig. 9.1   *Negative Income Tax and Social Dividend*

Under the SD scheme, based on the proposal of Rhys-Williams (1942, reprinted in 1953), everyone would receive a social dividend payment equal to *b* in Fig. 9.1. All income would then be taxed at a constant proportional rate. It is convenient to compare the two schemes algebraically as follows:

For NIT: $z = y - T(y) = y - t(y - a) = y(1 - t) + at.$ (9.1)
For SD: $z = b + y - T(y) = b + y - ty = y(1 - t) + b.$ (9.2)

Thus they are equivalent if $b = at$. Furthermore, it can be seen that the slope of the line TT is equal to $1 - t$.

It would be possible, under both schemes, to vary *b* according to family circumstances, although the issue is not examined further here. The schemes offer the apparent appeal both of huge simplification and of abolition of any type of means-testing (other than the income-testing inherent in assessment of taxable income), along with the use of a single marginal tax rate. The latter feature would also mean that taxation could be based on weekly income, since averaging of fluctuating incomes over a period would have no effect. These schemes have thus been attractive to both the 'intellectual right' (for the first reason) and the 'intellectual left' (for the second reason mentioned).

The major drawback of the NIT and SD schemes stems from the variety of special needs which are dealt with in the present system. To avoid some special groups becoming worse off under an inclusive scheme such as NIT or SD, the level of b would have to be relatively high. But given that some who are not in need also receive transfers under these schemes, a rather high marginal tax rate would be required in order to finance the scheme. This may be demonstrated easily. Consider only the revenue needed to finance the minimum income, b. The amount of tax raised per person from a proportional tax on all income is simply $t\bar{y}$, where $\bar{y}$ is arithmetic mean income. Thus the value of t must be at least as large as the ratio of b to $\bar{y}$: a minimum income of 50 per cent of average income would need a tax rate of 0.50 before any tax for general revenue could be raised. An increase in the ratio $b/\bar{y}$ must be matched by an equal increase in t for any given total income. The average (effective) tax rate would however be quite low for a large proportion of individuals, and the dispersion of z would be considerably lower than that of y.

For these reasons, the NIT and SD schemes have not generally been regarded as practicable proposals. Either the basic minimum must be too low, thereby defeating its objective (as was the case with the 1972 Tax Credit scheme described in section 9.4 below), or the marginal tax rate must be unacceptably high, as has proved to be the case with more generous proposals, such as Meade (1972) and Meade *et al.* (1978). Alternative proposals have therefore involved some non-linearity in the relationship between gross income and after-tax-and-transfer, or disposable income. This non-linearity may be achieved by having higher marginal rates of tax at the two extremes of the income distribution, as discussed in the following section.

9.2 A Minimum Income Guarantee

The most basic form of minimum income guarantee (MIG) involves raising the incomes of all those with gross incomes below a specified level, y_0, to a fixed minimum, b. This means that the effective marginal tax rate is 100 per cent for incomes below y_0; any marginal

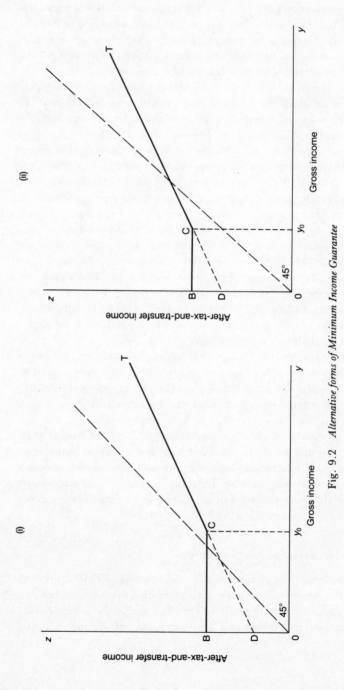

Fig. 9.2 *Alternative forms of Minimum Income Guarantee*

increase in income is matched by a reduction in transfer payments, leaving disposable income unchanged. Alternative forms of MIG are shown in Fig. 9.2. The desired relationship between z and y could be achieved using several administrative procedures. For example, a fully integrated tax and benefit scheme could be used (as with the basic NIT); a conventional tax system could be combined with means testing; or one of the schemes examined in section 9.1 could be used to produce the line DCT, with a means-tested supplement to shift DC up to BC.

The main advantage of MIG is that it allows a higher minimum income to be paid than with SD or NIT, for any given value of t. This is because it is less generous to the not-so-poor, since most of the transfers go to raising the poor to the poverty line; in the terminology of Beckerman and Clark (1982), MIG has a high poverty reduction efficiency. The great disadvantage of MIG is that the 100 per cent effective marginal tax rate at the lower end of the income distribution is thought by many to have strong disincentive effects on labour supply, and there is little reason to believe that these effects will be offset by the lower overall tax rate needed to finance MIG, relative to the NIT or SD.

Under the NIT and SD there are two policy variables to be set, namely b and t. But the budget constraint means that only one variable can be set independently; as explained above there is a direct linear relationship between t and $b/\bar{y}$ (the position of the line depends on the amount of revenue needed for non-transfer purposes). With MIG there are three policy variables, b, y_0 and t, but only two 'degrees of freedom' because of the budget constraint. For any given value of y_0, there is also a linear relationship between the basic minimum and the constant marginal tax rate. This is because equal absolute increases in b, with y_0 unchanged, mean that equal increases in total benefits are required (assuming that the number receiving benefits and the income available for taxation are unchanged). The slope of the relationship depends on the general shape of the distribution of income. For higher values of the level below which the guaranteed minimum is given, y_0, it is clear that the value of t must be higher in order to finance any given value of b. At higher values of y_0, the tax rate needed to finance given values of b increases *more rapidly* than when y_0 is relatively low. Further details of the relationship are given in section 9.3 below.

A modified minimum income guarantee

Criticism of MIG has concentrated mainly on the fact that effective marginal tax rates are so high for those at the lower end of the income distribution. A modification is shown in Fig. 9.3, whereby the effective marginal rate applied to those below y_0 is s. This scheme is therefore a compromise between the two extremes of NIT/SD and MIG. The modified scheme moves from NIT to MIG as s increases from t to 1. For any given values of y_0 and b, the tax rate applying to those above y_0 is higher than under MIG because of the greater generosity of the scheme to those just below y_0. However, for given values of s and y_0, the tax rate, t increases as b increases by exactly the same rate as under the basic form of NIG. For example an increase in b from b to $b + 1$ involves the same increase in total benefits as does an increase from $b + 1$ to $b + 2$; hence t increases at a *constant* rate. With the same distribution of income and value of y_0 as before, the rates of increase must also be the same although the modified scheme requires higher levels of t. The scheme proposed by Dilnot, Kay, and Morris (1984), although contingency related, is very similar in effect to a modified MIG.

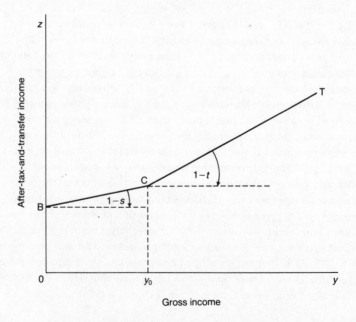

Fig. 9.3 *The Modified Minimum Income Guarantee*

9.3 Comparisons of Alternative Schemes

The previous sections of this chapter have outlined and compared in general terms the two major theoretical tax-and-transfer schemes: NIT/SD and MIG, emphasizing the extent to which taxes on income need to be increased in order to finance a given increase in benefits. It is clear that many alternative schemes could be examined, involving, say, more progressive tax structures with increasing marginal rates and a greater complexity of benefit levels and 'tapers' (the rates at which benefits are withdrawn as y is increased). At this stage, however, it is useful to illustrate some basic comparisons; these relationships, which are imposed by the budget constraint, are obtained using the analytical results in Creedy (1982b). The results are shown in Fig. 9.4.

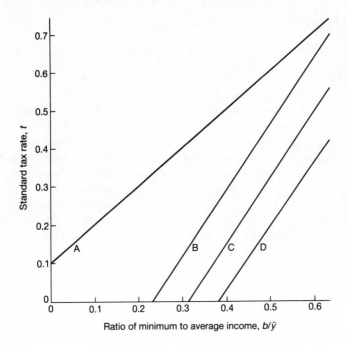

Fig. 9.4 *Relationship between tax rate and benefits in alternative systems*

Notes
A: NIT/SD
B: Modified MIG; $s = 0.8$
C: MIG
D: MIG with NI ($c = 0.10$)

These comparisons are derived for a distribution of gross incomes which has a mean of £6000 and a coefficient of variation of 0.5. In each case the value of y_0 is £2500. For the modified MIG scheme, the higher marginal tax rate, s, is set at 0.8. Comparisons are also made in which MIG is partially financed by the National Insurance contribution, c. The National Insurance contributory scheme has already been discussed at length, and is described in more detail in the next chapter; for the moment, it is sufficient to note that contributions are not paid if earnings are below a limit y_L, and are then proportional to gross earnings up to a limit y_U. The schedule of contributions, $C(y)$, is therefore:

$$C(y) = 0 \qquad\qquad y < y_L$$
$$C(y) = cy \qquad\qquad y_L < y < y_U \qquad\qquad (9.3)$$
$$C(y) = cy_U \qquad\qquad y < y_U.$$

In the comparisons given here, the values of c and y_U are 0.10 and £9000 ($1.5\bar{y}$) respectively. In each example it is also assumed that general tax revenue of 10 per cent of average income is raised in addition to that needed to pay for transfers.

Figure 9.4 illustrates the extent to which the required tax rate differs among the various schemes, and the 'cost' of increasing the minimum income. However, great care must be used when interpreting these simple comparisons, even setting aside the limitations imposed by the assumptions outlined in section 9.1. First, it should be noted that each scheme implies a very different distribution of disposable income. For example, when NI contributions are used to help finance transfers, the main tax burden falls on the middle incomes, and the overall effect is to make it less redistributive than the basic MIG scheme; see Creedy (1982b). In addition, the minimum income under NIT and SD is paid to very few people. Secondly, the tax rates shown are those needed to finance only the benefits plus the small addition of general revenue (of 10 per cent of $\bar{y}$). In fact the type of MIG scheme shown in Fig. 9.2(i), where b is *less* than y_0, can be financed with all of the revenue coming from those with incomes under y_0. This explains why the lines B, C, and D in Fig. 9.4 cut the horizontal axis: for even lower values of b the revenue is sufficient to pay the higher income groups as well, and so t becomes negative. The need for greater general revenue shifts all the profiles upwards by the same extent.

9.4 The UK Tax-and-Transfer Scheme

No explicit universal Negative Income Tax or Social Dividend scheme has been introduced in the United Kingdom, although a rather unambitious tax credit scheme was proposed by the Conservative government in 1972. Employees who paid tax were to be offered a tax credit, offset against tax liability and paid as a cash sum to those for whom the credit exceeded the tax liability. However, those below the tax threshold and the self-employed were excluded, along with all those solely in receipt of Supplementary Benefit. The scheme closest to the original NIT/SD proposal currently in operation is Family Income Supplement (FIS), introduced in 1971. FIS is a means-tested benefit, administered through the DHSS, by which low-income, working families may receive half the difference between their gross income, y, and a qualifying income level, analogous to the value a in equation (9.1), when $y < a$. However, as this section will demonstrate, the existence of a range of other means-tested benefits in addition to FIS for low-income, working families means that the line TT in Fig. 9.1 is far from linear in practice.

The nearest equivalent to MIG in the United Kingdom is Supplementary Benefit (SB), a means-tested benefit paid to those not in full-time work whose family income lies below the SB scale rate. For those in work, FIS and a range of other means-tested benefits are available and although none of these individual benefits has an effective marginal tax rate of 100 per cent, effective rates of 100 per cent or more are produced when the schemes are combined with the tax and National Insurance systems.

One of the characteristics of the actual tax-and-transfer system in the United Kingdom is its great complexity. First, there is a wide variety of benefits available to each type of claimant. Secondly, as mentioned previously, the relationship between gross and disposable income differs among the various sections of the population, when classified by household composition, age, marital status, and labour market status. One implication of this diversity is that it is extremely difficult to generalize about the effect of any given change in taxes or benefit levels on the population as a whole. A revealing example is contained in the DHSS *Tax/Benefit Model Tables*, which are frequently used in parliamentary debates, and from which Figs. 9.5 and 9.6(i) below are largely derived. These *Model Tables* calculate the relationship between gross and disposable earnings over a wide earnings range for several types of household, including single people, single parents, and married couples with various-sized families (all where the head of the household is in full-time work), plus several types of unemployed families. Yet Atkinson, King, and Sutherland (1983) argue, from an analysis of the Family Expenditure Survey, that the hypothetical family types described in the *Model Tables* account for only 4 per cent of actual families in the population. Hence it is not attempted here to describe the actual tax-and-transfer system covering a 'typical' family, but the relation between gross and disposable income for various family types is illustrated. The three following examples are therefore intended to give an idea of some of the complexities involved in practice when relating gross to disposable income.

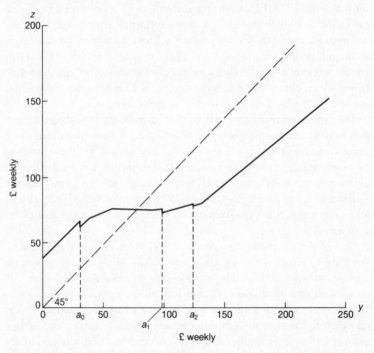

Fig. 9.5   *Hypothetical financial position of married couple, head of household working, with 2 children aged 4 and 6, April 1984*

Notes

$a_0 = y_L$ (National Insurance contribution)
$a_1 = $ Loss of free milk
$a_2 = $ Loss of free school meals

Source: DHSS *Tax/Benefit Model Tables* November 1983 (updated by authors to 1984 Budget).

The case of a married couple with two children, and with the head of the household in employment, is illustrated in Fig. 9.5. Here the main benefits available are Child Benefit (which is not means-tested) and a range of means-tested benefits (which include Family Income Supplement, housing benefits, welfare milk, and free school meals, all of which are gradually withdrawn as gross income rises, although the period of assessment varies). Figure 9.5 incorporates all these benefits, plus tax and National Insurance contributions, and deductions for rent, rates, and travel-to-work costs. It will be noted that over a wide range of gross income, from around £40 to £130 weekly, the effective marginal tax rate, as with MIG, is close to 100 per cent. This range of incomes, in which disposable income remains constant as gross income rises, has been termed the 'poverty trap' or 'poverty plateau'. Some further implications of the poverty trap will be discussed in Chapter 12.

The case of a single parent with one child under school age is shown in Fig. 9.6(i). A further complexity is revealed in this example, namely that single parents not only receive a higher rate of Child Benefit, but are also eligible for Supplementary Benefit so long as they work for less than 30 hours a week. Furthermore, earnings while in receipt of SB are not taxed at 100 per cent until they reach £20 a week, at which point a switch to the use of FIS becomes advantageous. There are thus several additional kinks in the relation between y and z; the net effect is to extend the range of incomes over which marginal effective tax rates are 50 per cent or more. Here the desire to be generous to single parents has to be combined with a choice between treating single parents in tax terms as equivalent to other Supplementary Benefit claimants (tax rate 100 per cent) or as married women working part-time (tax rate currently 39 per cent).

The case of a single pensioner affected by the Earnings Rule is shown in Fig. 9.6(ii). There are numerous factors underlying the determination of individual pension entitlements. A lifetime perspective is necessary in order to examine the earnings-related component of the state scheme (SERPS), as argued in Part 2. Nevertheless one regulation may be illustrated here. This concerns the choice of the male pensioner aged 65–9, or the female pensioner aged 60–4, among the alternatives of full retirement, part-time work, or pension deferral and continuing to work full-time (or indeed to return to full-time work having retired). This is conditioned by the operation of the Earnings Rule, by which pensioners are allowed to earn a certain sum without

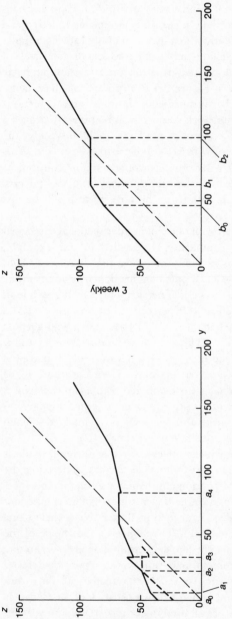

Fig. 9.6 (i) *Hypothetical financial position of single parent, one child aged 3, April 1984*

(ii) *Hypothetical financial position for single pensioner aged 65–9 (men) or 60–4 (women) receiving only flat-rate pension, April 1984*

Notes
a_0 = Supplementary Benefit payable at long-term rate
a_1 = SB earnings disregard threshold (effective tax rate, 50 per cent)
a_2 = End of earnings disregard; switch to FIS
a_3 = y_L (National Insurance contribution threshold)
a_4 = Loss of free milk.

Notes
b_0 = Tax threshold with single person age allowance
b_1 = Earnings Rule threshold
b_2 = Upper limit of application of Earnings Rule.

Sources: DHSS *Tax/Benefit Model Tables* November 1983; Ogus and Barendt (1982); update by authors to 1984 Budget.

losing basic pension entitlement, after which their pension is withdrawn as earnings increase at successive rates of 50 and 100 per cent. The resulting relation between y and z is depicted in Fig. 9.6(ii), from which it can be seen that the effective tax rate is 100 per cent over a segment of the curve.

These illustrations reveal that the actual tax-and-transfer system in the United Kingdom contains a number of complexities absent from schemes such as the NIT/SD and MIG, and that there are likely to be gains from some form of integrated tax-and-transfer scheme. Furthermore, as discussed in Chapter 12, there may be more general welfare gains from removing the various kinks and non-convexities contained in the relation between y and z. Nevertheless, quite apart from the disadvantages of NIT/SD and MIG outlined in previous sections, there are good reasons for treating different types of claimant in a variety of ways, albeit not necessarily in the manner illustrated in this section. As suggested in Chapter 1, the motives for state intervention may differ among groups of individuals, with the redistributive motive, for example, being given greater priority for one group relative to another. Consequently, as Akerlof (1978) argues, 'tagging' particular groups for special treatment has the advantage of allowing high benefit payments with relatively low overall marginal tax rates (although of course the 'tagged' characteristics must be easy to monitor).

The next chapter builds a more general model of the tax-and-transfer system in the United Kingdom. Chapter 11 will then examine the extent of redistribution resulting from this system.

10

The Finance of Transfer Payments in the UK

The previous chapter examined the relationships between benefits and tax rates in alternative schemes. It was assumed in the comparison of these schemes that all revenue was raised using direct taxation, with only a brief reference to the interaction of the schedules of income tax and National Insurance contributions which make up the system of direct taxes in the United Kingdom. The last section of that chapter contrasted these schemes with some of the complex tax-and-transfer schemes for various types of household in the United Kingdom.

The present chapter takes a step away from the rather stylized schemes outlined in Chapter 9, sections 1 to 3, and towards an analysis of the actual tax-and-transfer schemes in the United Kingdom. The framework of analysis constructed in this chapter is then used in Chapter 11 in order to investigate the redistributive implications of various tax functions and benefit levels on a revenue-neutral basis. The framework does not capture all the complexities of the actual tax-and-transfer system; this would require an analysis based on a greater disaggregation of household types by, for example, using the *Family Expenditure Survey*. However, it enables the main interdependencies in the system to be seen clearly; and is useful in examining some policy implications concerning, for example, the impact of merging the income tax and National Insurance systems and of increased reliance on indirect rather than direct taxes (stemming from the cut in the basic rate of income tax from 33 to 30 per cent in 1979, associated with the near-doubling of Value Added Tax from 8 to 15 per cent in the same Budget).

The basic framework of analysis is set out in section 10.1. This is followed in section 10.2 by an investigation of revenue-neutral tax changes, and the question of indexation is then considered in section 10.3.

10.1 A Basic Framework of Analysis

This section describes the main components of the model used to compare alternative rate structures. It is necessary to capture the main characteristics of the tax-and-transfer system in order to clarify the interdependencies without wishing to include all the complexities described in section 9.4.

National Insurance contributions

In the United Kingdom, National Insurance benefits are financed by a payroll tax levied on employers and employees, topped up by a subsidy from the central Exchequer. The latter, expressed as a proportion of the receipts of the National Insurance Fund, has declined in recent years, from 18 per cent of total receipts in 1979–80 to 12 per cent in 1984–5.

The National Insurance contribution schedule has been described earlier in this book. The value of the upper earnings limit, y_U, is set at approximately 1½ average earnings and the ratio of y_U to the lower earnings limit, y_L (also equal to the basic rate of the flat-rate state pension) lies between 6½ and 7½. As described in section 9.4, the schedule produces a kink in the relation between gross and disposable income at y_L, where the marginal contribution rate is well over 200 per cent. In contrast, the marginal contribution rate is zero above y_U. The regressive effect of this feature is examined further in Chapter 11.

Section 9.4 concentrated on the impact of y_L, and the effect of y_U is considered further here. If NI contributions are used along with income taxation to finance a scheme such as MIG, then y_U will produce a kink in the section CT in Fig. 9.2. The effect on the relationship between t and the level of the MIG, b (for a given value of y_0) is however fairly straightforward. The required level of t is reduced by the same amount for all levels of b, since the net contribution to finance made by NI is the same so long as y_0 is unchanged.

The more interesting implications follow when revenue-neutral changes in t and c are considered, involving a shift towards different methods of financing a given minimum income for a specified proportion of the low paid. For example, it has often been suggested that NI should be abolished and that transfers should then be financed by increasing the tax rate, t. Meade *et al.* (1978, pp. 374–5) has suggested that it is reasonable to calculate the new tax rate required simply by adding the values of t and c used in the combined system. However, the fact that for each person NI is based on *gross* earnings, but income tax is based on *taxable* income (that is, income less the value of allowances), means that a reduction in c by one percentage point must be met by an increase in t by more than one percentage point.

The relevant comparison can easily be made for a single individual who has allowances equal to a, and has earnings below the upper limit y_U. His total income tax and NI contributions, R, are thus $t(y - a) + cy$. If the individual is to pay the same total amount after a reduction in the value of c by one percentage point, then t must increase by $y/(y - a)$ percentage points. For someone with earnings of double the level of allowances ($y = 2a$), then t must increased by two percentage points. Comparisons are more difficult to make for *aggregates*, but it has been shown by Creedy (1981b, 1982d) that the abolition of NI contributions would require a tax rate significantly higher than the sum of previous values of t and c. The precise difference depends on the rates operating before the change and on the level of tax allowances assumed, but it is likely to be at least five percentage points for current values.

When this characteristic of the system is not always understood, and emphasis is placed on the separate rates, it is not surprising that in recent years NI contributions have been used in preference to income tax in order to increase revenue. Indeed the cut in the basic rate of income tax announced in the 1979 Budget, from 33 per cent to 30 per cent, has in aggregate been more than offset by a rise in the NI contribution rate on employees, from 6.5 per cent in 1979–80 to 9 per cent in 1983–4.

Income taxation

The analysis uses a non-linear tax schedule and considers only income from employment, which forms over 70 per cent of average household income in Britain. This limitation is made so that income taxation and National Insurance contributions apply to the same measure. If $T(y)$ is the tax paid by an individual with income y, the schedule is as follows

$$
\begin{aligned}
T(y) &= 0 & y &< a_1 \\
&= t(y - a_1) & a_1 &< y < a_2 \\
&= t(a_2 - a_1) + (y - a_2)(d - hy^{-k}) & a_2 &< y
\end{aligned}
$$
with $h = (d - t) a_2^k$ and $k < 1$. \hfill (10.1)

The tax schedule in (10.1) has a standard tax rate of t over the range of income from a_1 to a_2, and thereafter has rising marginal rates up to a maximum rate of d. The parameter k governs the rate of increase in the marginal rate between t and d. The same threshold levels a_1 and a_2 apply to all individuals and although this assumption is not entirely realistic the schedule can be used to approximate the British structure closely, as shown in Creedy and Gemmell (1982). For present purposes the schedule may be assumed to apply to a particular type of household, and individual variations in allowances (arising for example because of differences in mortgage and other payments) are ignored. The values of d and k may be estimated using regression analysis, and values of 0.95 and 0.65 are used for d and k respectively. These values are based on the UK tax schedule for the tax year 1977–8. The resulting relationship, from equation (10.1), is shown in Fig. 10.1, along with the actual schedule indicated by the series of 'steps' in the marginal tax rate.

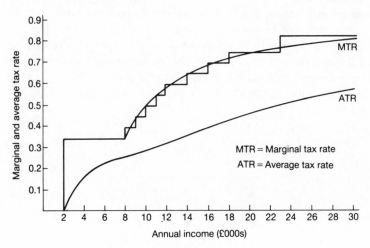

Fig. 10.1   *The income tax schedule*

Transfer payments

There is a significant proportion of individuals who pay little in the form of income tax and NI contributions but who pay indirect taxes in the form of Value Added Tax resulting from their expenditure. Much of this expenditure is in turn financed from transfer payments, so that it is necessary to specify a form of transfers before VAT is considered.

The variety of means-tested and other benefits in the United Kingdom were described in Chapter 9, section 9.4. Here, for simplicity, these are approximated by a simple 'minimum income guarantee' (MIG) whereby all those with a gross income below the level of y_0 have their net income brought up to the level b.

Some features of this system are illustrated in Fig. 10.2, which concentrates on the lower incomes. A comparison between Fig. 10.2 and Fig. 9.5 suggests that the stylized system is broadly similar to the actual system, although the relationship between net and gross income is smoother because the actual system is administered in a much more complex way. In Britain the typical situation in recent years has been for y_0 to exceed a_1, and for the latter to exceed y_L. Thus individuals with earnings below y_0 pay income tax and NI contributions *and* simultaneously receive transfer payments. This situation, which has been labelled the 'poverty trap', has sometimes been criticized although it is not necessarily a bad feature of a tax-and-transfer system. For example, raising a_1 above y_0 would be very expensive, and would actually benefit those with higher incomes more than those with lower incomes (if all other tax thresholds are adjusted in the same way). Nevertheless such a system must attempt to ensure that there is a smooth relationship between gross and disposable income (as in Fig. 9.2, for example). This imposes a constraint on the relationship between b, y_0, c, t, and a_1.

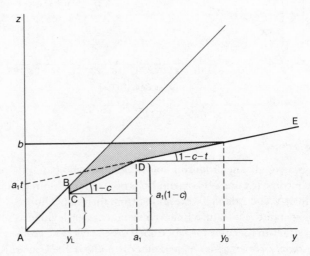

Fig. 10.2   *Direct taxes and transfers*

In Fig. 10.2 the line marked ABCDE shows the relationship between gross income, y, and income 'after income tax and NI', z. There is of course another kink in the schedule after y_U, and it becomes non-linear after a_2 ($a_2 > y_U$). If $y_0 > a_1$ then the value of b must be equal to the vertical distance from y_0 to the line segment DE. Thus

$$b = y_0(1 - c - t) + a_1 t. \qquad (10.2)$$

If b were set at a value greater than the right-hand side of equation (10.2), then a small increase in gross income from y_0 would result in a reduction in disposable income.

In practice, more emphasis may be given to the value of b, relative to average earnings. In this case equation (10.2) can be easily rearranged to express y_0 in terms of the other parameters of the system. The shaded area of Fig. 10.2, applying to those between y_L and y_0, shows the extent to which individuals both pay income tax and NI *and* receive transfers. In some cases the latter exceeds the former. One important implication is that a time-series of the total value of transfers may give a spurious indication of the extent of transfers to the relatively low paid. This is particularly relevant when considering the 'costs' of alternative methods of indexation, in section 10.3 below.

Value Added Tax

The taxes and transfers considered above provide a non-linear transformation between gross income and disposable (post-income tax NI and transfers) income. To complete the model it is necessary to specify a relationship between expenditure and the amount of VAT paid. In Britain a significant number of goods and services do not attract VAT, and the proportion of expenditure devoted to zero-rated goods varies as total expenditure varies. Furthermore, VAT is levied on the tax-exclusive price of goods and services.

If q denotes expenditure, $V(q)$ the VAT paid, v the VAT rate, and $r(q)$ the proportion of expenditure on zero-rated goods, then the relationship between $V(q)$ and q is given by

$$V(q) = q\{1 - r(q)\}\{v/(1 + v)\}. \qquad (10.3)$$

For present purposes it is necessary to specify the form of $r(q)$. Using *Family Expenditure Survey* data Creedy and Gemmell (1984) have shown that good results are obtained using a log-linear relationship between $r(q)$ and q. Using data for 1978, for all households, the ordinary least squares regression result was

$$\log r(q) = 0.654 - 0.302 \log q \qquad R^2 = 0.970 \qquad (10.4)$$
$$(0.0633)(0.0143).$$

These results apply to weekly expenditure, so that the relationship between $r(q)$ and q when the latter is in annual terms is given by

$$r(q) = 6.343 q^{-0.302} \qquad (10.5)$$

The effects of varying the rate of VAT may be examined by substituting (10.5) into (10.3) for alternative values of v. This method assumes that any substitution between zero and non-zero-rated goods, as v varies, is such as to leave the *proportion* of expenditure devoted to zero-rated goods unchanged at each expenditure level. In practice this assumption does not seem to be unduly restrictive. Estimates of the relationship in (10.4), using similar FES data for three other years (1973, 1975, and 1980), show that it is stable, despite changes in real incomes over the period and the large increase in the VAT rate in 1979. The value of the coefficient on $\log q$ in (10.4) was in the range -0.30 to -0.34 in all years, and the value of $r(q)$ at mean expenditure was roughly constant at 0.45.

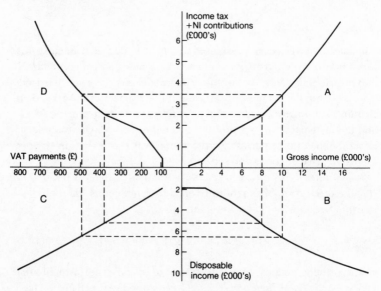

Fig. 10.3   *The tax-and-transfer model*

The complete tax-and-transfer model

The basic characteristics of the model are illustrated in Fig. 10.3, using a particular set of rates and thresholds, from Creedy and Gemmell (1984). The tax thresholds a_1 and a_2 are £2000 and £8000 respectively; the NI lower and upper earnings limits are £700 and £5000 respectively; and a guaranteed minimum disposable income of £1832 is received by individuals with a gross income below £2250; the standard tax rate is 0.32; and the NI contribution rate is 0.15. These values are representative of the British system in 1978, although they are rounded for convenience.

Quadrant A of Fig. 10.3 shows the relationship between the sum of income tax and National Insurance contributions, and gross income. The relationship consists of five sections. An individual with gross income below £700 pays no income tax or national insurance. Thereafter contributions are paid at the constant rate c until the £2000 income tax threshold is reached, where the rate is $t + c$ up to £5000. There is a further linear section between the upper earnings limits and £8000 (a_2). Above this level the non-linear section of the income tax schedule applies.

The resulting relationship between gross income, y, and $y - T(y) - C(y)$ is illustrated in quadrant B. This quadrant also shows the effects of the transfer system. The present analysis assumes that all disposable income is consumed. This assumption avoids the complexities of a savings model and the tax treatment of different methods of saving.

Quadrant C then shows the relationship between disposable income (expenditure) and VAT payments, from equation (10.3). Finally, quadrant D illustrates the relative magnitudes of direct taxes (income tax and NI) and indirect taxes (VAT), showing the extent to which the former is relatively more important than the latter at high income levels.

10.2 Revenue-Neutral Tax Changes

The method of analysis

With the above framework it is not possible to obtain convenient analytical results for total revenue. In order to examine the effects of variations in the parameters of the model it is therefore necessary to use a simulated distribution of gross income. The same distribution is used for each set of rates and thresholds considered, as no allowance is made for incentive effects. The results presented below are based on a simulated lognormal distribution of income, for which the mean and variance of the logarithms are μ and σ^2 respectively. Parameter values of $\mu = 8.0$ and $\sigma^2 = 0.2$ were used to obtain the incomes of a simulated sample of 1000 individuals. These values were chosen as corresponding closely to the distribution of gross annual earnings in Britain in 1978, though it should be stressed that the following results are not affected by the particular values used. Experiments with different sample sizes showed that a sample size of 1000 is more than adequate for present purposes, in order to avoid significant sampling variation. The sample arithmetic mean and coefficient of variation of gross income are £3276 and 0.482 respectively.

The procedure used in the calculations is as follows. First, the National Insurance contributions of each individual are calculated, having set the values of the lower and upper earnings limits. The total value of contributions per person, R_c, and the distribution of post-NI contributions income is obtained. Each individual's income tax is then calculated using the schedule (10.1), giving the total income tax revenue per person, R_t, and the distribution of 'after tax and NI contributions income'. Since income tax and NI operate quite separately, the order of these calculations is arbitrary.

Before examining VAT payments it is then necessary to apply the system of transfer payments. Under that system some individuals pay income tax and NI contributions *and* receive transfer payments to bring their gross income up to a specified level. The total value of transfer payments per person (that is, total transfers divided by the total population), denoted T, is obtained.

On the assumption that all disposable income is consumed, each individual's VAT payments are then calculated for a specified rate of VAT. Total VAT payments per person are denoted R_v. If VAT is then subtracted from disposable income for each individual, a distribution of what may be regarded as 'net consumption' is obtained.

With a given distribution of gross income, and a set of parameters for each component of the model, the implications of varying the three relevant rates c, t, and v may then be examined. Any change in either c or t will affect the total amount of transfer payments which need to be made, by changing the net incomes of those below y_0, and thereby altering the value of b as specified in equation (10.2) above.

Some numerical results

Using the same threshold values as those of Fig. 10.3, the effects of varying the various rates of tax can be examined numerically. A selection of results for variations in the standard rate of income tax and in the VAT rate are taken from Creedy and Gemmell (1984) and are shown in Fig. 10.4. The left-hand side of Fig. 10.4 shows how income tax revenue per person increases linearly, and how VAT revenue and total transfer payments decrease slightly (also at a linear rate), as t increases. Remember that in the present framework (unlike Chapter 9) increased tax revenue is not used to finance more generous transfer payments. T falls as a result of the operation of equation (10.2). The linearity of the R_t schedule is clear from the individual tax schedule, but that of R_v and T is not obvious. Similar relationships apply for variations in the NI contributions rate. The right-hand side of Fig. 10.4 shows a slightly non-linear relationship between R_v and v, when other parameters are unchanged, and this is clearly expected from the nature of VAT (being based on the tax-exclusive price).

The shares of the three different sources of tax in total revenue obviously change as the rates change. The proportions of income tax, NI, and VAT per person in total revenue are respectively 0.53, 0.37, and 0.10 when t, c, and v are respectively 0.32, 0.10, and 0.08. VAT's share increases to 0.17 when v increases to 0.16. The relatively high contribution of NI is explained by the fact that the 'tax' base is larger than the income tax base, despite the effect of the upper earnings limit.

Results such as those presented above can be used to obtain revenue-neutral changes in tax rates. Total net revenue per person, R, is equal to

$$R = R_c + R_t + R_v - T$$

and the total differential is then

$$dR = (\partial R_c/\partial c + \partial R_v/\partial c - \partial T/\partial c)dc + (\partial R_t/\partial t + \partial R_v/\partial t - \partial T/\partial t)dt + (\partial R_v/\partial v)dv. \qquad (10.6)$$

The examination of revenue neutral rate changes is considerably eased by the fact that, except for $\partial R_v/\partial v$, the partial derivatives are constant and in many cases the shifts in the relevant schedules, as other parameters change, are parallel. Some indication of the relevant orders of magnitude may be obtained as follows.

Consider revenue-neutral changes in the standard rate of income

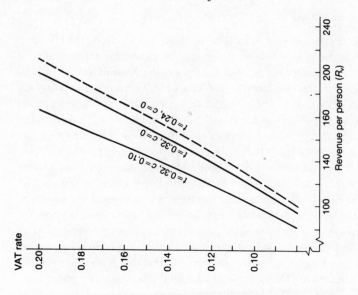

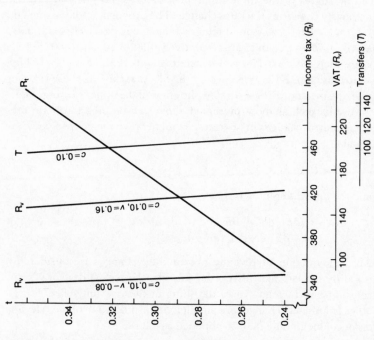

tax and the rate of VAT, with c unchanged. With c, t, and v of 0.10, 0.32, and 0.16 respectively, substitution into (10.6) gives $dv = -2.034$ dt. Thus if t is reduced by one percentage point the VAT rate v must be increased by just over two percentage points. Changes in c and t, with v unchanged, may be examined in the same way. It is found that for revenue neutrality, $dt = -1.686\ dc$, so that if c is reduced by one percentage point, t must be raised by about 1.70 percentage points. The effects of such revenue neutral changes on income *distribution* will be examined in Chapter 11.

10.3 Indexation of Tax Thresholds and Benefits

The question of the appropriate level at which a guaranteed minimum income should be set, and then subsequently adjusted, raises many complex issues. Governments have rarely made explicit their reasons for announced adjustments. However, between 1948 and 1973 pensions and Supplementary Benefits were approximately doubled in real terms, which is consistent with the assumption that governments took a 'relative' view of minimum standards. But since legislation allowing for *price* indexation was passed in the early 1970s there seems to have been a gradual transition towards an 'absolute' view. Such an inference is not however obvious from the current confused set of regulations concerning pensions and pensionable earnings, which were examined more closely in Part 2. Furthermore, in 1980 short-term benefits were adjusted by less than anticipated price inflation, the stated reason being that it was a temporary measure until plans to tax benefits could be completed. The fact that benefits are adjusted according to anticipated inflation over the following year can of course mean that the intention to maintain real benefits may not be fulfilled. The implications of adjusting only once per year have recently been examined by Beckerman and Clark (1982), and Harvey and Hemming (1983). Since November 1983, however, indexation depends on inflation in the preceding year.

The question of the appropriate method of indexation involves many complex issues (see, for example, Meade *et al.* (1978), Wilson (1982), and Wilson and Wilson (1982)). These involve questions relating to the maintenance of even real benefits when inflation has been affected by an adverse movement in the terms of trade (for example, the oil price rise of the early 1970s), whether indexation is part of an explicit redistribution policy, the extent to which there is reliance on certain built-in stabilizers, and also the particular type of price of earnings index used. (The use of average post-tax earnings, based perhaps on a form of tax-and-price index, would raise difficulties, for example.) If built-in or automatic stabilizers are used, then there will of course be some income redistribution. This implication is often ignored but, as shown in Chapter 11, can be very significant.

Any debate about the appropriate indexation of benefits will be largely affected by views about the 'costs' involved. Now, other things being equal, these costs will change largely as a result of changes in the dependency ratio. The indexation of all benefits and tax thresholds to an earnings index removes any built-in flexibility which otherwise exists, and there is no change in the 'burden' of financing the same relative benefits. This is satisfactory so long as the number and composition of those in receipt of benefits does not change. If an adverse movement in the dependency ratio is not met by changes in tax *rates* in order to raise more revenue, then differential indexation must be used.

An important point about the reliance on the built-in flexibility of progressive income taxes is that it cannot be used for an indefinite length of time. The revenue elasticity of a tax schedule gradually declines as fewer people can be brought into the 'tax net', and there are fewer movements into the higher marginal rate tax bands (see Creedy and Gemmell, 1982). It is not a straightforward matter to examine the implications of using different methods of indexation in Britain. This difficulty arises because of the complex interdependencies which exist within the system of taxes and transfer payments. In particular, the net cost of indexing all benefits using an earnings index (when tax thresholds are not fully adjusted) cannot simply be measured by the total value of transfer payments. Many individuals both pay tax *and* receive benefits because of the overlap in the system. Part of the increase in transfer payments is actually met by the higher tax payments of those receiving benefits. This has already been illustrated in Fig. 10.2. It is quite possible, when thresholds are adjusted by less than an earnings index (and earnings increase faster than prices), for *total* transfer payments to increase without this reflecting any greater 'generosity' of the system. 'Net transfers', allowing for the direct tax paid by those receiving transfers, will nevertheless be falling.

A further complication is raised by the fact that the expenditure of those receiving benefits will produce tax revenue from value added taxes. The changes in VAT revenue depend on a number of factors in addition to the $r(q)$ relationship. First, the form of indexation of income tax and NI, by altering the flexibility of income tax and NI revenues, changes the relationship between gross and net income and thus has differing effects on the VAT tax base. For example, price indexation of income tax thresholds reduces net relative to gross income (if earnings rise faster than prices) as incomes increase. This 'income effect', in turn, reduces VAT revenue relative to average earnings.

Secondly, VAT revenue depends on the way in which the guaranteed minimum income, b, is adjusted and, through income tax and NI, on changes in y_0. Increases in y_0, relative to average income, increase the proportion of the population eligible for transfers. Various forces will be in operation here. First, different forms of adjustment of b will have differing effects on the dispersion of disposable incomes. This 'redistribution effect' will depend on how the transfer system operates. An increase in b which increases the equality of disposable income by transfering income mainly from those with high incomes to those with low incomes, will increase the proportion of total expenditure on non-VAT-rated goods and hence reduce VAT revenue. Secondly, indexation of benefits also creates an 'income effect' by increasing disposable income of those below y_0, which increases VAT revenue.

These interdependencies have been examined in detail in Creedy and Gemmell (1984), who show that (with an unchanged income distribution) the 'burden' of financing transfers, measured by *net* transfers, can 'at worst' remain fixed, although total transfers increase slightly when benefits are indexed to earnings and tax thresholds are indexed to prices. Revenue flexibility is dominated by income taxation, since real ·income growth leads to very little change in VAT revenue per person whatever form of indexation is used. If NI earnings limits are adjusted by less than the growth of earnings, then revenue falls and the dispersion of post-contribution earnings increases. The concentration on total, rather than *net*, transfers can give a very misleading impression of the policy options available. It therefore seems that the most important policy considerations involve the extent to which the dependency ratio is expected to change (resulting from demographic factors, unemployment, or changes in labour force participation), and judgement about the desired redistribution resulting from the system. The redistributive implications are therefore examined in the following chapter.

11

Income Redistribution

Comparing distributions

The measurement of income or wealth 'inequality' raises many complex issues. These concern, for example, the choice of appropriate unit of analysis (individual, family, household), the concept of income (including the time-period over which income is measured), and the statistical measure itself. There has been a great deal of research, especially since the early 1970s, into the properties of various statistical measures of a single dimensional variable, and the relationships among a large number of measures are now fairly well understood. It is not proposed to examine these issues here, but it should be recognized that the measurement of *redistribution* involves a further set of complications.

The main problem is that the assessment of redistribution immediately implies a comparison between two distributions, one of which may not actually be available for observation. There is obviously little sense in allocating all taxes and benefits (including transfer payments and implied benefits from, say, education expenditure) to income groups and describing the difference between the observed distributions of gross income and a resulting measure of 'net' income as the 'redistributive effect of government as a whole'. Much government expenditure directly gives rise to incomes, for example of government employees, and of course government intervention has important indirect effects on the process of income generation. The same qualification applies to specific policies, such as a state pension scheme, since the absence of the state scheme would not be expected to imply a complete lack of private provision, or retirement at such a uniform age. This kind of argument has led some economists to be extremely sceptical of any attempt to measure redistribution. The case has been put most forcefully by Prest (1955, 1968, 1976), though the comments by Musgrave (1976) and Atkinson (1976), both of whom have made significant contributions to the analysis of redistribution, are instructive. If a nihilistic view is not taken, then comparisons must at least be made with great caution. No attempt will be made here to assess the 'overall' impact of tax and expenditure policies, but some general implications of income support programmes are examined.

Tax incidence

In measuring redistribution it is also necessary to recognize explicitly that the effects of a tax depend on the possibility that the person who is in direct contact with the Inland Revenue authorities (and who bears the legal or 'formal' incidence) may to some extent 'shift' the tax to other people.

The question of who bears the 'burden' of taxation raises one of the oldest problems to be discussed in public finance literature. It played a major role in the first really systematic treatise on taxation, by McCulloch (1845), though it was many years before even the concept of incidence was clarified in a satisfactory way; see especially the works of Seligman (1899) and Musgrave (1959, pp. 227–31).

The distinction between 'direct' and 'indirect' taxes has varied over time, but the former is perhaps best defined as including those taxes which may be adjusted to the individual characteristics of the taxpayer, and the latter as those levied on transactions irrespective of the circumstances of buyer or seller. At one time the distinction rested on a simple and incorrect view of incidence; that direct taxes were borne by the person on whom they were levied, while indirect taxes could be shifted (see Mill, 1848, reprinted in 1920, p. 822). It was generally held that income taxation, the prime example of a direct tax, could not be 'passed on'. This question was much discussed by the Colwyn Commission (1920), and is the subject of a classic monograph by Black (1939). The extent to which the income tax is 'borne' by employees, employers, or consumers who face higher prices is very difficult indeed to determine, especially when the 'deadweight loss' (see Chapter 12) is taken into account.

Because of the difficulty of determining incidence empirically, most studies have assumed that income taxes are borne in full by employees and that commodity taxes result in a straightforward increase in the prices which consumers have to pay (although Musgrave *et al.* (1951) provided a sensitivity analysis using alternative incidence assumptions). However these assumptions are not strictly compatible, since inelastic commodity demands are not consistent with an inelastic supply of labour. Atkinson and Stiglitz (1980, p. 291) have shown, using a general equilibrium framework of analysis, that the extent to which these elasticity assumptions are mutually incompatible depends on differences in factor intensities across industries.

Incidence of National Insurance contributions

Similar problems also arise in the treatment of employers' National Insurance contributions. In its annual analysis of the effects of taxes and benefits on household incomes, the Central Statistical Office have assumed since 1969 that employers' contributions can be 'treated as an indirect tax included in the prices of goods and services produced in the UK' (*Economic Trends*, 1969, p. xviii). It had previously been regarded as part of the employee's income, but the CSO offered no justification either for its earlier position or its change.

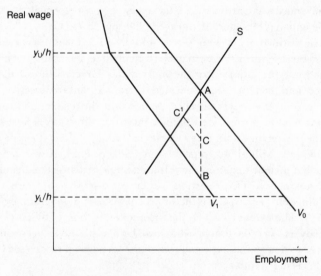

Fig. 11.1 *Effect of employers' NI contribution*

Notes: y_L = lower earnings limit
y_U = upper earnings limit
h = hours worked

As the quotation suggests, indirect taxes are assumed to be fully passed on to consumers in the form of higher prices and this assumption of 'forward shifting' is usually made in studies of redistribution.

In contrast, studies of the shifting of payroll taxes, such as the National Insurance contribution, examine the more general case in which such taxes may be forward shifted, or 'backward shifted' on to wage-earners.

Payroll taxes imply a difference between the marginal value product of the worker and the cost of the worker to the firm. In Fig. 11.1, the imposition of an employer's contribution, with wages and prices unchanged, reduces the effective marginal value product of the worker to the firm, for wage rates above the lower earnings limit, from V_0 to V_1. The impact tapers off at high wages given the declining average contribution rate above the upper earnings limit.

Early evidence across countries, as in Brittain (1972), suggested that the whole burden of the employer's contribution was shifted by employers, although the mechanism of shifting was not identified. However Beach and Balfour (1983) argued not only that the econometric methods of previous studies were faulty, but also that the degree of observed shifting may be considerably lower, especially if labour supply is not perfectly inelastic. Full shifting with a perfectly inelastic labour supply is indicated by a movement from A to B in Fig. 11.1; this can stem from either lower nominal wages or higher prices. Beach and Balfour actually estimated the 'shifting coefficient' to be less than 1, say from A to C, but the coefficient which they estimated, 0.6, may be better·interpreted as a coefficient showing the *speed* with which employers are able to adjust real wages in the short period. However if labour supply is not completely inelastic, as illustrated by curve S, then the reduction in real wages is even less, from A to only C^1, with a corresponding reduction in employment. It is apparent therefore that the redistributional impact of changes in payroll tax rates is difficult to identify, and that simple procedures, such as those of the CSO, are based on 'extreme' assumption.

It has been seen in Chapter 10 that the nature of revenue neutral changes in income tax and National Insurance contribution rates are far from obvious, because of the difference in their 'tax bases'. A reduction in the standard rate of income tax of one percentage point, accompanied by an increase in the NI contributions rate of one percentage point, will actually lead to an increase in total revenue. Thus a government may wish to continue using the myth of social insurance for general revenue purposes. This point is in addition to the very different argument which supports the use of special hypothecated contributions for revenue purposes, and which states that people are

more willing to pay higher taxes if they *think* that they are also paying
for their own future benefits. This view is clearly expressed by Prest
(1979, p. 253), who acknowledged the mythical nature of the 'insurance' component and stated, 'but this does not stop a lot of people
from *thinking* that the benefits they receive are related to the contributions they pay. And was it not Jonathan Swift who said that the secret
of happiness is to be perpetually deceived.' There is a suspicion here
that Swift's brilliant satire is again acting as a 'non-reflecting mirror'.
But the uncertainty about the incidence of the National Insurance
'tax' provides another reason why governments are attracted to it if
they are preoccupied with the problem of raising revenue. With such
an uncertain incidence, so that different people can (inconsistently)
believe they are passing the burden of the tax to others, 'taxable
capacity' is thereby raised. At least no government has seriously considered adopting Swift's major proposals for raising tax revenue,
according to which the government should

tax those qualities . . . for which men chiefly value themselves, the rate to be
more or less according to the degree of excelling, the decision whereof should
be left entirely to their own breast. The highest tax was upon men who are the
greatest favourites of the other sex, . . . for which they are allowed to be their
own vouchers. But . . . honour, justice, wisdom and learning . . . should not
be taxed at all, because . . . no man will either allow them in his neighbour, or
value them in himself. (*Gulliver's Travels.*)

The conceptual problems associated with measuring incidence and
redistribution cannot be discussed at length here, although they must
of course be recognized. They are not the only problems, and the following section briefly considers some of the more technical aspects of
measuring redistribution.

11.1 Some Measurement Problems

Progressivity and flexibility of taxes

The general acceptance in parliament, during the last quarter of the
nineteenth century, of income redistribution as an explicit part of the
role of government led naturally to the acceptance of progressive
taxation. The general idea of a progressive tax schedule, as one in
which the average tax rate increases as income increases (so that the
marginal rate exceeds the average rate), is not however sufficient for

comparisons of the *degree* of progressivity. While the statement that one tax schedule is 'more progressive' than another is nearly always meant to imply a comparison between the distributions of post-tax income, there have been many attempts to define progressivity with reference only to the nature of tax schedules. This desire is understandable, since judgements would require much less information.

A number of alternative measures of progressivity were compared in an early paper by Musgrave and Thin (1948). They examined four different measures (average rate, marginal rate, liability, and residual income progression) which depend only on the tax schedule, and compared them with 'effective progression' which they defined in terms of shifts in Lorenz curves. The rankings of income tax schedules using the various measures were very different. Furthermore, Musgrave and Thin showed that comparisons should not be made without reference to the tax yield (the *distribution* of tax revenue would of course need to be considered in a more comprehensive treatment, but this is not the relevant issue here). Many new measures of progressivity, such as Kakwani (1977) and Suits (1977), compared in Formby *et al.* (1981), have therefore been formulated explicitly in terms of inequality comparisons.

More recently, however, Hemming and Keen (1983) have returned to the question of finding conditions, based only on the tax schedule, under which the relevant distributions may be unambiguously ranked in terms of their Lorenz curves. Jakobsson (1976) had shown that Lorenz comparisons can be unambiguously related to comparisons between tax schedules according to their schedules of the elasticity of post-tax income with respect to pre-tax income (which must not cross). However, Hemming and Keen (1983) obtained the result that Lorenz rankings could be made unambiguously if (for equal yield comparisons) the *tax* schedules cross only once. If the tax schedules cross more than once then there are distributions of pre-tax income for which the progressivity ranking is reversed, and when non-equal yield comparisons are being made the tax schedules simply have to be appropriately normalized.

Now there is a clear connection between the 'progressivity' of a tax system and its built-in flexibility. The extent to which inflation or real income growth leads to an increase in total revenue relative to average income, when tax thresholds are not changed, depends on the extent to which people are moved into income ranges for which higher marginal tax rates apply. The flexibility properties therefore depend, like degrees of progressivity, on the tax schedule *and* on the pre-tax income distribution. Flexibility is measured by the 'revenue elasticity' of a system; that is, the elasticity of total revenue with respect to average income. By extending the 'crossing point' analysis of Hemming and Keen, Hutton and Lambert (1983) were able to show that 'elasticity neutrality' ensures 'distribution neutrality'.

The practical value of these results is that Hutton and Lambert were then able to derive combinations of tax rate changes and threshold changes required, when changing the relative importance of income tax and NI contributions in total revenue, in order to achieve revenue *and* distribution neutrality. The conditions may thus be used in considering certain types of tax reform which are required to achieve fairly limited objectives, such as simplifying the system or changing only the balance between different taxes.

However, if the main purpose of an investigation is to examine explicitly the changes in the *degree* of inequality which are implied by certain types of tax change, the results mentioned above are of limited value. To what extent has a shift towards NI contributions involved an increase in the dispersion of after-tax-and-contributions income? To what extent has under-indexation of tax thresholds and transfer payments increased the dispersion of disposable income? These questions can only be answered by direct consideration of changes in a measure (or preferably a number of measures) of income dispersion.

Linearized tax systems

A more direct approach to the problem of measuring the distributional effects of tax changes was used by Kay and Morris (1979). Their main objective was to examine the consequences for income distribution of a major shift towards indirect taxation (mainly from VAT) in the 1979 Budget. The feature of their approach is that, within specified ranges of the income distribution, the tax schedules can be treated as being linear. Below the NI upper earnings limit, which is within the standard tax rate band, both NI and income tax are linearly related to pre-tax income. The basic approach can be illustrated using income taxation and VAT only, as follows.

Suppose that the standard rate of income tax is 0.30 and that personal allowances are £1500. Then for those with income, y, above 1500 the tax paid $T(y)$ is $0.30 (y - 1500)$. This can be rearranged as

$$T(y) = -(0.30)(1500) + 0.30y \qquad (11.1)$$
$$= -450 + 0.30y.$$

Thus individuals effectively receive a 'tax credit' of £450 and pay tax at a fixed marginal rate (see also the simple analysis of the Negative Income Tax in Chapter 9). Kay and Morris specify a linear relationship between the amount of VAT paid, $V(q)$, on expenditure of q. (This may be contrasted with the treatment in Chapter 10.) The effects of the various exemptions on items such as food, which form a higher proportion of the total expenditure of low-income families, is that there is also an effective tax credit with the VAT schedule. Suppose that

$$V(q) = -100 + 0.10q. \qquad (11.2)$$

It is necessary to translate the values in (11.2) to those which apply to income, y, rather than expenditure, q (ignoring the possible effects of savings). Since only a proportion equal to $1.0 - 0.30 = 0.70$ of an additional £1 is available for consumption, the effective marginal rate of VAT in this example is $(0.70)(0.10) = 0.07$ (or 7 per cent). But since the income tax credit of £450 is all available for consumption, the amount of VAT which is paid on this is equal to £$(0.10)(450) =$ £45. Hence the effective VAT tax credit is reduced to £$(100 - 45) =$ £55. The combined effect of income tax and VAT in this example is that there is a tax credit of £505 $=$ £$(450 + 55)$ and a marginal rate of $0.37 = 0.30 + 0.07$.

The basis of comparisons of tax progressivity is the argument that, 'other things being equal, the higher the tax credit and the higher the marginal rate, the more progressive the system' (1979, p. 3). Kay and Morris calculated the effective tax credits and marginal rates for a variety of household types (within specified income ranges) before and after the 1979 Budget. Since there was little change, they concluded that the Budget was almost neutral in its redistributive effect. This procedure provides an attractive and simple procedure in the convenient case where both parameters move in the same direction, otherwise an explicit treatment of redistribution is required. Kay and Morris (1979, p. 4) suggest that, 'there is a "balanced package" . . . of threshold increase and rate reduction, which is more or less distributionally neutral in its effect'.

Judgement about a 'balanced package' requires however an explicit measure of dispersion. For example, if the coefficients of variation of post- and pre-tax income are denoted η_z and η_y respectively, and if the tax credit and marginal tax rate are b and t respectively, then it can be shown that

$$\eta_z = \eta_y \left\{ 1 + b/(1 - t)\bar{y} \right\}^{-1} \qquad (11.3)$$

where $\bar{y}$ is arithmetic mean pre-tax income. From this result, the combination of changes in b and t which leave η_z unchanged is given by

$$dt = -db\{(1 - t)/b\}. \qquad (11.4)$$

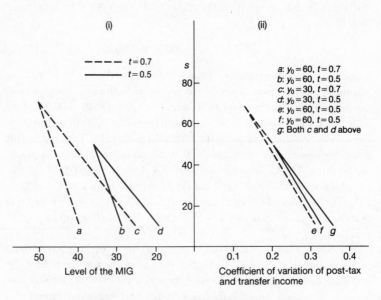

Fig. 11.2   *The modified MIG and dispersion*

Despite the simple interpretation of changes in a linear tax schedule applied to a specified section of the distribution of pre-tax income, the progressivity of the complete system cannot easily be assessed in terms only of the changes *within* each section. With a number of linear sections it is quite possible for the dispersion of after-tax income within each section to be reduced, but for the complete distribution the dispersion will also depend on the effect of the *between*-group components of dispersion. For linearized tax schedules the coefficient of variation of the complete distribution of post-tax income, allowing for between- and within-group components, can be in fact derived algebraically.

Results are given in Creedy (1978) for the Minimum Income Guarantee and modified MIG discussed in Chapter 9 above, and in Creedy (1982d) for the MIG which is financed by various combinations of income tax and National Insurance contributions. Examples from the former are shown in Fig. 11.2, for alternative modified MIG schemes. For convenience, the required tax rates are also shown.

These examples are in terms of weekly income, and the pre-tax and transfer distribution was assumed to have an arithmetic mean and coefficient of variation of £71.9 and 0.402 respectively (that is, the distribution of the logarithms of income is assumed to follow the Normal distribution with mean and variance of logarithms of income of 4.2 and 0.15 respectively). The effect of using NI contributions in addition to income tax in order to finance the MIG is to increase the value of η_z for any given minimum income. Dispersion increases as the contribution rate increases because of the effect of the upper earnings limit in reducing marginal rates on higher incomes. In all cases the coefficient of variation, η_z, is linearly related to the marginal tax rate, t.

A problem with the studies just mentioned is that they do not include Value Added Tax, and a further problem with the method of Kay and Morris is that it does not include transfer payments. This means that the 'tax credit' calculated for VAT overstates the progressivity of the indirect tax, since much of the expenditure by the lower-income groups is financed from transfer payments. VAT should be compared with disposable, rather than pre-tax and transfer income. It is therefore useful to return to the 'basic framework' presented in Chapter 10. This framework has the additional advantages of not being restricted to linearized tax schedules, and allowing a large variety of measures of dispersion to be calculated. Non-linear income tax and VAT schedules are used.

Consider equation (10.3), which relates VAT payments $V(q)$ to expenditure, q, via the proportion of expenditure devoted to zero-rated goods. This stated that $V(q) = q\{1 - r(q)\}\{v/(1 + v)\}$. The use of a linear relationships between $V(q)$ and q, as in Kay and Morris, can be seen to imply that $r(q)$ is related to the reciprocal of q. Since if

$$r(q) = \delta - \gamma/q \qquad (11.5)$$

then

$$V(q) = \{(1 - \delta)v/(1 + v)\}q - \{\gamma v/(1 + v)\}. \qquad (11.6)$$

The log-linear form for $r(q)$ reported in Chapter 10 provides better results (in a statistical sense) than the reciprocal form of (11.5).

11.2 Comparisons Using the Basic Framework

The framework of analysis described in Chapter 10, and used to examine changes in revenue and transfer payments, can also be used to calculate a variety of measures of dispersion. The relevant distributions to be considered are those of gross income, post-tax income and National Insurance contributions, disposable income (that is, after the receipt of transfer payments), and what may be called 'net consumption' (that is, expenditure less the amount of VAT paid).

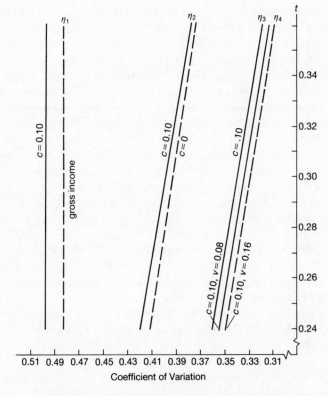

Fig. 11.3 *Changes in the standard rate of income tax*

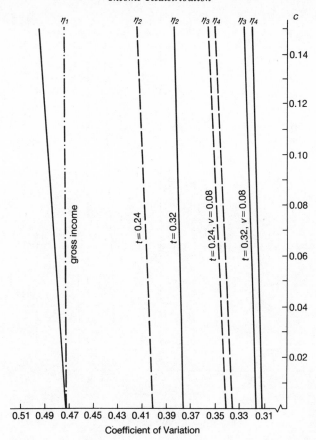

Fig. 11.4 *Changes in the NI contributions rate*

Results for the coefficient of variation are shown in Figs. 11.3, 11.4, and 11.5. These are taken from Creedy and Gemmell (1984), and are directly comparable with those shown in Chapter 10. Creedy and Gemmell obtained other measures of dispersion, and showed that the coefficient of variation behaved in just the same way as 'Atkinson's measure' (for various 'inequality aversion parameters'; see Atkinson, 1970). The coefficient of variation of pre-tax and transfer income (gross income) is 0.482, and the corresponding measures for each of the distributions mentioned above are denoted η_1 to η_4 respectively.

The progressive effect of the income tax system can be seen in Fig. 11.3 by the shift from η_1 to η_2. This can be compared with the

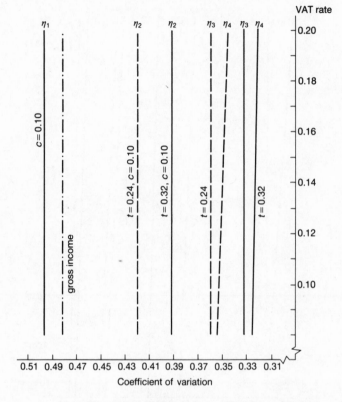

Fig. 11.5 *Changes in the rate of VAT*

progressivity of VAT. Although increases in the rate of VAT have a
large effect on total revenue R_v (as seen in Chapter 10), the shift from
η_3 to η_4 in each of the cases of $v = 0.08$ and 0.16 is rather small. Indeed
Fig. 11.3 shows that a doubling of the VAT rate from 0.08 to 0.16, at
any given income tax rate, does not even outweigh the regressive effect
of NI contributions, when the latter rate is 0.10. The rather low effect
of increasing the VAT rate on the dispersion of net consumption can
also be seen by the steepness of each of the η_4 schedules shown in
Fig. 11.5.

The regressive effect of NI contributions, caused by the upper earnings limit, is shown by the positive slope of each of the schedules in
Fig. 11.4. This also shows how the regressivity of NI is in most cases
not outweighed by the progressivity of VAT, as reflected in the shift

from η_3 to η_4. These three figures show that, with a given set of tax thresholds, NI limits and structure of VAT zero-rated goods, variations in the *rates* do not have a large effect on the dispersion of net consumption relative to gross income. In each case the *gradients* of the schedules are rather steep. But it is clear, by comparing the *positions* of the schedules for the various distributions examined, that income taxation and the system of income transfers to the low paid make the largest contributions to overall redistribution. NI contributions are of course regressive, but the progressivity of VAT, measured by its contribution to the reduction in the dispersion of net consumption, is very low.

A reduction in the income tax threshold a_1 (below which no tax is paid) to £1500 reduces the redistributive effect of income taxation, as expected. For example, η_4 rises from 0.327 (when $t = 0.32$, $c = 0.10$, $v = 0.08$) to 0.348, compared with the coefficient of variation of gross income of 0.482. The results of varying the parameters of the VAT schedule showed that there is very little scope for changing the progressivity of VAT payments. A similar conclusion was also reached by Sah (1983), who used a theoretical analysis which extended some of the results in Atkinson and Stiglitz (1980) relating to direct and indirect taxes.

Distribution-neutral changes in tax rates

Chapter 10 showed how revenue-neutral changes in tax rates could be obtained using the basic framework, this problem being simplified by the fact that the relevant schedules were linear. The same approach can be applied to distribution-neutral changes, since the coefficient of variation of net consumption, η_4, can be written as a function of c, t, and v, for fixed values of the other parameters of the model. Thus

$$d\eta_4 = (\partial\eta_4/\partial c)dc + (\partial\eta_4/\partial t)dt + (\partial\eta_4/\partial v)dv. \qquad (11.7)$$

Consider, first, changes in the standard rate of income tax and the rate of VAT, with c unchanged. It was shown in Chapter 10 that (with c, t, and v of 0.10, 0.32, and 0.16), revenue-neutral changes required $dv = -2.034 \, dt$. This may be contrasted with the changes required to ensure distribution neutrality, where it is found that

$$dv = -7.70 \, dt. \qquad (11.8)$$

The change in v in this case is much larger than that required for revenue neutrality. Nevertheless a revenue-neutral change has a rather small effect on the coefficient of variation of net consumption. If $dv = -2.034$ dt is imposed on (11.7) with $dc = 0$, it is found that $d\eta_4 = -0.0033$ dt. Conversely, a reduction in t, accompanied by a distribution-neutral change in v, would require a significant increase in the total amount of revenue raised.

For changes in c and t, with v unchanged, it was found in Chapter 10 that for revenue neutrality $dt = -1.686$ dc. However, if it is required to ensure distribution neutrality, then

$$dt = 0.133 \ dc, \qquad (11.9)$$

and the standard tax rate must be increased if the NI rate is increased, and vice versa. Again, distribution neutrality can only be achieved by raising total revenue, if only the rates are changed. Nevertheless the effect of revenue-neutral change on dispersion is given by $d\eta_4 = 0.0086$ dc.

12

Transfer Schemes and Labour Supply

The previous three chapters in this Part have compared alternative tax-and-transfer schemes using the assumption that total gross income and its distribution are fixed irrespective of the system in operation. There is in fact nothing unusual about making this assumption; it has been made in virtually all studies which have attempted to assess the cost, in terms of the tax rates required, of any recommended scheme of benefits. It would of course be unrealistic to maintain that the distribution of gross income would be completely unaffected by any policy change. Adjustments to labour supply and demand (influenced by, for example, employers' contributions, or general equilibrium effects on the structure of demand for goods and services) may be expected to take place. Incentives to shift sources of income, or hold wealth in alternative forms, may also result from policy changes. Furthermore, household formation and population growth may well be influenced by the nature of benefits and the conditions concerning eligibility. The processes involved are obviously very complex indeed, and in a much wider framework the distribution of income must be regarded as being endogenous rather than fixed. Nevertheless the previous results can usefully be interpreted as showing the 'limiting' cases. In other words the extent of redistribution implied by any particular scheme, as shown in Chapter 11, is an indication of the limits to redistribution. Any responses, such as increases in the number eligible for benefits or reductions in the tax base, would lead to a smaller amount of redistribution than shown.

In the practical design of systems of poor relief and social insurance, considerable emphasis has always been given to the possible effects on incentives. Very often this emphasis has involved insistence on benefits being strictly at a 'subsistence' level, and well below the amount which could be obtained in employment Examples include the role of 'less eligibility' in the Poor Law, and more recently the use of the 'wages stop'.

In the discussion of moral hazard in Chapter 1, it was stressed that this arises because of the difficulty of monitoring the behaviour of benefit recipients. Previous systems have indeed attempted to overcome this problem in various ways. These include the restriction to indoor relief, or the control of administration at a narrow local level (which makes both monitoring and the collection of information about employment prospects and the 'character' of the recipients much easier). The linking of benefit payments with labour exchanges until 1983 also reflected a concern with incentives, as did the need, again until 1983, for a doctor's certificate for the receipt of short-term sickness benefits. Other features of the British social insurance scheme are easily traced to a concern with incentives. Thus, those who are dismissed by their former employer, or leave voluntarily, may receive no Unemployment Benefit for six weeks; only a limited number of 'reasonable' job offers can be refused; and local Supplementary Benefit officers have a significant amount of discretion in the assessment of claims.

Participation and labour supply

It has proved extremely difficult to measure the responsiveness of labour supply to changes in the tax-and-transfer system; (see Killingsworth, 1983). This is true even of the extensive income maintenance experiments carried out in the United States (see Burtless and Greenberg, 1984). Earlier studies have often been concerned with separate aspects of the general problem. Thus there are analyses of the effects of high marginal tax rates on hours of work supplied by those in employment; for a survey, see Ashworth (1982). Other studies have concentrated on the impact of the benefit system. There have been fairly basic and highly aggregative time-series analyses of the relationship between the 'unemployment rate' and the 'replacement rate', and more detailed studies of the effects of benefits on the probability of leaving the unemployment register, using cross-sectional data. They have not, however, produced a set of unequivocal and widely accepted results, and there is still much controversy; for a review of several methodological problems see Atkinson (1981).

In Britain in recent years much attention, such as Hemming (1984) and Dilnott, Kay, and Morris (1984), has been focused on two features of the tax-and-transfer system which are closely related to the question of labour supply. The first aspect concerns the poverty trap, mentioned in Chapter 9 as arising from very high marginal tax rates (sometimes exceeding 100 per cent) applying to households with low earnings from employment. The second aspect is concerned with the definition and measurement of replacement rates for the unemployed. The existence of very high replacement rates is said to give rise to a second 'trap', the 'unemployment trap'. The calculation of marginal tax rates for low earners, and of replacement rates, along with the estimation of the likely number of people affected, has turned out to be much more complex than was initially supposed. Marginal tax rates depend on which household member is assumed to receive an income increase, the time-period of assessment (many benefits are assessed at long intervals, and do not therefore instantly disappear when earnings increase), and the size of the increase. Calculations based on a hypothetical increase of only £1 are of little relevance. Similarly, replacement rates vary according to the length of time in employment, previous earnings and employment experience, the amounts assumed for 'travel to work' costs, and many other factors. The problem in measuring marginal tax rates are described in Atkinson, King, and Sutherland (1984), and on replacement rates see Dilnot and Morris (1983).

Such studies have helped to clarify the concepts, and have provided a much richer range of information. It must be stressed, however, that they do not actually indicate the likely effects on labour supply of any policy regime; they simply provide more appropriate measures of factors affecting incentives. There still remains much room for dispute as to the relative orders of magnitudes of these labour supply responses, a factor which is considered in section 12.4 below. In the meantime, section 12.1 briefly presents the basic labour supply model which is often used to examine the effects of taxes and transfers, and explains the concept of excess burden in this context. Section 12.2 then considers some features of the current British scheme using the basic model, and section 12.3 identifies some of the implication of a *transition* from an existing tax-and-transfer system to an alternative scheme.

12.1 Labour Supply Theory and Transfer Schemes

The basic neoclassical model of labour supply which is applied to transfer schemes is a simple extension of the utility theory of demand, in which the individual is assumed to be entirely free to vary the number of hours worked. Utility is regarded as a function of real (disposable) income and leisure, and is maximized subject to a budget constraint which is determined by the wage rate (or rates, allowing for

overtime), the price level, non-wage income, the structure of taxes
and transfers, and of course the number of potential working hours. A
complication is therefore introduced by the fact that the actual wage
rate received is to some extent endogenous and depends on the section
of the generally non-linear budget constraint at which utility is maximized. For simplicity, the following discussion will consider only a
simple proportional tax system, and a single wage rate. A change in
the real wage rate (which may be brought about by a change in the
price level, a change in the money wage, or a change in the tax rate)
will result in a change in the budget constraint. Following the conventional demand theory this can be shown to lead to a negative substitution effect and an indeterminate income effect. Thus the effect on the
number of hours offered for work cannot be predicted without detailed
information about the structure of preferences. Despite this important
point, empirical studies generally use a fairly *ad hoc* form of utility
function.

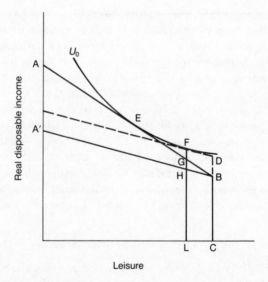

Fig. 12.1   *Dead-weight loss from a tax-and-transfer scheme*

Consider Fig. 12.1, which shows a single individual with non-wage
income w_n, facing a wage of w, and a price level of p. The budget
constraint is the line ABC, and the optimal position is at point E. Now

suppose that a proportional tax is levied on employment income only, at the rate t. The budget constraint shifts to A'BC, and the slope of A'B is equal to $(1 - t)w/p$. The new optimal position is somewhere along the new constraint, and the individual is obviously on a lower indifference curve (unless he is in both cases at the corner solution, B, when there is no change). The tax revenue can however be used to increase the individual's non-wage income. If the latter is raised to DC it can be seen that the tax-and-transfer system leaves the individual on the initial indifference curve U_0, but supplying less labour. In terms of utility, the income effect of the tax has been exactly balanced by that of the increase in non-wage income. The problem with this is that when CL hours of work are supplied only GH is raised in revenue, which is insufficient to raise non-wage income to DC. Thus a tax-and-transfer system applied to the single individual must lead to a 'dead-weight' welfare loss because the individual will be on a lower indifference curve. The dead-weight loss therefore arises from the substitution effect of the change in the slope of the budget constraint. With a large number of individuals, the aggregate tax revenue may of course be redistributed in such a way that some individuals gain, and are able to reach higher indifference curves. But there will be an overall dead-weight loss, by the preceding argument. The design of a policy which minimizes the aggregate dead-weight loss (requiring a cardinal concept of utility) thus requires a considerable amount of knowledge on the part of the policy-maker. This knowledge includes complete information about all individuals' utility functions. In practice, policies are therefore not surprisingly assessed on the basis of the distribution of net income rather than utility, by no means a straightforward task.

12.2 Labour Supply and the Current UK Scheme

Section 9.4 of Chapter 9 gave several examples of the relationship between gross and disposable income stemming from the scheme of taxes and transfers in the United Kingdom. Given that in all the cases illustrated, the relation between gross and disposable income implied effective marginal tax rates close to 100 per cent over a part of the earnings range, many authors have concluded that the actual tax-and-transfer scheme implies a substantial excess burden, especially when contrasted with schemes such as NIT/SD which, although having high *average* tax burdens, have relatively low *marginal* tax rates.

Nevertheless, important qualifications must be made. First, as suggested earlier, it is very difficult indeed to know how many individuals are potentially affected by the 'theoretically' high effective tax rates. In this respect, it is insufficient simply to examine how many individuals are in specified ranges of earnings, since some individuals may have altered their labour supply in order to avoid the impact of high marginal rates. Furthermore, although many studies refer only to earnings increases of £1, the effects can be very different for larger increases, or indeed for *decreases*.

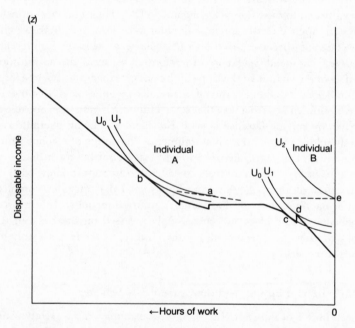

Fig. 12.2   *Labour supply in the presence of kinks in the budget line*

Notwithstanding these qualifications, it is perhaps useful to examine briefly the existing tax-and-transfer scheme in the United Kingdom. Figures 9.5 and 9.6(i) gave examples of budget lines facing working families. In the case of a family with two children and head of household working (Fig. 9.5) there was an earned income range at April 1984 figures of between approximately £30 and £130 weekly, between which effective marginal tax rates were close to 100 per cent. The number of families estimated to be in this 'poverty trap' has varied over the years but has increased in recent years as real tax thresholds have fallen. The Low Pay Unit (1983) suggested a rise in the number of families affected from 15,000 in 1974 to 105,600 in 1981. It seems likely that the numbers continued to increase until the rise in real tax thresholds in the 1984 Budget.

These numbers are relatively small as a proportion of working households (ranging between 0.2 per cent and 2.0 per cent) but this is not the full story of the effect on labour supply, or the excess burden problem. In Fig. 12.2 the budget line in Fig. 9.5 is redrawn showing two labour supply responses which put the household outside the range of the 'poverty trap', but which nevertheless indicate a wider impact. Individual A chooses point *b* with an earned income above the poverty trap range. But it is apparent that were that poverty trap segment of the budget line to be replaced by a linear schedule with a lower effective tax rate, point *a* on that segment would be preferable. Here the poverty trap makes the individual work more hours. Conversely, individual B avoids the poverty trap by working fewer hours at point *d*. This is at the kink in the schedule, stemming from the lower limit for National Insurance contributions. This behaviour seems less plausible for primary workers in the family than for married women and single parents. Blundell *et al.* (1984) provide estimates suggesting that gross incomes, and therefore labour supply, for married women have been affected by this threshold. More generally, individual B may be eligible for a benefit while out of work, such as Unemployment Benefit. If this is incorporated in Fig. 12.2, the high marginal effective tax rates at the lower end of the budget line will deter the person from participating at all, choosing point *e*. This is an example of unemployment trap mentioned above, and which has been further discussed in Chapter 7.

Another example was given in Fig. 9.6(ii) which illustrated the operation of the Earnings Rule. Evidence from a Retirement Survey in 1977 suggested that only 1 per cent of pensioners in the relevant age categories were directly affected by the Rule. But it would again be misleading to limit the impact of the Rule to this small proportion, since its more general impact is to encourage individuals in that age-group to work part time rather than full time. To judge the full effect, it is necessary to know labour supply elasticities with sufficient precision to calculate the proportion of the elderly who would have worked sufficient hours to be in that range of gross earnings in the absence of the Earnings Rule. Zabalza, Pissarides, and Barton (1980) impose a utility function on a sample from the Retirement Survey and use this to simulate the labour supply response of the elderly, both with and without the Earnings Rule. They find that its abolition would indeed increase the number of full-time workers in this age category relative to part-time workers, although the effect is rather small.

The discussion has so far ignored the existence of administrative costs. Otherwise optimal tax-and-transfer schemes (from the point of view of minimizing excess burdens) may not be optimal when administrative costs are taken into account. The classic example is where optimal commodity taxation implies different tax rates for different commodities according to the various price and income elasticities of demand and of supply. Yet where the administrative costs involved in differentiating tax rates are high, these may outweigh the welfare losses associated with a single uniform tax rate such as Value Added Tax. By analogy, the great simplicity of, say, NIT/SD, is the administrative ease of operating a uniform and universal tax-and-transfer system. If the labour supply effects and excess burdens associated with actual United Kingdom schemes are rather small, the advantage of simplicity offered by alternative schemes may be substantial.

12.3 The Transition to an Alternative Scheme

This section examines the labour supply effects associated with a switch from the existing United Kingdom tax-and-transfer scheme to a NIT/SD scheme. This particular transition encapsulates many of the issues associated with any extensive reform of the scheme which, it may be assumed, would try to reduce the present complexity of administrative procedures and minimize incentive effects, subject to revenue constraints. Unlike many other analyses of the effects on labour supply of income support schemes, comparisons are not made with the unreal situation in which no tax-and-transfer scheme exists.

Some insights of both the tax and social security literature and the labour supply literature may nevertheless be used in assessing the effects of a transition from the existing tax-and-transfer scheme in the United Kingdom to a NIT/SD. The ensuing analysis takes as its model the tax-credit scheme proposed to the 1982-3 Treasury and Civil Service Committee by Vince (1983). The ubiquitous married couple with two children, head of household working, is again taken as the basis of the comparison. Figure 12.3 therefore shows both the budget line under the existing tax-and-transfer scheme and the budget line with the tax-credit scheme. The latter proposes a personal credit for both adults, a child credit at a higher rate than existing Child Benefit, and a housing credit with a proportional taper. The values of the proposed benefits are updated to 1983–4; the hourly wage is assumed to be £5 up to 40 hours a week; rent, rates, and travel-to-work expenses from the DHSS *Model Tables* are also incorporated. The tax rate required to finance benefits, without allowing for labour supply changes, is assumed to be 47 per cent (that is, 1 per cent higher than that assumed by the proponents of the scheme).

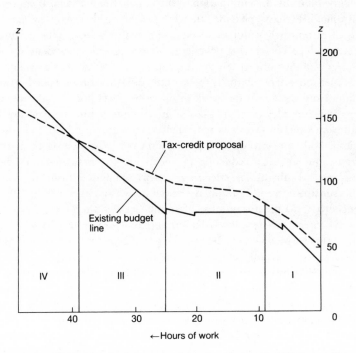

Fig. 12.3 *Comparison of existing tax-and-transfer scheme with 1983 tax-credit proposal (couple with 2 children)*

It is apparent from Fig. 12.3 that there are a number of non-linearities in the tax-credit budget line, stemming from the treatment of housing costs. Nevertheless the general impact of the scheme is to smooth out the budget constraint and eliminate a number of kinks. Reducing the extent of the non-convexities would be expected to reduce incentive effects, while administrative costs will be reduced by the simplification of the tax-and-benefit structure. To examine labour supply effects further, the budget constraint is divided into four segments, within each of which the labour supply changes consequent upon the transition to the tax-credit scheme differ. The direction of these effects may be obtained using standard indifference curve analysis. In segment I, in Fig. 12.3, the transition to the tax-credit scheme will produce an income effect encouraging fewer hours and, in some cases, non-participation, coupled with a minimal substitution effect operating in the same direction. This general shift to reduced effort will be offset by the elimination of the kink at the National Insurance threshold. Strictly speaking, the comparison on this segment should be of income when not in work, which will depend on the relation between levels of existing benefits such as Supplementary Benefit and the level of the non-earners credit proposed in the tax-credit scheme.

Over most of segment II, the income and substitution effects stemming from the transition work in opposite directions. Again the tax credit induces fewer hours via the income effect, but induces a substitution effect in favour of more hours. In segment III, on the other hand, both the income and substitution effects stemming from the transition suggest a reduction in effort. Finally, in segment IV the income and substitution effects again work in opposite directions with the substitution effect inducing fewer hours and the income effect encouraging a greater number of hours. Overall, therefore, there are two segments where a lower labour supply is predicted and two segments over which no net effect can be signed a priori. Note that even if the restrictive assumption were made that income effects cancel out, the overall substitution effect could not be signed a priori either, since the presumption that leisure will be substituted for work in segments I, III, and IV may be offset by the reverse substitution in segment II.

The immediate conclusion which stems from this analysis is that unlike a simple comparison with a situation in which no scheme exists, the overall impact on labour supply from the change to the tax-credit scheme is uncertain. Furthermore the impact on the aggregate excess burden cannot be predicted a priori.

Additional information is therefore needed in order to judge the net effect on labour supply of this transition and therefore whether the tax rate under the 'static' comparison remains constant after the allowance for substitution effects. The first evidence which might be useful here is to know how many households come within each segment. The classification of households by composition and by income range by Morris (1983) suggests that the majority of households of this composition come into segment III (approximately 48 per cent) and segment IV (33 per cent). Only 2 per cent come into segment 1 and 17 per cent in segment II. Half the households therefore come into segments where the net effect on labour supply cannot be signed.

The overall impact on labour supply depends on the relative size of the income and substitution effects at the two ends of the earnings distribution. If the uncompensated supply elasticity is constant across the earnings distribution, then no clear statement can be made. If the income effect dominates the substitution effect at higher incomes, and vice versa for lower incomes, there is a presumption that the transition to a NIT/SD will increase labour supply. If, in contrast, the substitution effect dominates at higher incomes and vice versa for lower incomes, the transition to NIT/SD will tend to reduce labour supply and therefore raise the tax rate necessary to finance a given level of transfers. No precise answer can be given, although recent econometric evidence which take account of non-linearities in the supply response suggests that the latter may be the more likely outcome (see Blundell *et al.*, 1984).

12.4 Analytical Extensions

The previous section suggested that calculating the labour supply effects of transitions between different tax-and-transfer schemes raise complex problems which are concealed in the deceptively simple framework of section 12.2. These difficulties stem from a number of causes. In the example depicted in Fig. 12.2, the problem was the non-linearity of the budget constraint, but other problems include the heterogeneity of household preferences and the fact that models designed to estimate labour supply responses to marginal changes are not well equipped to deal with the large discrete changes associated with major reforms of the tax-and-transfer system.

At present, increasingly sophisticated techniques are being utilized to obtain estimates of labour supply response to reforms of the whole or parts of the tax-and-transfer system which take account of some of these problems: see, for example, King (1983), Blundell *et al.* (1984), and Dilnot, Kay, and Morris (1984). The results suggest that labour supply responses to particular reforms may be quite significant: for example, the abolition of the lower earnings limit on National Insurance contributions consequent upon a revenue-neutral merger of the income tax and National Insurance contribution schedules may induce non-marginal effects on female participation.

Nevertheless, although these studies undeniably provide the basis for a more realistic account of the impact of changes in the tax-and-transfer system than is the case in the static comparison, the pitfalls involved in obtaining a definitive measure of the labour supply response are numerous. These pitfalls were illustrated by the variation in measured labour supply responses obtained from the income maintenance experiments conducted in the United States, as mentioned above. In evaluating reforms to the tax-and-transfer system which take account of the labour supply effects, it is necessary to know the extent to which the measured labour supply responses are sensitive to the following factors.

  (i) The sample characteristics: in particular, biases may arise from non-reporting and the way in which the labour supply variables are constructed (see Killingsworth, 1983, pp. 67–100).
 (ii) The specification of the budget constraint: in particular, whether non-linearities are incorporated and in what form they are introduced into the model.
(iii) The specification of household utility functions: a variety of forms are available which satisfy a number of criteria to varying degrees (see Stern, 1984).
 (iv) The extent to which involuntary unemployment and under-employment, as well as fixed hours of work, force households 'off their supply curve', and thereby distort their measured labour supply response (see Ashenfelter, 1980 and Ham, 1982).

In Britain research on these issues is still in its early stages. No sufficiently definite results have yet been obtained, or consensus of judgements reached, for application in transfer models of the kind used in this book. Thus, no explicit allowance for labour supply responses has been made in the various estimates reported in this book. It is important that discussions of incentive effects do not dominate the 'centre stage' in examining social security, to the exclusion of other important economic aspects of social insurance which influence the assessment of policies, namely those outlined in Part 1.

PART 5

Social Insurance in Transition

Problems and Prospects for Social Insurance

13.1 Major Themes of the Book

This book has been concerned with the principles and practice, mainly in the United Kingdom, of state involvement in schemes designed to overcome several types of risk. These are the risk of becoming unemployed, of being temporarily unable to work through sickness or permanently ceasing work due to disability, and of being unable to provide for old age. In the past three-quarters of a century the state has gradually come to dominate provision in all these areas through the operation of a largely contributory social insurance system. Within its short life, the system has undergone many changes, mainly resulting from the need to respond to changes which were unforeseen at the time of planning. These include the enormous effects of the two World Wars, along with the inter-war depression. The rapid inflation of the 1970s, followed by the high and rising unemployment of the late 1970s and 1980s, gave rise to further developments. Other significant influences have been the ageing population, the changing pattern of labour force participation (especially of married women), and changing household structure (the increase in single-person households and single-parent families).

The National Insurance scheme, a major component of United Kingdom social security provision, has come under increasing attack from numerous pressure groups. At the same time the government has been pursuing a vigorous policy of retrenchment, frustrated to some extent by the high level of unemployment. Therefore it is inevitable that there will be further changes in the future. However, in the present economic climate it seems unlikely that any reform of the social security system would involve a significant increase in planned expenditure. A difficulty in predicting what reforms will take place is that the majority of criticisms or policy proposals for reform have concerned particular aspects of the system, which is not surprising given the activities of pressure groups. Nevertheless, some commentators have proposed a major restructuring of the whole system. Of course any policy proposal will involve not only a set of value-judgements but also a set of assumptions about their implications. Unfortunately these values and assumptions are not always made explicit and, when they are, sometimes remain confused or contradictory. Proposals continue to be presented in the media, sometimes with only a brief estimate of methods of financing extra expenditure, and often without a serious analysis of their likely implication for the distribution of income.

A primary purpose of the present book has been the attempt to provide a basis for discussion of the complex policy issues. The implications of adopting certain policies and points of view were investigated, following the framework of economic analysis described in Chapter 1. There, policies were assessed in terms of their relation to fairly standard economic arguments. These concerned the role of the state in the provision of insurance, of which the main elements included the nature of and response to the 'failure' of insurance markets, paternalism, redistribution, revenue raising, and administrative efficiency. However the implications of these arguments for state policies are not always particularly straightforward, as Chapter 1 and the ensuing discussion has illustrated.

An important feature of a rational policy analysis is the explicit consideration of the relevant trade-offs involved in policy choices. Constraints are imposed on policy choices, and not all policies give mutually consistent results, so some trade-off among policy objectives must inevitably be made. A crucial aspect of such trade-offs involves the government budget constraint; for any system of benefits and taxes the constraint results in the loss of a degree of freedom in policy choices. The budget constraint played an important part in the analysis of alternative systems in Part 4. It should be emphasized that a detailed appraisal of this kind is really a prerequisite to any criticism of the existing system and suggestions for its reform or supersession.

In judging the performance of the present system, it is also important to try to be clear about the objectives and value-judgements behind the system. An attempt must be made to examine the consistency of a scheme within its own terms of reference, although the rationale for policies is seldom made explicit by governments and the process of decision-making is itself extremely complex. A good example of the difficulties involved is provided by the issue of income redistribution, the measurement of which gives rise to many conceptual and practical problems. As seen in Chapter 1, social insurance policy may be in favour of some kind of redistribution for two reasons: as the outcome of risk-pooling insurance (without risk-rating) and/or using 'pure' transfers as a separate policy objective. These two aspects are seldom distinguished in policy debates despite the fact that they raise quite different issues. It has not been possible in this study to decompose redistribution into two such components empirically, although much attention has been given to distributional aspects. In particular this book has emphasized the need to take a longer-term perspective.

In examining the internal consistency of the National Insurance system in the United Kingdom, however, it was suggested in Chapter 2 that an explicit redistributive motive did not appear to underlie many of the extensions of the social security system. Furthermore, many aspects of the unemployment and sickness insurance schemes do not allow for population heterogeneity, the regulations being based on the tacit assumption that experience is widely dispersed, rather than concentrated among particular groups some of whom experience repeated spells (see Chapter 6). Thus it seems that little redistribution arising from an 'insurance' motive seems to have been anticipated by planners. Part 3 of this book suggested that, when redistribution has been sufficiently clearly defined, the unemployment and sickness insurance schemes do contain a significant redistributive component in practice. In contrast, one of the few innovations in social insurance which seems to have been introduced explicitly for its redistributive content, the state earnings-related pension scheme, turns out, according to Part 2, to have an extremely limited redistributive potential. The rationale for these particular forms of state intervention which have evolved therefore have to be judged in the light of this evidence.

One of the difficulties in analysing the social security system is its increasing complexity. In view of this complexity, it is not surprising that many people have attempted to use a single unifying theme in appraising the social security system and in judging its performance; to reduce this complexity of needs and methods of provision to a single 'indicator' of failure or success. Recent contributions, such as Beckerman and Clark (1982), Hemming (1984), and Dilnot, Kay, and Morris (1984) have to a large extent concentrated on the relief of poverty as their sole indicator or criterion by which to judge the system. The discussion has unfortunately been somewhat confused by the tendency for many investigators to adopt as their poverty line the 'level' of Supplementary Benefits (there is, of course, no single level).

Too often this is justified only by the remark that it reflects the 'views of society' about the level of income to be judged adequate. That the basic level of National Insurance benefits has for long been slightly below the Supplementary Benefit level has therefore been used to criticize the system unequivocably for failing in its objective of avoiding poverty, while spending more than would be required for that objective alone. Furthermore, increasing the generosity of state provision by increasing the level of Supplementary Benefits therefore has the curious result of leading to the judgement that poverty has increased. Several issues stem from this discussion of poverty; for example whether poverty should be defined 'absolutely' or 'relatively' and whether the 'poverty gap' of Beckerman and Clark is a better measure of poverty than the 'headcount' method are two such issues. Nevertheless the point to be reiterated here is that the concentration of resources on the alleviation of measured poverty, however defined, at a point in time may not be the sole criterion by which to judge the performance of the system. Admittedly, if the existing system fails to alleviate poverty, or is wasteful in redistributing resources over and above those necessary to alleviate poverty, and no overrriding rationale can be found under any other criterion for a particular regulation of provision of the social security regime, the case against that regime is strengthened.

Finally, a theme which has been emphasized is the need for an approach in which it is revealed how the various components of the social security system interract; in particular how the combined tax-and-transfer system generates *ex post* distributions of income for households as a whole and for particular groups. In order to make such calculations, it is necessary to make simplifying assumptions. Some of those made in Part 4 are quite stringent. Nevertheless it has been argued that this is a useful exercise; there is a danger of producing optimal tax-and-transfer schemes in a 'black box' framework when the assumptions involved—which may be equally stringent—are concealed from the general reader. In addition to stressing these interdependencies in the tax-and-transfer system, it is perhaps also worth emphasizing here the general point that public expenditure on transfer payments needs to be seen in a very wide context. It was of course explicit in Beveridge's proposals that their success depended to a large extent on a government policy of full employment. Social security systems may perform very differently under different macroeconomic conditions (although it might be argued that the robustness of social security systems in relation to varying economic conditions is another test of optimal provision) and apparent priorities, or criteria underlying state provision, may be distorted by current macro-economic policies. It should also be recognized that transfer payments are not the sole means of attaining given ends. In particular, policies concerning education, the operation of the labour and capital markets, housing standards, and health care are in some ways more fundamental methods of redistributing income (see Le Grand, 1982).

13.2 Problems with the Present Scheme

Section 13.1 described how the National Insurance scheme has come under increasing fire in recent years. Some critics have argued that the scheme, the cornerstone of Beveridge's conception of social insurance, be replaced by an entirely new tax-and-transfer scheme, choosing a variant of one of the schemes described in Chapter 9. In contrast, other commentators have argued that a return to the 'pure' Beveridge concept is the optimal solution, with universal contingency benefits extended to a wider range of eventualities at present only covered by a variety of means-tested benefits. Some, such as Dilnot, Kay, and Morris (1984), with a scheme providing both tax credits and contingency-related 'benefit credits', have attempted to combine the two. These various proposals will be examined briefly in the next section. However, it is first useful to summarize some of the problems of the present system which have been identified in the course of this book.

The 1942 Beveridge scheme envisaged a single flat-rate National Insurance contribution financing a range of flat-rate contingency benefits. Eligibility for these benefits would be dependent on obtaining a certain number of weekly contributions. In the context of long-term benefits, notably the old age pension, this requirement would involve a state subsidy to the National Insurance Fund in the interim period as the scheme built up to a 'steady state', during which people reached pensionable age without having accumulated sufficient contributions over their working lifetime. This scheme of 'social insurance' would be supplemented by a scheme of family allowances and a means-tested benefit, National Assistance, for what were, it was later hoped, the 'residual categories'.

The problems which emerged with this scheme, and the changes that occurred in the 25 years after 1946, have been described in the text and elsewhere: see, for example George (1968), Atkinson (1969),

Kincaid (1973), and Dilnot, Kay, and Morris (1984) for a variety of interpretations. The problems which emerged are best illustrated by comparing the original Beveridge proposal with the present situation. On the revenue side, any 'quasi-insurance' component of the National Insurance scheme has been eliminated by its reformulation as a 'pay-as-you-go' scheme, despite DHSS published material and evidence of its officials to the recent Treasury and Civil Service Committee (1983) which still refer to the scheme as if it has a pseudo-actuarial component. For pension eligibility, the contribution conditions now merely serve the function of defining an explicit 'contract' which, it is thought, will morally bind future generations. For the unemployed, in contrast, the eligibility conditions, including the contribution requirements, have operated so that less than a third of the unemployed currently receive Unemployment Benefit (Table 7.1). For the sick, the contribution conditions have become increasingly peripheral to the determination of benefit eligibility, particularly since Statutory Sick Pay was introduced (see Chapter 8).

The difficulties involved in raising sufficient revenue to finance growing numbers of pensioners and steady rises in benefit levels through a flat-rate contribution has necessitated a switch to earnings-related National Insurance contributions. Since 1975 these have been levied in more or less the same way as other direct taxes, with a large proportion of revenue raised in conjunction with the PAYE income tax system. However, there are important differences: allowances against income tax are not permitted for National Insurance contributions and there are upper and lower earnings limits to contributions. Overall these facets introduce a highly non-linear element to the overall rate structure of personal taxation which make calculations of, for example, fiscally neutral tax changes or the redistributive impact of tax changes quite complex, as illustrated in Chapters 10 and 11. Certainly the consequent rate structure accords neither with the requirements of optimum tax theory nor with administrative simplicity.

On the side of benefits, it might be anticipated that a shift to earnings-related contributions would require, in the context of a 'pseudo-social insurance' scheme, a shift to earnings-related benefits. Indeed in the period 1966 to 1978 just such a shift occurred. However, as Part 2 illustrated, the consequent post-1978 scheme of pension benefits is highly complex, with both a flat-rate and an earnings-related component, and with the inconsistent indexation of the earnings limits and past earnings suggesting that the actual relation between contributions paid and benefits received for individual contributors will be extremely complex and quite arbitrary. In any case, it seems quite unlikely that the present scheme will survive for any length of time without further amendment. Furthermore, modifications since 1980 have ensured that Unemployment Benefit is no longer earnings-related, although as Chapter 7 suggested, benefit levels and contributions have never been very closely related anyway. Finally, the Sickness Benefit scheme is also now very complex. From 1983, payments of Statutory Sick Pay are earnings-related but unrelated to contributions, while eligibility for Sickness Benefit will be determined by contributions paid but benefits will be flat rate. As suggested in Chapter 8, no other country has managed to evolve such a complex scheme of sickness insurance. All these developments, of course, reflect the increasingly short-term perspective within which social security has come to be viewed, with financial exigency coming to dominate its provision.

The core of the present social insurance scheme is therefore very different from that proposed by Beveridge in 1942 and instituted by the post-war Labour government. Few of the original proposals have stood the test of time and indeed in the last few years there have been almost annual changes in major aspects of the scheme. In addition, side by side with the social insurance scheme, a whole range of benefits have been introduced financed out of general taxation. In the Beveridge conception, this sector outside the social insurance scheme was to have a peripheral role. However recent growth in expenditure has, with the exception of the state pension, been almost entirely in this non-contributory and, other than Child Benefit, means-tested sector (Table 1.1). In part this growth has stemmed from newly perceived areas for state intervention such as poverty among working families and one-parent families, but a major reason has been that means-tested benefits have continued to supplement and indeed replace National Insurance benefits in areas where social insurance provision was intended to dominate. In 1984–5, for example, pensioners took a large share of the £3.9 billion expended on Supplementary Benefit at the long-term rate, while of nearly £6 billion spent in total on the unemployed, only £1.5 billion comprised payments of the National Insurance benefit, Unemployment Benefit.

However, as is well known, the non-contributory sector of social security provision is not without its share of problems. Benefits which are cheap to administer because they are universal for all who are eligible, notably Child Benefit, are extremely expensive to the taxpayer and have a low 'Poverty Reduction Efficiency'. Benefits which are in contrast directed at the poor, such as Family Income Supplement, are costly to administer, have substantially less than 100 per cent take up and seem to have low 'targeting efficiency' (Dilnot, Kay and Morris 1984). Finally, the combination of tax and contribution rates on the one hand and benefit withdrawal on the other, as income rises, leads to the notorious 'poverty trap' described in Part 4. Although there is increasing evidence that few families are directly affected by this 'trap', its effect on optimal participation and labour supply may be somewhat greater, as described in section 12.2. However, as Chapter 12 suggests, it is an exceedingly complex problem to estimate the incentive effects of a shift to an alternative tax-and-transfer scheme.

These problems with the present system of social security are substantial; so much so that many commentators would now apparently seek to abandon the whole conception of social insurance and complexity of non-contributory benefits in order to start again from a completely new scheme. Again, however, it is necessary to emphasize the need for a rational analysis of policies, and for proposals for reform to be guided by a set of explicit criteria which both facilitate an analysis of possible outcomes and which would gain a widespread degree of popular approval. As the next section suggests, with such a wide range of possible reforms on view and given the apparently transitory nature of many modifications of the system in the recent past, the reform of social security is a Herculean task.

13.3 Policy Choices

It is apparent from this book, and the last section in particular, that there is much that is wrong with the social security system in the United Kingdom, whatever the criteria chosen in order to appraise its operation. Given the different ways of ordering these criteria, however, it is likely that no single major restructuring of the system would receive general support. Futhermore, any reform would be mediated through a series of pressure groups and vested interests who would seek to offset the particular innovatory aspects of the new policy, especially any modifications which would imply rationalizations of tax-and-benefit structure and other administrative simplifications.

For example, in recent years the Inland Revenue have argued that almost any reform in the system would require extra civil servants, although the inherent resistance to almost any change on these grounds is not always justified by any objective analysis or evidence. The general problem of policy implementation is nothing new in social security provision, as well illustrated by Gilbert (1966); that it is still a major problem is illustrated by pension planning over the last 20 years or so. Agreement was finally reached by all major parties, resulting in the Social Security Act of 1975. Nevertheless the new state pension scheme was found to be extremely complex and has since become subject to a great deal of adverse criticism. The existence of such a complex, far-reaching and long-term scheme then imposes considerable constraints on subsequent policy.

Therefore it seems essential that whatever new policies are advocated, it must be recognized that consensus will only be achieved subject to a degree of complexity in provision and obscuring of original aims. Indeed, in discussing various recent proposals for integrated tax-and-transfer schemes, Atkinson has argued that: (These schemes). . . are more ambitious in their attempt to simplify. . . . By sweeping away the present benefits, the authors are indeed able to start with a clean slate. But it is evident from the details of the schemes . . . . that complexity all too easily re-enters the scene (1984, p. 10).

Furthermore, the history of social insurance provision in the United Kingdom has suggested that the implemented scheme will always be in transition, in the sense that it will be subject to constant subsequent amendment. What is required is a social security system which has the built-in flexibility to be adjusted at minimum administrative cost to take account of a changing economic environment (such as a change in the dependency ratio for pension analysis) and changing policy goals of politicians and administrators (such as a change in the allocation of public expenditure). It is apparent, for example, that the Beveridge 'social insurance' scheme proved to be rather inflexible as circumstances changed and priorities altered, even though it received a degree of popular support at the time unparalleled by any subsequent reform proposal.

These factors suggest that the possibility of wholesale social security reform is more limited than many commentators are prepared to accept. Nevertheless there are certain aspects of the social security system which appear ripe for reform. The remainder of this section therefore presents some possible avenues for reform (concentrating in particular on the social insurance scheme) which appear to be consistent with the discussion of motives for state intervention outlined in Chapter 1 and developed in subsequent chapters, especially in Parts 2 and 3. Again it must be emphasized that the particular package presented here is only one of several possibilities and that further research and evidence on specific issues, which will be described, are a necessary prerequisite for implementation even if such proposals were to be accepted. Most notably, the cost of the various proposals is omitted. Finally, a brief discussion of alternative proposals which have been put forward recently, and which imply a wholesale reform of the social security system, is presented.

Pensions

The present state pension scheme in the United Kingdom was analysed in Part 2. The criticisms presented there were threefold: the complexity of the scheme (notably its indexation and revaluation provisions); the lack of redistributive content; and the high cost of the mature scheme given its provisions and undesirable demographic and economic trends. This last point, it has been argued, would necessitate sharp rises in rates of direct taxation in the early part of the next century. The government has recently been reviewing pension provision, but although commentators have been almost unanimous in their criticisms of the present scheme, there is, predictably, very much less agreement on its reform: in particular on the major issue of whether a reformed scheme would retain an earnings-related component. The Institute for Fiscal Studies (Dilnot, Kay, and Morris, 1984) and Parker (1983) favour abolition, although they differ in their preferred alternative, whereas Vince (1983) and the Graduated Tax/Improved Social Insurance Option discussed by Atkinson (1984) retain the earnings-related scheme.

Abolition of the earnings-related component is also bound up with the issue of whether the contributory aspect of social insurance should be maintained. Even if a separate payroll tax were retained, many commentators would wish to eliminate the contributory aspects of the scheme, such as the maintenance of contribution records. It would presumably be possible to retain an earnings-related pension by using tax records although this would involve a greater degree of integration of the tax and social insurance schemes than at present (see Kay and King, 1983). As argued in the previous section, and in Chapters 10 and 11, the present combination of tax and contribution rates is complex and analysis of major tax reforms is not a central ambit of this book. It was one of the issues discussed by the Treasury and Civil Service Committee's Sub-Committee (1983) and proved intractable there, as evinced by the Final Report of that committee.

None the less, the case for maintaining an earnings-related scheme at all is not particularly convincing. The case relies either on the paternalist motive (that people should be forced to save more than they would voluntarily) or market failure (there is no index-linked alternative form of saving available). Neither of these arguments seems particularly convincing. It is not clear what evidence can be adduced for the paternalist case given the existence of both public and private pension provision. Nor is there a clear reason as to why pension provision is a superior alternative to capital market intervention in the case of market failure (which is itself open to doubt given recent provision of index-linked securities for occupational pension schemes). Furthermore, the calculations in Part 2 show that it is extremely difficult to introduce a redistributive content into a scheme which pays earnings-related benefits; on this count a flat-rate scheme with earnings-related contributions is always superior, subject to special provisions such as the transfer of contribution rights between spouses in the present scheme. This leaves only the revenue-raising case for present provision: that the state is in essence raising current finance for pensioners by the simpler means of earnings-related contributions, while postponing the payment of earnings-related benefits on a large scale for the future. However there seems little likelihood that this state of affairs can persist once the cost of the scheme builds up.

Although this would seem to tip the balance in favour of abolition, it is also important to emphasize that the cost calculations are complex, and highly sensitive to the set of assumptions used, as made in clear in Part 2 and, in more detail in Creedy (1982a) and Altmann and Atkinson (1982). Previous pension reforms were implemented after long debates on principles, but insufficient evidence as to likely future financial requirements. In particular, evidence concerning lifetime earnings profiles was lacking, while the implications of various clauses and regulations such as the indexation rules for these calculations was largely ignored. So even if the earnings-related components were to be retained, there is a strong case for considerable simplification of the regulations, most notably concerning indexation and earnings revaluation provisions. Even this alone would facilitate public discussion of pension reform. Proposals could then be presented, as they can and have been with rather greater difficulty in the immediate past, which could for example show the degree of systematic redistribution associated with any pension plan within a range of assumptions as to lifetime earnings profiles, the dependency ratio, or the unemployment rate. It might then be possible to encourage a greater degree of public participation in achieving a consensus on pension reform and a greater awareness of the impact of changes in variables on pension finance. Furthermore, there is no reason why pensioners should not be paid currently according to whatever pension scheme is chosen, given the pay-as-you-go nature of the state pension scheme in practice. Instead debate is shrouded in a fog of spurious pseudo-actuarial language and a concept of intergenerational contracts which render rational analysis, as well as public debate, extremely difficult.

Unemployment Insurance

In some respects, the issue of short-run social insurance benefits is less complex than that of pensions. Less than 40 per cent of expenditure on unemployment, sickness, and invalidity benefits are now financed by contributions (Table 1.1). This suggests a strong case for taking short-term earnings replacement out of the contributory insurance scheme altogether, irrespective of whether the National Insurance scheme is separately maintained or not. In the case of unemployment insurance, the historical analysis in Chapter 2 and the analysis of the present scheme in Chapter 7 suggest that it has proved impossible to design a mix of contribution conditions and eligibility requirements compatible with efficient and adequate provision of state unemployment insurance, in any period other than one of very low unemployment.

The most controversial issue in state unemployment insurance has been that of moral hazard, although the balance of evidence is that, in the last few years at least, levels of earnings replacement have not been high enough to induce substantial disincentive effects. It is suggested here, however, that the main criterion which should underly provision of unemployment benefit is the 'availability for work' criterion (see Chapter 7). It does not seem rational, for example, to allocate claimants between two distinct sectors of benefit provision, with the majority in the administratively costly means-tested sector, according to criteria such as value of contributions attained or length of duration unemployed. There would seem to be an overwhelming case therefore for financing Unemployment Benefit out of general taxation, abolishing the contribution requirement (subject to minimum residential laws) and paying Benefit to claimants so long as they are 'available for work'. There would of course be distributive consequences for a shift from a contribution-related measure of eligibility to a pure household need/labour market attachment criterion. More research is needed into these distributive effects. The argument which has been presented against this proposal in the past—that the contributory scheme of Unemployment Benefit at least confirms the 'right' of claimants to a guaranteed level of benefit in line with their contributions—is not only spurious in theory but has turned out to have little practical effect in recent years when short-term benefits have been cut quite sharply.

Sickness and Invalidity Insurance

The reform of sickness and invalidity insurance raises other issues. The present scheme has become excessively complex since the introduction of Statutory Sick Pay (SSP) for short spells of sickness. There are contributory, non-contributory, and employment-related benefits; some are flat-rate while others are earnings-related (see Chapter 8 for more details). Although both unemployment insurance on the one hand and sickness and invalidity insurance on the other raise several related issues, there are two distinct features associated with the latter. First, there is the extreme bimodality in spell distributions, with 90 per cent of notified sickness spells terminating within six weeks but with a small proportion of claimants, albeit representing a large share of weeks spent in sickness or invalidity, experiencing long spells often only completed by retirement from the labour force. Secondly, there is an extensive although not universal system of private provision through occupational sick-pay schemes.

Recent reforms of state sickness and invalidity insurance provision have shifted the allocation of resources *within* the scheme away from the short-term sick (since SSP was introduced) and towards long-term claimants. However, given the real cuts in benefit stemming from SSP, the *total* provision for sick and invalids has declined. Given three motives for state provision: paternalism, market failure, and redistribution, the shift in the allocation of resources within the scheme seems more justified than the shift of resources away from the scheme as a whole. This in turn suggests an avenue for further reform:

to continue the shift but to increase resources devoted to these contingencies as a whole. Such an outcome might be facilitated by a move towards compulsory private insurance through occupational sick-pay schemes for the short-term sick, coupled with more generous and administratively simplified provision for the long-term sick and disabled through a move towards a comprehensive scheme of disability income and invalidity pensions. These proposals will now be discussed in more detail although again the qualification is necessary that further evidence is required in some key areas of incidence and cost before such a reform might be implemented.

The move to full compulsory private insurance represents a more radical step along the road taken by the government in the original Green Paper (HMSO, 1980), and is the solution adopted by other countries such as West Germany. The general criticisms of present state provision through SSP are its low levels of income replacement and the substantial and rising cost of full refunds of claims for SSP to employers. Whether compulsory private insurance would alleviate the former depends on the minimum acceptable standards of private sick-pay schemes set by the government. Most employers would presumably relate sick-pay provision to earnings as at present and, as Tables 8.3 and 8.4 indicated, sick-pay provision is considerably more generous than provision through SSP. Although a scheme of fully earnings-related occupational sick-pay provision would be technically less redistributive than SSP at present, since the latter only links pay to earnings across three broad bands, the government could insist on standards of sick-pay provision which would increase resources devoted to the short-term sick as a whole. Furthermore, the government would of course save on refunds of SSP to employers, currently budgeted at well over £500 million a year.

The major criticisms of this proposal are, naturally, the extra burden of cost on some employers who do not currently offer sick-pay schemes and the related ending of cross-subsidization among employers. It is almost certain that employers will argue against this compulsory insurance on the grounds that it will raise labour costs and reduce employment, representing just another extension of protective regulations imposed on firms by the state. There is very little evidence, however, that recent extensions of employee rights to what were previously more 'marginal' parts of the labour market have had employment effects (Disney and Szyszczak, 1984). Furthermore, there is the important issue of incidence in this context, and so far studies of this question have failed to come up with definitive answers (see Chapter 8). The cross-subsidization point is potentially more serious. Individuals with a greater propensity to short-term sickness (it seems less plausible to argue that there are industry-specific differences in *short-term* sickness incidence, but this needs to be investigated in more detail) would presumably face greater difficulties in finding employment whereas any employers who ignored individual histories of recurrent sickness would face adverse selection problems. How extensive these problems would be is less clear. More important, there has been very little discussion of the merits of regulatory policies designed to give greater opportunities to those with histories of chronic ill-health or invalidity (for example, mandatory employment quotas for the disabled) relative to the use of cross-subsidization through benefit provision. It is well known that quotas are rather unsuccessful in times of economic recession (and enforcement would involve the state in some cost). But it is arguable that, had the government of the day showed the same energy in implementing employment quotas for those with disabilities or histories of chronic ill-health that it showed in conceding to pressure groups arguing for a continuation of cross-subsidization of the *short-term* sick, the redistributive potential of state intervention in this area would have been much greater.

One consequence of saving in this area is that provision for the long-term sick and disabled could be much more generous than at present. In the light of the preceding discussion, and that contained in Chapter 8, there seem to be good grounds for moving towards a comprehensive scheme, such as that proposed by the Disability Alliance (1975) and Wilson (1981). This scheme proposes a set of non-contributory benefits: a disablement allowance, an invalidity pension, and additional special allowances paid at the rate of benefit for industrial injuries. This reform shifts eligibility away from the criterion of contributions and entirely towards medical certification and assessment, which share the same function as the 'availability for work' regulation would in the suggested reform of the unemployment insurance regime. Wilson estimates that a reform of this kind would cost £1600 million at 1980–1 prices, so the cost of full implementation is now almost certainly well over £2000 million. More research is needed on the question of cost, as well as concerning the issues of differential risk and the redistributive implications of the shifts in benefit provision suggested here.

Overall, therefore, there seems to be a strong case for preserving a system of contingency benefits for interruptions to employment but for financing the whole scheme out of general taxation. A greater transfer of resources will be required given the extension of duration for claimants in receipt of Unemployment Benefit, and the more generous treatment of the intermediate and long-term sick and disabled. On the other hand, taking the state out of benefit provision for the short-term sick (although there will be regulatory costs), the elimination of the contributory requirement for benefits, and the administrative savings from moving claimants out of the means-tested sector would partially offset this higher cost.

Integrated tax-and-transfer schemes

So far, the emphasis of this section has been on optimal provision of each of the various social insurance contingency benfits. In contrast, Part 4 of the book considered the tax-and-transfer system as a whole. Various alternative forms of tax-and-transfer schemes were considered in Chapter 9, while Chapters 10 and 11 estimated the distributional effects of the existing system and the sensitivity of these results to shifts in the important parameters. Chapter 12 examined incentive effects in more detail and also the difficulties involved in estimating the consequences of shifts to alternative integrated tax-and-transfer schemes.

This book has not been intended as a tract on the optimal structure of taxation in the United Kingdom; there has been an extensive literature on this issue including, in recent times, Meade *et al.* (1978), Kay and King (1983), and the deliberations of the Treasury and Civil Service Committee Sub-Committee (1983). Questions of tax structure have only entered the analysis here in so far as they are connected with the provision of various social security benefits, notably those associated with the contingencies of old age, unemployment, and sickness and invalidity. However some recent proposals for reform treat the issues of social security provision and tax reform explicitly as interdependent decisions. Most notable among such proposals are those involving reform of the tax-and-transfer system as a whole along the lines of some of the schemes discussed in Chapter 9. The final part of this section therefore considers some of these reforms in a little more detail.

'Back to Beveridge'

This is a misleading name for set of options which are presented with regularity: recent proposals in this vein include several reports by the

National Consumer Council (including its evidence to the Treasury and Civil Service Committee, 1983) and the Graduated Tax/Improved Social Insurance option discussed by Atkinson (1984). The misleading nature of the title stems from the fact that no serious proposals presently advocate a return to the original 1942 Beveridge package including flat-rate National Insurance contributions. Instead, such reforms advocate increases in the value of contingency benefits and a sharp reduction in the degree of means-testing in the social security system, perhaps accompanied by a more progressive tax structure, the possible treament of benefits as taxable income, and the merger of the direct tax and contribution schedules.

Although some of the avenues of reform suggested earlier in this section are similar to these proposals, it is apparent that extension of the package to working families, for example by 'floating' families off Family Income Supplement and housing benefits through more generous Child Benefit payments, makes this an expensive option. Atkinson suggests that such a proposal would raise rates of direct tax by a minimum of three percentage points, and this takes no account of disincentive effects particularly if, as in the Graduated Tax/Improved Social Insurance package, the proposal were to be accompanied by a more graduated rate structure of direct taxation. Although this package maintains its adherents, it is hard to see any likelihood of its implementation in the foreseeable future. The case made in this section for more generous treatment of certain contingencies (for example, disability) or for taking certain claimants out of the means-tested sector on grounds of administrative efficiency as much as social grounds (for example, the unemployed) seems logically distinct from a *general* move away from means-tested benefits in all sectors.

Social dividend/negative income tax

Recent proposals for a tax credit scheme by Vince (1983), and a Basic Income Guarantee by Parker (1983), raise again the possibility of a fully integrated tax-and-transfer scheme such as that described in Section 9.1 of this book. Both schemes involve replacing the current system of social security benefits by a system of tax credits which can either be paid as cash or serve to reduce tax liability. Vince proposes an additional non-earners' credit and an income-related low-income credit, and there are various additional credits under both schemes. In general, however, the Parker scheme is rather less generous in relation to benefit levels (other than for children) and rather more radical in abolition of various reliefs and other benefits such as the state earnings-related pension. Direct taxes are then levied on all income through a combined rate of tax and National Insurance contributions.

The main problem with these schemes has already been mentioned in Chapter 9: the high average tax rate necessary to finance them. Atkinson (1984) estimates that the average combined tax rate would have to be between 47 and 50 per cent in order to finance the Parker scheme, and 47.5 to 51 per cent for the Vince scheme. Furthermore, this takes no account of disincentive effects, although as Section 12.3 suggested in the context of the Vince scheme, it is difficult to determine the exact extent, if any, of the disincentive effects stemming from a switch from the present system to a new scheme, even for one household type. Such calculations are extremely complex when extended to all household types and a variety of major reforms (see, for example, Blundell *et al.*, 1984). The more general point, made in their different ways by Akerlof (1978) and Dilnot, Kay, and Morris (1984), is that fully integrated schemes reduce administrative costs in many respects, but fail to use important contingent information which might be a way of targeting resources to particular groups at lower overall cost. A fully integrated scheme could only be introduced in the present economic environment (at existing average tax rates) at the expense of much lower benefit levels. It would then be almost impossible to protect the real living standards of those in particular contingencies (such as unemployment, disability, or old age). Yet the integrated framework makes it difficult to direct resources to particular contingencies without reintroducing some of the administrative 'complexities' which integration was designed to avoid.

'Modified Minimum Income Guarantee/Social Dividend' Schemes

Both the 'Back to Beveridge' and the SD/NIT proposals suffer from the high average tax rates involved in their implementation. In section 9.1, the 'Modified Minimum Income Guarantee' scheme was described (as one of a family schemes also called 'Modified' or 'Two-tier' schemes), in which the imposition of a higher tax rate on incomes below a particular income level, y_0 was shown to be a way of reducing the basic tax rate. Dilnot, Kay, and Morris (1984) have recently proposed a similar scheme. Indeed the Institute for Fiscal Studies has traditionally advocated this type of approach to tax reform (see Meade *et al.*, 1978). In addition they retain the principle of contingency benefits as a way of targeting benefits at particular group. The essence of the IFS proposal is a tax credit, set at a much lower rate than in the basic SD/NIT schemes, but combined with 'benefit credits' for each contingency. These 'benefit credits' are then withdrawn at a higher rate than the basic tax credit, as income rises, so giving a combined budget constraint with a single kink, as in Fig. 9.3. The 'poverty trap' is alleviated by the combined rate of withdrawal always being less than 100 per cent, but on the other hand the scheme extends the range of incomes over which there are marginal rates greater than the basic combined tax and contribution rate.

The attraction of this proposal in the present financial environment is that combined basic tax and contribution rates need not be increased, although poverty and the 'extreme' poverty trap (i.e. where implicit tax rates exceed 100 per cent) are alleviated. There are significant distributional effects since, for example, the earnings-related pension is abolished and Child Benefit is replaced by a child credit which is withdrawn as income rises. The extent of 'vertical' redistribution is, however, likely to be rather less than the other integrated tax-and-transfer schemes, although this depends on the rate at which 'benefit credits' are withdrawn as income rises. The apparent attraction of the scheme is that it is more flexible than some proposals in relation to changes in political priorities and financial constraints. For example, a change in priorities can be reflected by changes in the magnitude of the various 'benefit credits'; a change in the fiscal stance of the government by a change in the rate at which 'benefit credits' are withdrawn. In particular, by reducing the benefit withdrawal rate and raising the tax credit withdrawal rate, a 'Back to Beveridge' solution can be approached, although any other outcome under this scheme in effect implies extending the range of means-testing (albeit through the tax system rather than the DHSS) to a wider range of household types and income levels.

It is apparent from this brief discussion of recent proposals that a variety of reforms of the social security system as a whole can and have been constructed in recent years. Some seem rather rigid in their reliance on a more favourable economic environment than seems likely in the near future; others seem to involve political considerations, such as an extension of means-testing, which may be resisted in some quarters. There is now extensive analysis of these and other reforms under way, and it may be that a particular scheme is constructed which obtains widespread agreement. In the meantime, as this chapter has made clear, there is still a large amount of systematic analysis which needs to be done. Furthermore, a central argument of this book, and this final chapter in particular, is that improvements in the way the existing social insurance contingency benefits are operated can be made without prejudicing the case for a reform of the social security system as a whole. The proposals to simplify the administration of unemployment insurance, to consider the case for full insurance of the short-term sick and more generous provision for the long-term sick, and to remove these benefits from the contributory sector altogether, are compatible with several recent proposals for integrated schemes. In addition, it is suggested that a rationalization of the state pension and a fuller analysis of its implications on both financial and redistributive grounds is an urgent priority in order to facilitate public debate. It may be that these proposals are the best hope for the immediate future.

References

Aaron, H. (1966). 'The social insurance paradox', *Canadian Journal of Economics*, 32, 371-9.

Aaron, H. (1967). 'Benefits under the American Social Security System', in *Studies in the Economics of Income Maintenance* (ed. O. Eckstein), pp. 49-72. Washington: The Brookings Institution.

Aaron, H. J. (1977). 'Demographic effects on the equity of social security benefits', in *The Economics of the Public Services* (ed. by M. Feldstein and R. P. Inman), pp. 151-73. London; Macmillan.

Akerlof, G. A. (1978). The economics of "tagging" as applied to the optimal income tax, welfare programs and manpower planning', *American Economic Review*, 68, 8-19.

Altmann, R. M. and Atkinson, A. B. (1982). 'State Pensions, Taxation and Retirement Income 1981-2031', in *Retirement Policy: The Next 50 Years* (ed. M. Fogarty), pp. 72-97. London: Heinemann.

Ashenfelter, O. (1980). 'Unemployment as disequilibrium in a model of aggregate labour supply', *Econometrica*, 48, 547-64.

Ashworth, J. (1982). 'The Supply of Labour', in *The Economics of Labour* (ed. J. Creedy and B. Thomas), pp. 42-90. London: Butterworths.

Atkinson, A. B. (1969). *Poverty in Britain and the Reform of Social Security*, Cambridge: Cambridge University Press.

Atkinson, A. B. (1970). 'National superannuation: Redistribution and value for money', *Oxford Bulletin of Economics and Statistics*, 32, 171-85.

Atkinson, A. B. (1976). Comment, in *The Market and the State* (ed. T. Wilson and A. S. Skinner), pp. 324-9. Oxford: Clarendon Press.

Atkinson, A. B. (1981). 'Unemployment benefits and incentives', in *The Economics of Unemployment in Britain* (ed. J. Creedy), pp. 128-49. London: Butterworths.

Atkinson, A. B. (1984). 'Review of the UK social security system: Evidence to the National Consumer Council', *ESRC Programme on Taxation, Incentives and the Distribution of Income*, Discussion Paper 66.

Atkinson, A. B. *et al.* (1984). 'Unemployment benefits, duration and incentives: How robust is the evidence?' *Journal of Public Economics*, 23, 3–26.

Atkinson, A. B., King, M. A., and Stern, N. (1983). 'The structure of personal income taxation and income support', evidence to *Treasury and Civil Service Committee, Sub-Committee*, 1982–3, 20-II, 3–30.

Atkinson, A. B., King, M. A., and Sutherland, H. (1983). 'The analysis of taxation', *ESRC Programme on Taxation, Incentives and the Distribution of Income*, Discussion Paper 51.

Atkinson, A. B. and Stiglitz, J. E. (1980). *Lectures on Public Economics* London: McGraw-Hill.

Atkinson, J. A. (1977) 'The developing relationship between the state pension scheme and occupational pensions', *Social and Economic Administration*, 11, 216–25.

Baily, M. N. (1978). 'Some aspects of optimal unemployment insurance', *Journal of Public Economics*, 10, 379–402.

Beach, C. M. and Balfour, F. S. (1983), 'Estimating payroll tax incidence and aggregate demand for labour in the United Kingdom', *Economica*, 50, 35–48.

Beckerman, W. and Clark, S. (1982). *Poverty and Social Security in Britain since 1961*. Oxford: Oxford University Press.

Benjamin, D. K. and Kochin, L. A. (1979). 'Searching for an explanation of unemployment in inter-war Britain', *Journal of Political Economy*, 87, 441–78.

Beveridge, W. H. (1930, new edn.). *Unemployment: A Problem of Industry*. London: Longmans.

Beveridge, W. H. (1936). 'An analysis of unemployment, I', *Economica*, 3, 357–86.

Beveridge, W. H. (1942). *Social Insurance and Allied Services*. London: HMSO, Cmd. 5404.

Black, D. (1939). *The Incidence of Income Taxes*. London: Macmillan.

Blundell, R. *et al.* (1984). 'A labour supply model for the simulation of tax and benefit reforms', Department of Econometrics, University of Manchester (mimeo).

Bosanquet, H. (1914). *Social Work in London 1869 to 1912*. London: John Murray.

Briggs, E. and Deacon, A. (1973). 'The creation of the unemployment assistance board', *Policy and Politics*, 2, 44–62.

Brittain, J. A. (1972). *The Payroll Tax for Social Security*. Washington: The Brookings Institution.

Browning, E. (1975). 'Collective choice and general fund financing', *Journal of Political Economy*, 83, 377–90.

Buchanan, J. M. (1963). 'The economics of earmarked taxes', *Journal of Political Economy*, 71, 457–69.

Buchanan, R. E. (1967). *Public Finance in a Democratic Process*. Chapel Hill: University of North Carolina.

Burns, E. M. (1941). *British Unemployment Programs 1920–1938*. Washington: Social Science Research Council.

Burtless, G. and Greenberg, D. (1984). 'Measuring the impact of NIT experiments on work effort', *Industrial and Labour Relations Review*, 36, 592–605.

Clark, K. B. and Summers, L. H. (1979). 'Labour market dynamics and unemployment: A reconsideration', *Brookings Papers*, no. 1, 13–72.

Clark, M. (1978). 'The unemployed on Supplementary Benefit: making ends meet on a low income', *Journal of Social Policy*, 7, 385–410.

Creedy, J. (1978). 'Negative income taxes and income redistribution', *Oxford Bulletin of Economics and Statistics*, 40, 363–9.

Creedy, J. (1980a). 'The new government pension scheme: A simulation analysis', *Oxford Bulletin of Economics and Statistics*, 42, 51–64.

Creedy, J. (1980b). 'Pension schemes and the limits to redistribution: some policy alternatives', in *Income Distribution: The Limits to Redistribution* (ed. D. Collard, R. Lecomber, and M. Slater), pp. 103–18. Bristol: Scientechnica.

Creedy, J. (1981a). Introduction to *Economics of Unemployment in Britain*. London; Butterworths.

Creedy, J. (1981b). 'Taxation and national insurance contributions in Britain', *Journal of Public Economics*, 15, 379–88.

Creedy, J. (1982a). *State Pensions in Britain*. Cambridge: Cambridge University Press.

Creedy, J. (1982b). 'Some analytics of income tax/transfer systems', *Journal of Economic Studies*, 9, 30–9.

Creedy, J. (1982c). 'The British state pension: contributions, benefits and indexation', *Oxford Bulletin of Economics and Statistics*, 44, 97–112.

Creedy, J. (1982d). 'The changing burden of National Insurance contributions and income taxation in Britain', *Scottish Journal of Political Economy*, 29, 127–38.

Creedy, J. (1984). 'Public finance', in *Economic Analysis in Historical Perspective* (ed. J. Creedy and D. P. O'Brien), pp. 84–116. London: Butterworths.

Creedy, J. and Disney, R. (1981a). 'Eligibility for unemployment benefits in Great Britain', *Oxford Economic Papers*, 33, 256–73.

Creedy, J. and Disney, R. (1981b). 'Changes in labour market states in Great Britain', *Scottish Journal of Political Economy*, 28, 76–85.

Creedy, J. and Gemmell, N. (1982). 'The built-in flexibility of progressive income taxes: A simple model', *Public Finance*, 37, 361–71.

Creedy, J. and Gemmell, N. (1984). 'Income redistribution through taxes and transfers in Britain', *Scottish Journal of Political Economy*, 31, 44–59.

Creedy, J. and Hart, P. E. (1979). 'Age and the distribution of earnings', *Economic Journal*, 89, 280–93.

Cripps, T. F. and Tarling, R. J. (1974). 'An analysis of the duration of male unemployment in Great Britain 1932–1973', *Economic Journal*, 84, 289–316.

Cullis, J. G. and Jones, P. R. (1983). 'The welfare state and private alternatives: towards an existence proof', *Scottish Journal of Political Economy*, 31, pp. 97–113.

Culyer, A. J. (1980). *The Political Economy of Social Policy*. Oxford: Martin Robertson.

Deran, E. (1966). 'Income redistribution under the social security system', *National Tax Journal*, 19, 276–85.

DHSS (1969). *National Superannuation and Social Insurance*, Cmnd. 3833. London: HMSO.

DHSS (1974). *Better Pensions: Proposals for a New Pension Scheme*, Cmnd. 5713. London: HMSO.

DHSS (1975). *Social Security Pensions Bill 1975, Report by the Government Actuary on the Financial Provisions of the Bill*, Cmnd. 5928. London: HMSO.

DHSS (1977). *Report of a Survey of Occupational Sick Pay Schemes*. London: HMSO.

Diamond, P. A. (1977). 'A framework for social security analysis', *Journal of Public Economics*, 8, 275–98.

Dilnot, A. W., Kay, J. A., and Morris, C. N. (1984). *The Reform of Social Security*. Oxford; Clarendon Press for Institute for Fiscal Studies.

Dilnot, A. W. and Morris, C. N. (1983). 'Private costs and benefits of unemployment: Measuring replacement rates', *Oxford Economic Papers*, 35, Supplement, 321–40.

Disability Alliance (1975). *Poverty and Disability*. London: Disability Alliance.

Disney, R. (1976). 'The distribution of unemployment and sickness among the U.K. population', *University of Reading Dept. of Economics Discussion Paper*, no. 87.

Disney, R. (1979). 'Recurrent spells and the concentration of unemployment in Great Britain', *Economic Journal*, 89, 109–19.

Disney, R. (1981). 'Unemployment insurance in Britain', in *The Economics of Unemployment in Britain* (ed. J. Creedy), pp. 150–85. London: Butterworths.

Disney, R. (1982). 'Theorising the welfare state: the case of unemployment insurance', *Journal of Social Policy*, 11, 35–58.

Disney, R. (1984a). 'The regional impact of unemployment insurance in the United Kingdom', *Oxford Bulletin of Economics and Statistics*, 46, 241–54.

Disney, R. (1984b). 'Social Security', in *Public Expenditure Policy, 1984–85* (ed. P. W. Cockle). pp. 149–71. London: Macmillan.

Disney, R. and Szyszczak, E. (1984). 'Protective legislation and part-time employment in Britain', *British Journal of Industrial Relations*, 22, pp. 78–100.

Doherty, N. (1979). 'National Insurance and absence from work', *Economic Journal*, 89, 109–19.

Dunn, A. T. and Hoffman, P. D. R. B. (1983). 'Distribution of Wealth in the United Kingdom: Effect of including pension rights, and analysis by age-group', *Review of Income and Wealth*, 29, 243–82.

Fenn, P. (1981). 'Sickness duration, residual disability, and income replacement', *Economic Journal*, 89, 158–73.

Flemming, J. S. (1978). 'Aspects of optimal unemployment insurance', *Journal of Public Economics*, 10, 403–25.

Flux, A. (1934). 'Comment', *Journal of the Royal Statistical Society*, 97, 105.

Formby, J. P. *et al*. (1981). 'A comparison of two new measures of tax progressivity', *Economic Journal*, 91, pp. 1015–19.

Friedman, M. (1962). *Capitalism and Freedom*. Chicago: University of Chicago Press.

George, V. (1968). *Social Security: Beveridge and After*. London: Routledge & Kegan Paul.

Gilbert, B. B. (1965). 'The British National Insurance Act of 1911 and the commercial insurance lobby', *Journal of British Studies*, 4, 127–48.

Gilbert, B. B. (1966). *The Evolution of National Insurance in Great Britain*. London: Michael Joseph.

Gilbert, B. B. (1970). *British Social Policy 1914–1939*. London: Batsford.

Ginsburg, N. (1979). *Class, Capital and Social Policy*. London: Macmillan.

Gosden, P. H. J. H. (1973). *Self-Help: Voluntary Associations in Nineteenth Century Britain*. London: Batsford.

Gough, I. (1979). *The Political Economy of the Welfare State*. London: Macmillan.

Government Actuary (1982). *National Insurance Fund Long-Term Financial Estimates*. Report of the Government Actuary on the First Quinquennial Review under section 137 of the Social Security Act 1975. London: HMSO.

Ham, J. (1982). 'Estimation of a labour supply model with censoring due to unemployment and underemployment', *Review of Economic Studies*, 49, 333–54.

Hamermesh, D. S. and Rees, A. (1984). *The Economics of Work and Pay*. New York: Harper & Row.

Harris, J. (1972). *Unemployment and Politics: A Study in English Social Policy 1886–1914*. Oxford: Clarendon Press.

Harvey, E. C. (1965). 'Social Security taxes—regressive or progressive', *National Tax Journal*, December, 408–14.

Harvey, R. and Hemming, R. (1983). 'Inflation, pensioner living standards and poverty', *Oxford Bulletin of Economics and Statistics*, 45, 195–204.

Heckman, J. J. and Borjas, G. J. (1981). 'Does unemployment cause future unemployment?', *Economica*, 47, 247–84.

Hemming, R. (1984). *Poverty and Incentives: The Economics of Social Security*. Oxford: Oxford University Press.

Hemming, R. and Kay, J. A. (1982). 'The costs of the state earnings-related pension scheme', *Economic Journal*, 92, 300–19.

Hemming, R. and Keen, M. J. (1983). 'Single crossing conditions in comparisons of tax progressivity', *Journal of Public Economics*, 20, 373–80.

HMSO (1980). *Income During Initial Sickness: A New Strategy*, Cmnd. 7864. London: HMSO.

HMSO (1984). *Government Expenditure Plans 1984–5 to 1986–7*, vol. II, Cmnd. 9143-II. London: HMSO.

Hockley, G. C. and Harbour, G. (1983). Revealed preferences

between public expenditures and taxation cuts: Public sector choice', *Journal of Public Economics*, 22, 388–99.

Hutchens, R. (1981). 'Distributional Equity in the Unemployment Insurance System', *Industrial and Labour Relation Review*, 34, 377–85.

Hutton, J. P. and Lambert, P. F. (1983). Inequality and revenue elasticity in tax reform', *Scottish Journal of Political Economy*, 30, 221–34.

Jackson, P. M. (1983). *The Political Economy of Bureaucracy*. Oxford: Philip Alan.

Jacobsson, U. (1976). 'On the measurement of the degree of progression', *Journal of Public Economics*, 5, 161–8.

Kaim-Caudle, P. R. (1973). *Comparative Social Policy and Social Security*. Oxford: Martin Robertson.

Kakwani, N. C. (1977). 'Measurement of tax progressivity: an international comparison', *Economic Journal*, 87, 71–80.

Kay, J. A. and King, M. A. (1983). *The British Tax System*. Oxford: Oxford University Press.

Kay, J. A. and Morris, C. N. (1979). 'Direct and indirect taxes; some effects of the 1979 Budget', *Fiscal Studies*, 1, 1–10.

Killingsworth, M. R. (1983). *Labor Supply*. Cambridge: Cambridge University Press.

Kincaid, J. C. (1973). *Poverty and Equality in Britain*. Harmondsworth: Penguin.

King, M. A. (1983). Welfare analysis of tax reforms using household data. *Journal of Public Economics*, 21, 183–214.

Kitagawa, E. M. and Hauser, P. H. (1973). *Differential Mortality in the U.S.A. A Study in Socioeconomic Epidemiology*. Cambridge, Mass: Harvard University Press.

Kunreuther, H. (1976). Limited knowledge and insurance protection. *Public Policy*, 23, 939–56.

Lancaster, T. (1979). 'Econometric methods for the duration of unemployment', *Econometrica*, 47, 939–56.

Land, H. (1975). 'The introduction of family allowances: An act of historic justice?', in *Change, Choice and Conflict in Social Policy* (ed. P. Hall, H. Land, R. Parker, and A. Webb), pp. 157–230. London: Heinemann.

Le Grand, J. (1982). *The Strategy of Equality*. London: George Allen & Unwin.

Leimer, D. R. and Petri, P. A. (1981). 'Cohort-specific effects of social security policy', *National Tax Journal*, 34, 9–28.

Lewis, R. (1982). 'The privatisation of sickness benefit', *Industrial Law Journal*, 11, 245–54.

Lewis, R. (1983). Policing the sick', *Industrial Law Journal*, 12, 48–51.

Low Pay Unit (1983). Evidence to Treasure and Civil Service Committee, in *The Structure of Personal Income Taxation and Income Support*, pp. 3–40. London: HMSO.

Marin, A. and Psacharopoulos, G. (1982). 'The reward for risk in the labour market: evidence from the UK', *Journal of Political Economy*, 90, 827–53.

Marston, S. T. (1976). 'Employment instability and high unemployment rates', *Brookings Papers*, 1, 169–203.

McClements, L. (1978). *The Economics of Social Security*. London: Heinemann.

McCulloch, J. R. (1845). *A Treatise on the Principles and Practical Influence of Taxation and the Funding System*. Edinburgh: Adam & Charles Black.

Meade, J. E. (1972). 'Poverty in the Welfare State', *Oxford Economic Papers*, 24, 289–326.

Meade, J. E. *et al.* (1978). *The Structure and Reform of Direct Taxation*. London: Allen & Unwin.

Metcalf, D., Nichell, S. J. and Floros, N. (1982). 'Still searching for an explanation of unemployment in inter-war Britain. *Journal of Political Economy*, 91, 396–9.

Mill, J. S. (1845). *Principles of Political Economy*, repr. in 1920 with editorial material by W. J. Ashley. London: Longmans.

Minford, P. (1983). *Unemployment: Cause and Cure*. Oxford: Martin Robertson.

Morris, C. N. (1983). The structure of personal income taxation and income support', *Fiscal Studies*, 4, 210–18.

Mueller, D. C. (1979). *Public Choice*. Cambridge: Cambridge University Press.

Musgrave, R. A. (1959). *The Theory of Public Finance*, pp. 16, 227–31. New York: McGraw-Hill.

Musgrave, R. A. (1976). 'Adam Smith on Public Finance and Distribution', in *The Market and the State. Essays in Honour of Adam Smith* (ed. T. Wilson and A. S. Skinner), pp. 297–319. Oxford: Clarendon Press.

Musgrave, R. A., Carroll, J. J., Cook, L. D., and Frane, L. (1951). 'Distribution of Tax Payments by Income Groups: A Case Study for 1948', *National Tax Journal* 4, 1–54.

Musgrave, R.A. and Thin, T. (1948). Income Tax Progression', *Journal of Political Economy* 56, 498–515.

Narendranathan, W., Nickell, S. J., and Metcalf, D. (1982). 'An investigation into the incidence and dynamic structure of sickness and unemployment in Britain 1965–1975', *London School of Economics: Centre for Labour Economics*, Discussion Paper 142.

National Consumer Council (1983). Memorandum to the *Treasury and Civil Service Committee Sub-Committee* 1982–3, 20-II, pp. 64–75.

Nickell, S. (1977). 'Trade unions and the position of women in the industrial wage structure', *British Journal of Industrial Relations*, 15, 192–210.

Nickell, S. J. (1979). 'Estimating the probability of leaving unemployment', *Econometrica*, 47, 1249–66.

Nickell, S. J. (1980). 'A picture of male unemployment in Britain', *Economic Journal*, 90, 776–94.

Ogus, A. I. (1975). 'Unemployment benefit for workers on short-time', *Industrial Law Journal*, 4, 12–23.

Ogus, A. I. and Barendt, E. M. (1982). *The Law of Social Security*, 2nd edn. London: Butterworths.

Parker, H. (1983). 'Basic Income Guarantee scheme', *Treasury and Civil Service Committee Sub-Committee 1982–3*, 20-I, pp. 424–453.

Pauly, M. V. (1968). 'The economics of moral hazard: Comment', *American Economic Review*, 58, 531–7.

Prest, A. R. (1955). 'Statistical calculations of tax burdens', *Economica*, 22, 234–45.

Prest, A. R. (1968). 'The budget and interpersonal distribution', *Public Finance*, 23, 80–98.

Prest, A. R. (1970). 'Some redistributional aspects of the national superannuation fund', *Three Banks Review*, 86, 3–22.

Prest, A. R. (1976). Comment, in *The Market and the State* (ed. T. Wilson and A. S. Skinner), pp. 319–23. Oxford: Clarendon Press.

Prest, A. R. (1979). 'The structure and reform of direct taxation', *Economic Journal*, 89, 243–60.

Revell, J. R. S. (1967). *The Wealth of the Nation*. Cambridge: Cambridge University Press.

Rhys-Williams, J. (1953). *Taxation and Incentive*. London: William Hodge.

Richards, J. (1984). 'The use of the unemployment benefit system for short-time working in Great Britain', *ESRC Short-time working*

Project, University of Kent. Working Paper, no. 8.

Rimlinger, G. V. (1971). *Welfare Policy and Industrialisation in Europe, America and Russia*. New York: John Wiley.

Room, G. (1979). *The Sociology of Welfare*. Oxford: Martin Robertson.

Sah, R. K. (1983). 'How much redistribution is possible through direct taxes?' *Journal of Public Economics*, 12, 83–102.

Salant, S. W. (1977). 'Search theory and duration: a theory of sorts', *Quarterly Journal of Economics*, 91, 39–57.

Samuelson, P. A. (1958). 'An exact consumption-loan model of interest with or without the social contrivance of money', *Journal of Political Economy*, 66, 467–82.

Sandford, C. (1980). 'Taxation and social policy: An overview', in *Taxation and Social Policy* (ed. C. Sandford, C. Pond, and R. Walker), pp. 1–12. London: Heinemann.

Seligman, E. R. A. (1899). *The Shifting and Incidence of Taxation*. New York: Macmillan. Repr. 1969, New York: August M. Kelley.

Sen, A. R. (1973). *On Economic Inequality*. Oxford: Oxford University Press.

Shimono, K. and Tachibanaki, T. (1982). 'Lifetime income and public pension: An analysis of redistribution effects with a two-period analysis', *Kyoto University, Institute of Economic Research Discussion Paper*, no. 182.

Slovic, P. *et al.* (1977). 'Preference for insuring against probable small losses', *Journal of Risk and Insurance*, 44, 237–58.

Smith, A. (1982). 'Intergenerational transfers as social insurance', *Journal of Public Economics*, 19, 97–106.

Stead, F. H. (1909). *How Old Age Pensions began to be*. London: Methuen.

Stern, N. (1984). 'On the specification of labour supply functions', *ESRC Programme on Taxation, Incentives and The Distribution of Income*. Discussion Paper 50.

Stewart, C. M. and Young, A. G. (1982). 'Calculating the best years of your life', *Employment Gazette*, September, 396–9.

Stiglitz, J. E. (1983). 'Risk, incentives and insurance: The pure theory of moral hazard', *Geneva Papers on Risk and Insurance*, 8, 4–33.

Suits, D. (1977). 'Measurement of tax progressivity', *American Economic Review*, 67, 747–52.

Thane, P. (1978). Non-contributory versus insurance pensions 1878–1908', in *The Origins of British Social Policy* (ed. P. Thane), pp. 84–106. London: Croom Helm.

Treasury and Civil Service Committee (1983). *The Structure of Personal Income Taxation and Income Support* (Third Special Report). London: HMSO.

Treasury and Civil Service Committee Sub-Committee (1983a). *The Structure of Personal Taxation and Income Support. Minutes of Evidence.* London: HMSO.

Treasury and Civil Service Committee Sub-Committee (1983b). *The Structure of Personal Income Taxation and Income Support. Appendices.* London: HMSO.

US Department of Health, Education and Welfare (1975). *Social Security Programs Throughout the World.* Washington: US Government Printers.

Varian, H. R. (1980). 'Redistributive taxation as social insurance', *Journal of Public Economics*, 14, 49–69.

Vince, P. (1983). 'Combined benefits and taxation', evidence to *Treasury and Civil Service Committee Sub-Committee*, 1982–3, pp. 38–46.

Wagner, R. E. (1976). 'Revenue structure, fiscal illusion, and budgetary choice', *Public Choice*, 25, 45–61.

Whiteside, N. (1980). 'Welfare legislation and the unions during the First World War' *Historical Journal*, 23, 857–74.

Wilson, J. (1981). 'A comprehensive disability income scheme', *Poverty*, April, pp. 25–32.

Wilson, T. (ed.) (1974). *Pensions, Inflation and Growth.* London: Heinemann.

Wilson, T. (1980). 'Welfare economics and the welfare state', *Swedish Journal of Political Science*, 5, 367–73.

Wilson, T. (1982). 'The finance of the welfare state', in *The Political Economy of the Welfare State* (ed. by A. T. Peacock and F. Forte), pp. 94–117. Oxford: Basil Blackwell.

Wilson, T. and Wilson, J. (1982). *The Political Economy of the Welfare State.* London: Allen & Unwin.

Yeo, S. (1979). 'Working class association, private capital welfare and the state in the late nineteenth and twentieth centuries', in *Social Work and the State* (ed. N. Parry, M. Rustin, and C. Sayraymurti), pp. 48–71. London: Edward Arnold.

Zabalza, A., Pissarides, C., and Barton, M. (1980). 'Social security and the choice between full-time work, part-time work and retirement', *Journal of Public Economics*, 14, 245–76.

Author Index

Subject Index